T

THE **Past** AND ITS PRESENTERS

an introduction to

issues in historiography

JOHN WARREN

Hodder & Stoughton

A MEMBER OF THE HODDER HEADLINE GROUP

The publishers would like to thank the following for permission to reproduce material in the volume:

Basic Books, Inc. for extracts from *Style in History* by Peter Gay (1975); Cambridge University Press for extracts from *Montesquieu*, quoted in *The Transformation of 'The Decline and Fall of the Roman Empire'* by David Womersley (1988); Harcourt Brace and Co. Ltd. for extracts in *Polybius, Histories* in *Selections from Greek and Roman Historians* translated by Evelyn Shuckburgh (1957); Harvard University Press for extracts from *Sallust, The War with Catiline* in *Sallust* translated by JC Rolfe (1960) and *Cicero, De Oratoreain* translated by Sutton and Rackham (1959); JM Dent at Orion Publishing Group for extracts from *Thucydides, History of the Peloponnesian War* translated by Richard Crawley (1910) and *The Anglo-Saxon Chronicle* translated by GN Garmonsway (1972); Penguin Putnam Inc and Edward Gibbon for extracts from *The History of the Decline and Fall of the Roman Empire* by Edward Gibbon (1983); Penguin Putnam Inc for extracts from *Tacitus, The Annals of Imperial Rome* translated by Michael Grant (1959) and *Livy, The Early History of Rome* translated by Aubrey de Selincourt (1971), *Herodotus, The Histories* translated by Aubrey de Selincourt (1972), *Cuthbert's Letter on the Illness and Death of the Venerable Bede, Priest*, in *Bede, Ecclesiastical History of the English People* translated by Leo Sherley-Price (1990); SAMS for extracts from *The Theory and Practice of History* by Leopold von Ranke (1973); University of Chicago Press for extracts from *Ranke: The Meaning of History* by Leonard Krieger (1977); AP Watt for extracts from *Recessional* in *The Norton Anthology of English Literature* by Rudyard Kipling (1968).

Every effort has been made to trace and acknowledge ownership of copyright. The publishers will be glad to make any suitable arrangements with copyright holders whom it has not been possible to contact.

Orders: please contact Bookpoint Ltd, 39 Milton Park, Abingdon, Oxon, OX14 4TD, UK. Telephone: (44) 01235 400414; Fax: (44) 01235 400454. Lines are open from 9.00–6.00, Monday to Saturday, with a 24-hour message answering service. Email address: orders@bookpoint.co.uk

British Library Cataloguing in Publication Data
A catalogue record for this title is available from the British Library

ISBN 0 340 69934 4

First published 1998
Impression number   10 9 8 7 6   5 4 3 2 1
Year   2004 2003 2002 2001 2000 1999 1998

Cover photo shows 'The Conqueror' by Paul Klee, reproduced courtesy of Paul-Klee-Stiftung Kunstmuseum, Bern.

Typeset by Wearset, Boldon, Tyne and Wear.
Printed in Great Britain for Hodder & Stoughton Educational, a division of Hodder Headline Plc, 338 Euston Road, London NW1 3BH by Redwood Books, Trowbridge, Wilts.

Contents

Preface

Writing a preface for a book like this is rather a tense affair. One has the image of the reader – or should I say potential purchaser – picking the book up from the bookshop shelves (having been attracted, I trust, by the carefully chosen title and cover), noting the price (a real bargain) and then, after flicking through, quickly scanning this preface. My next few words, then, may be crucial: will this copy of *The Past and its Presenters* be heading for the cash-desk or back to the shelves? Perhaps a few words of judicious flattery might be in order – such as congratulating the reader on his or her obvious intelligence in choosing a work on the nature and purpose of history? After all, this would recognize the fact that it is, unfortunately, perfectly possible to study history at university level, or to have a genuine non-academic interest in history, without ever worrying about what history is. It is not only possible, but also rather convenient. One can choose to ignore those irritating questions which surface from time to time, like 'What is the point of studying history?' or, even more fundamentally, 'What is history?'

But such flattery would be misplaced. This book was written with the assumption that it is foolish to ignore such questions. Foolish, and fundamentally unhistorical. After all, those interested in history demonstrate their interest by asking questions of the past. So, if we are ready to ask these questions, why refuse to ask what it means to study history? We have no way of recreating the past to experience it ourselves. We cannot look at it as if through clear glass. We have to look at it through that special form of inquiry we call history. So we need to know what history in that sense actually is.

Of course, thinking about what it means to study history may well prove to be vexing, time-consuming, unsettling, provoking and provocative, and perhaps even a hindrance to getting on with the nitty-gritty of the activity itself. Some historians have been reluctant to engage in such matters for this reason, and tend to be antagonistic towards those who want to consider history from a philosophical standpoint, in which history might be seen as a particular system of knowledge with methods which distil or distort the past in identifiable ways. And yet, nobody can write history without taking a stance, implicit or explicit, on what history actually is, and what it is for. This is why *The Past and its Presenters* tackles the distinctly vigorous modern debate on the nature of history, discusses the writings of historians from the founding of the discipline of history up to the present day, and then considers the different views on the value of history. Its final chapter is a transcript of interviews with two practising historians at British universities, who bravely voice their opinions on some of the vital themes raised in the book.

Of course, one might argue that it is not necessary to look at the way in which past historians have tackled the writing of history. By this argument, studying historiography (historical writing) is largely irrelevant: one can discuss the necessary issues at a theoretical level without disturbing the dust of ages, which lies deep on the tomes (and tombs) of historians long dead. This would be arrogance at its most short-sighted and unattractive. There is no reason to assume unquestioningly that modern historians have transcended their predecessors, or that there is nothing we can learn from writers who have faced similar issues and tackled problems which exercise all historians. I found my own assumptions challenged and very often found wanting when faced with the writings of historians like Gibbon, whose work has all too often been commended as eighteenth-century literature but disparaged as history.

This is not to say that *The Past and its Presenters* attempts a survey of world (or even European) historiography. There are such books, often written with what appears to be frightening erudition: but they are also frequently unmanageable for the reader. The wide-ranging, encyclopaedic book can be very useful for reference, but rarely gives the reader a feel for the work of historians who, due to constraints of space, have been expeditiously labelled and hustled into an appropriate context. On the other hand, I am of course open to the charge of being heavily eurocentric – or even anglocentric – in my choice of historians. This is true enough. But I have at least given myself the chance to discuss historians in rather more detail than would otherwise have been the case, and to offer extracts which should encourage the reader to delve into the historians' works themselves.

One of the pleasures of writing this book has been the element of risk. Even if I had wanted to, it is difficult to make a work on the nature of history bland. *The Past and its Presenters* is certainly personal and opinionated, and no doubt correspondingly presumptuous. I have put myself in the position of daring to evaluate and disagree with historians of far greater experience and expertise than my own. Or, to put it more bluntly, what right has a comprehensive school teacher to venture into such treacherous waters and to sail across the bows of the well-armed galleons of Academe? Time (and reviewers) will no doubt tell. But I would argue that teachers of history in school have been forced to think very carefully about the nature and value of their subject. We have been buffeted by the disagreements over the National Curriculum, and obliged to justify history to those who have the choice to bid it farewell at the ages of fourteen or sixteen. Astute would-be sixth-formers can identify waffle and have the right to demand intellectual rigour in any explanation of what history is and does. If teachers are not prepared to provide such explanations, then the long-term effect on university history will be unfortunate to say the least.

I have benefited from help and advice from several quarters. I am very grateful to my publishers, Hodder & Stoughton, for encouraging me to chance my arm in a new field. Their generosity enabled me to take up the offer of a temporary education fellowship at Keble College, Oxford. My thanks are due to the Warden and Governing body of Keble for that opportunity, and also to Professor Averil Cameron and Dr Ian Archer for their helpful comments on the early chapters. Professor Colin Richmond of Keele University kindly read the whole MS, and I greatly appreciated his support. Together with Dr Michael Mullett of Lancaster University, Professor Richmond also agreed to take part in what must have seemed like a distinctly odd undertaking – the interviews that form the content of Chapter 6. The quality of their responses speaks for itself. The quality or otherwise of the rest of the book is, of course, my responsibility.

My final thanks are due to my family. I suspect that my daughters Elizabeth, Hannah and Ruth must have developed an unusual image of what constitutes fatherhood. Daddies, it would seem, spend their spare time hunched over word processors or riding mountain bikes to try to offset curvature of the spine. But my wife Margaret has had to put up with most. She has watched me type my way through doctorate, teaching certificate and three books with a patience and understanding which fly in the face of all reason.

Defining History

THE NOISE OF BATTLE

A definition of history? Is it really worthwhile? Surely this chapter ought to be uncontroversial, and maybe even a total waste of time. Perhaps so: in which case let me offer a straightforward definition. History is the past, and historians are those who study and write about history. At first sight, this seems reasonable, if a little dull. But this simple – and actually rather misleading – definition leads us straight into a bitterly-contested war zone, full of sound and fury, riven by the violent disagreements of those who write about what history is. You might think that my military metaphor is hopelessly overblown. Surely historians can conduct a reasonably urbane debate on a subject which, after all, ought to have been sorted out long ago? In fact, the debate is a very real one, accompanied by some rather violent and unscholarly language as historians see their cherished assumptions subjected to destructive irony. And that military metaphor is not the product of my fevered imagination. A recent book by Richard Evans is entitled *In Defence of History*: the very blurb on its dust-jacket talks of the 'disintegrative attack' to which the writing of history has been subjected. Evans speaks (a little tongue-in-cheek) of the 'invading hordes' of scholars from other disciplines.[1] Sir Geoffrey Elton was not satisfied with the language of war alone. Defending the historian's right to hold the 'fortress of truth' against such interlopers, he described his opponents as drug dealers.[2]

What, then, are the issues which generate such controversy? Let us start with my simple and apparently incontrovertible definition of history and identify some of the problems with it.

Firstly, it is all very well saying that history is the past, but, in practice, is it not the actual writing about the past by historians, rather than the past itself? After all, the words of historians are virtually all we have. Granted, there are traces of the past all around us, in buildings, landscape, memories and documents. But when we try to explain, to give some structure to the past, then our words do not actually let the past live. We impose ourselves on it. Historians cannot recreate the past. If they could, then our lives would be very strange and frightening.

So, one could argue that there is no such thing as history in the sense of 'the past' at all. All we have is what we write about it. Taking this a stage further, it has been argued that when we study history, we are merely studying historiography: the past as seen in the words of historians. We then end up with the problem of what historians do to the past. This means that the past is in the hands of people who are going to shape it to reflect their own political, social, cultural, religious and educational stances. In other words, the past is never handed on to us directly and objectively.

On the other hand, are we not forgetting the original sources themselves – the primary evidence or traces, as they are often called? Might we not let them speak to us, and thereby get the real thing with an absolute minimum of interference from our increasingly discredited historian? This sounds plausible enough, but there are a number of problems here. Firstly, such sources are themselves compromised by the distortions of the original writers – distortions which we cannot always detect. In any case, one cannot simply lump together a group of sources on, say, England under William the Conqueror and pronounce, 'Right! This is what it was like.' Sources are not designed with the needs of future generations in mind. There will be massive gaps. In the case of eleventh-century England, there will be almost nothing about the majority of the population. So, the sources are pre-selected by their incompleteness. And then, of course, along comes the historian to make a selection to suit himself. In any case, if the writing of history involves some sort of explanation, then this is where the historian comes in. He is our guide, and gives us the context into which these sources fit. He sifts, analyses, makes something coherent out of traces which are not in themselves coherent. What we get is the historian's view of eleventh-century England, even if he has given us little more than a set of sources with a linking text. What we do not get is eleventh-century England.

There is a final argument, and one which is potentially devastating to the pretensions of historians who claim the right to plant their flags in the fortress of truth. Briefly, it is not so much that we cannot possibly detect the truth about the past – although, of course, we cannot. It is more that we cannot detect truth anyway. To believe that humankind can do so is hopelessly outmoded. It is therefore best to see history as a set of texts on the subject of the past which are, in essence, fictional. The historian is therefore akin to a type of literary scholar who takes a text to pieces to show how it works rather than claiming that it reflects reality in any way.

Alternatively, perhaps we can dismiss much of all this as unhelpful philosophical posturing which denies the common-sense view that historians do use the traces of the past to create a picture which is close to, but never the ultimate, truth. Get yourself down to the archives, and stop worrying about the nature of reality. Leave it to the philosophers, who never do anything useful anyway.

As I said, a battlefield. The reader might hope that this chapter will act as a guide to the campaign, a way of avoiding it altogether or as the chance to get one's hands on some decent weapons with which to enter the fray. At the very least, we should be able to alight on a workable definition of history. Perhaps!

Postmodernism

To squeeze the last drops out of my military metaphor, this important section should be seen as the biting of the bullet. Postmodernism is perhaps the most radical and significant challenge to the 'common-sense' view of what the historian does. It is also a challenge to those who set out to write genuinely introductory books on history. This is partly because there is no such thing as a postmodern school of historians with a convenient and single approach which one can describe in a straightforward way. It is partly because postmodernism is interdisciplinary and feeds upon ideas from such fields as linguistics and anthropology in which the historian rarely has expertise. The main problem, though, is easily stated: postmodernist theory is difficult to understand. To be frank, some of the major theorists revel in provocative stances and elliptical statements in the process of dousing the reader in irony. It does not always help when the same reader is presented with invented words (like the philosopher Derrida's term *différance*) which arguably work in French but not in English. Depending on your viewpoint, this sort of thing can be stimulating. But it is not easy to follow. So, I propose to tackle this by adopting an approach which some would find hard to swallow. Firstly, I will offer a briefish summary of postmodernist views on history. This will, of course, lay me open to the charge of simplification and over-generalization. I might also be accused of setting up my own target at which to aim. Subsequent sections will – hopefully – repair some of the damage by giving me the chance to expand upon and discuss the issues raised.

Postmodernism and history: an introduction

We should start with what the word 'postmodern' actually means. The term was first applied to particular approaches in the creative arts in the 1970s. As the word suggests, it involves a deliberate rejection of 'modernism'. Postmodern architects, for example, poked fun at the systematic, regular, rational, 'style-fits-use' buildings constructed by their modernist colleagues. Postmodernist buildings were whimsical, ironic, irregular. In philosophy, postmodernism also represents an attack on so-called modernist thinking. Modernism was seen as a set of assumptions which held that it was possible for the fundamentally rational humankind to discover systematically certain scientific laws about the way the world operated. Such discoveries would allegedly lead to progress. In history, this would include theories like Marxism, which argued that struggle between classes was the factor which explained the development of the past, present and future. Postmodernism questions the validity of such theories, on the grounds that they are simply the product of a mistaken belief (characteristic of modernism) in what human reason is and can do. We may think we are objective, rational, able to look at our world, describe what it actually is, analyse what makes it tick and suggest ways of making it tick better and faster. But this is a delusion, for two main reasons. Firstly, what we claim as objective knowledge about society is very often just a way of getting power over other people. We decide what makes 'true' knowledge and then control access to it. This can range from denying a particular type of education to women, to assuming that Western democracy is more civilized than any other form of political life and that non-Western societies need help (or control) to be 'civilized'.

In any case, say postmodernists, can we really see ourselves as rational, scientific and objective when those supposed guardians of our civilization, the scientific community, encouraged the development of weapons of mass destruction? Where has technological advance led us? To the pollution of our planet and even greater inequality of wealth throughout the world? To the postmodernist, all the old certainties about progress or even religious belief have been exploded. We are the better for their departure. It is liberating to realize that 'truth' may be out of our reach.

There is a further reason for arguing that our belief in the all-conquering power of human reason is a delusion. Quite simply, we are all prisoners of language. We can know most things only indirectly, and only through words. This is particularly true for history, of course, because we can have no direct experience of the past. Being so dependent on words would not matter so much if we were in control of the words used by others or even by ourselves. But we are not. If we settle down to write, say, an accurate, calm, factual and objective account of some event in history, then what we

produce can never be the truth about the past. We have been using documents – texts – from the past. We have also been using the texts of other
historians. And now we have produced our own text. But each text, including our own, is anything but an objective and factual account. Texts,
whether we like it or not, are full of metaphors, symbols, signs, gaps, deliberate and accidental omissions and distortions. And where do these come
from? They reflect the power relationships of the given society, the conscious and unconscious attitudes of the author towards those relationships;
the position of the author within that society – and a host of distortions both
personal and public which cannot be allowed for in any typical and superficial analysis of 'bias'. If we take these texts to bits – subject them to a
process of deconstructive literary analysis – we can hope to identify some of
these symbols, gaps and distortions. But we are going to use words ourselves in writing up our conclusions, and so are going to be the prisoners of
language in the same way. The most honest approach in writing history is to
accept that the closest our work will get to the 'truth' is to put across our
own version of what the 'truth' is. If this is useful to us and to people who
share our particular set of ideals or prejudices, all well and good. In fact,
there is really no such thing as 'history', just 'historiography'. We must
never forget that historians who claim to be writing about the past as it actually happened are almost laughably naïve. In any case, their belief that the
truth is there to be found in an objective and 'scientific' sense is the kind of
modernist illusion we need to do away with in the postmodernist era. The
history we write is really fiction. Let us be honest, at least.

There are other implications of postmodernism. Historians are supposedly fond of building up – and then sheltering behind – barriers between
themselves and other disciplines as if there is something unique about what
they do. There is not. Historians are individuals who work on the texts produced by other people and then produce their own. They simply cannot
afford to ignore the contributions of, say, new ideas in linguistics, since
those ideas account for the way texts develop in the first place.

It is sometimes argued that history can teach us lessons, in that we can
learn from mistakes made in the past. This makes no sense in postmodernist terms. You can only learn in this direct way if you have actually succeeded in finding out the truth in the first place. As we have seen, this
allegedly cannot be done. Some postmodernists argue that writing, reading
and studying history are useful in an indirect way. Studying the development of postmodernism might help you gain the maximum from its liberating ironies and the debunking of modernist illusions. It can be fun to expose
the alleged limitations of the run-of-the-mill traditionalists who believe that
historians just let the past speak for itself. Also, if you see yourself as a
member of an exploited group, you might use its approaches to unmask the
techniques of power and exploitation to which you are currently subjected.

So far, I have suggested that defining history is massively controversial. I have also suggested that postmodernism currently represents the most far-reaching and radical attempt to define history, and one which short-circuits traditional definitions. We now need to clothe the skeleton by expanding on the summary. (By the way, I am sure that much might be made of the metaphors I use when discussing postmodernism – like battles, wars and skeletons.)

The origins of postmodernism

A Modernism

Since, as we have seen, postmodernism exists in opposition to so-called 'modernism', we should look at the charges made against modernism. Remember, though, that there is no obligation on us to accept that 'modernism' is a meaningful term in practice.

Modernism, we recall, is a world-view which assumes that human reason can detect reality or truth, and that we are capable of judging ideas by comparing them to that reality. There is, incidentally, nothing self-evident about this. One could equally argue that human reason is weak: that human beings are too violent, too emotional, to be able to find truth even if it walked up to them and introduced itself.

The optimistic view of human reason and potential lies at the heart of Greek philosophy from the time of Plato and Aristotle, but its more modern manifestation can be seen in the period known as the Enlightenment. This eighteenth-century European philosophical movement claimed that the power of human reason was sufficient to identify scientific laws – including those governing human behaviour – which would lead to the progress of humankind. If one was to curb the oppression of organized and superstitious religion (largely through appropriate education), then startling scientific, political and moral improvement would follow. And progress of a kind did seem to follow. Industrialization had a massive and transforming effect on much of the Western world, and was complemented by huge advances in science and technology. This was, in fact, the heroic age of the scientist: the objective, disinterested, white-coated seeker for truth before whom the laws of nature stood revealed. Small wonder that thinkers reacting for and against such changes looked for and claimed to find laws of progress in human society to parallel newly-discovered physical laws. The nineteenth-century French thinker Auguste Comte, for example, claimed to have uncovered the laws whereby human society had developed and would develop through history. Comte believed that the 'Positivist' age was about to dawn, where science would reign supreme, Christianity would fade and women would take on their supposedly appropriate roles as priestesses of the new morality.

A far more influential 'science of society' was that of Karl Marx (1818–83). Marx and Marxism are discussed in greater detail in Chapter 4. Briefly, in the concept of 'class struggle' lies Marx's explanation for change in history. Class struggle – the struggle of the bourgeoisie or middle-class capitalists against the feudal or land-owning classes, the struggle of the oppressed industrial workers or proletariat against the bourgeoisie – was based on economic relationships between the classes. Fundamental change in who controlled society and how its ideals were shaped came about due to change in society's economic structure. The political power, say, of the monarchs and the land-owning classes would be destroyed once the economic structure of society was no longer based on wealth from land and agriculture. Marx's friend and collaborator Friedrich Engels significantly claimed that Marx's discovery of the law of development of human history was a scientific breakthrough comparable to Charles Darwin's theory of evolution.

The impact of Marx's thought is undeniable. Although the Communist revolution he predicted came neither in the expected time nor place, the various Communist movements and a (decreasing) number of states throughout the world claim allegiance to his ideas. So do whole legions of scholars, including historians. Not that Marxism carried all before it in historiography. The British historical tradition in the twentieth century has been much enlivened by the works of Marxists, but has largely remained antagonistic to the concept of identifiable laws in history. But this does not mean that those who rejected Marxism were not 'modernist'. After all, they held the view that intellectual study must be objective and concerned with 'reality'. The belief in disinterested scholarship and freedom of inquiry was part and parcel of Western liberal culture. And behind all this, of course, lay the modernist assumption that it was possible to identify reality and explain it to others.

Modernism is, of course, more than a set of intellectual attitudes. Religious ideals can be part of it. In fact, modernism is supposedly strong on codes of morality which are 'true' across time since they reflect 'eternal truths'. A feeling of optimism and even certainty about human progress can also be translated into an increased certainty about God's benevolence, although one has to accept that there may well be a tension between faith, reason and science. Nevertheless, modernism in general is supposed to be characterized by the existence of optimism and a sense of certainty about what the human condition is and can be. It is possible for this to extend beyond the confines of the natural world into the world to come.

Why, then, did some thinkers come to identify and so reject what they called modernism?

B The rejection of modernism

(i) The historical background

Those who came to reject modernism did not exist in a kind of timeless bubble. Whilst it would be fatuous to claim that their ideas were the direct result of political experience, it would surely be perverse to deny the influence of historical events on their thought. Our first theme should be a change in attitude towards the once-esteemed scientist. That technological advance – which owed so much to scientists – was not necessarily a good thing was starkly revealed by what machine-guns could do to human bodies in the First World War. Some scientists were prepared to serve the cause of Nazism and even contribute towards providing the technology of genocide in the death-camps. The atomic bomb attacks on Hiroshima and Nagasaki were all too obviously facilitated by scientific endeavour, and all too difficult to present as signs of optimism and progress. Neither was studying post-war Soviet Russia very comforting. As Appleby points out,[3] the country had built up a massive technological and scientific establishment which had prostituted the ideals of scientific objectivity and had treated the environment and the living conditions of the people with scant regard. As historians of the 1960s turned their attention to the Western scientific establishments, it became clear that scientists, instead of being shut up in the laboratories in a suitably detached and objective manner, were anything but remote from the political, economic and social pressures surrounding the 'ordinary' citizen. Their science and even some of their 'results' and 'discoveries' were distorted by demands far different from those of truth. That historians should actually be looking at the issues of scientific objectivity is significant, and reflects a disenchantment with some of the seedier and more sinister aspects of capitalist Western culture: its racism and its readiness to impose itself on other cultures and countries through imperialism and colonialism. Many of those scholars important to postmodernist thought reacted strongly against the aggression of the Western powers, be it American involvement in Vietnam or French suppression and exploitation in her colony of Algeria. Of course, some people reacted against the capitalist West by following the thought of Marx. But there was plenty about the contemporary Communist states to object to as well. There was also the disillusionment following the failure of the May 1968 revolution in France where millions of workers had joined intellectuals and students in an attempt to overthrow de Gaulle's capitalist and imperialist Fifth Republic. The linguistic theorist Roland Barthes commented on the failure of May 1968 in very significant terms:

> **Make a revolution to destroy it, power will spring up again. And the reason why power is invincible is that the object in which it is carried for all human eternity is language: the language that we speak and write.**[4]

What is the origin of Barthes' comments on the relationship between power and language?

(ii) Saussure, structuralism and language

A fundamental assumption of modernism was that language reflected our thought, which in turn reflected reality 'out there'. But the work of the Swiss linguist Ferdinand de Saussure (1857–1913) denied this. Language had a set of laws, or a structure, true enough (hence 'structuralism'), but it operated by a system of signs which were not tied to an external reality. For example, take the English word 'sheep' and the French word 'mouton'. The word (or 'sign' in Saussure's terminology) 'sheep' conveys a particular meaning (Saussurean term, 'signifier') to the British; to the French, the word 'mouton', although clearly describing the same animal, has a subtly different meaning. This is because, in French, it means both the animal and the meat that comes from it. The British city dweller's view of sheep as attractive rural accessory would make no sense in French. So, meaning and words vary in an arbitrary way and reflect a different sense of reality. They cannot reflect a single, all-encompassing reality.

Poststructuralism

Poststructuralists accepted with structuralism the view that language did not reflect reality, but denied that there were any laws (even of the structuralist type) behind language. Yet language is all we have to establish what we think is real. But remember that we only *think* it is real: we have no way of accessing reality except through language, and language is incapable of doing it. This links conveniently with a dislike of the certainties of modernism and its assumptions that human reason can identify and therefore describe what is real. This is impossible, given the limitations of language.

Poststructuralist historians reject any theory of history which claims to identify or explain a law of development. In this way, poststructuralism is a variety of postmodernism. Both display what the French philosopher Lyotard (b.1925) calls 'incredulity towards metanarratives'.[5] A metanarrative is not just a theory of historical change, but any type of framework which human reason imposes on the past (perhaps to explain or describe a development through time). So, poststructuralism and postmodernism would object, not only to a typical Western liberal attempt to account for the rise and glory of parliament, but also to the Marxist law of history. As Robert Young puts it, 'poststructuralism challenges not just the politics and institutions of the right but also the politics and theoretical systems of the left'.[6]

What we now need to do is to look at some of the major intellectuals associated with poststructuralism to expand upon our understanding of the movement.

Jacques Derrida and deconstruction

Deconstruction is a way of handling texts whereby we do far more than try to understand what the author is saying. In any case, Derrida (b.1930) argues that meaning is elusive. Language is full of signs which do not carry a single meaning: gaps, omissions and metaphors are just as important in establishing the various meanings there might be as the content is. The author is not in control of the language she or he uses because language does not operate on a series of rational rules. In fact, authors are absent from their texts. There can be no one true reading of any text. You might think that this is an interesting way of looking at a poem or a novel, but Derrida argues that the technique applies to all texts. After all, it must do, since there is nothing outside the text. It is simply a false assertion of Western philosophy that there is a measurable, comprehensible reality against which texts can be judged. Texts are just based on other texts ('intertextuality').

What Derrida is doing is applying deconstruction to the standard texts of Western philosophy from Plato on down. In doing so, he claims to uncover not the workings of cool, calm reason and logic, but *rhetoric*: argument using the techniques of persuasion, like imagery and dominant metaphors, to convince the reader of a 'truth' which is no truth. Derrida also claims to identify within Western philosophical texts the reprehensible traits of ethnocentrism (belief in the superiority of one's own race) and colonialism – an argument fuelled to some extent by his experience as an Algerian Jew under French colonial rule.

Sidney Monas provides a useful summing-up of Derrida's main contribution to poststructuralism:

> **Post-structuralism ... pushed the idea of linguistic autonomy to radical and extreme conclusions ...**
>
> **Authorial intent was not a presence in the text, but an absence. The language of the text became a free play of signifiers, and the game they played was with each other, not with any putative 'objective world'. Derrida accompanied his campaign of textual liberation with a radical skepticism of the metaphysical assumptions of western philosophy.**[7]

Michel Foucault and power/knowledge

Derrida had professed himself to be wary of history as a discipline and has little to say about it directly, although it was, in his view, subject to the same constraints of textuality as any other form of study. The French philosopher Foucault (1926–84) shared Derrida's poststructuralism, but wrote some works which are clearly historical in theme, including *Madness and Civilization* (1961); *The Birth of the Clinic: An Archaeology of Medical Perception* (1963) and *Discipline and Punish* (1977).

Whilst Foucault accepted that language was not the communicator of reality, his main focus was how it communicated *power*. Power works through language by presenting a certain type of knowledge as if it were reality or truth. Let us take the way traditional historians claim that what makes sound historical writing is objectivity, achieved through the calm application of reason and training in the historian's craft at university level. Texts which do not match that particular model are attacked by them as unacceptable and the bearers of knowledge which is 'untrue'. So, upholding a particular system of knowledge is a tool for upholding power.

Foucault's *The Birth of the Clinic* is an attack on the standard assumptions made in the study of the history of medicine: namely, that modern medicine has thankfully triumphed over the alleged superstition and wild speculation of the irrational past. Modern medicine is, in this way, the heir to the objective, rational and progressive spirit of the Enlightenment. This rational system of knowledge (Foucault uses the word *episteme* for 'system of knowledge') is imposed by creating new categories of sickness, deviance or madness. Those who threaten to undermine the *episteme* are labelled as sick, deviant or mad and rendered powerless. What better method of tackling your opponents than having them categorized as mad? In *Discipline and Punish*, Foucault starts with a revolting contemporary account of the execution of a regicide and follows it with details of a prisoner's daily schedule. We are being invited to examine both *discourses* (sets of statements implying particular versions of 'truth') to identify how power is revealed through the language. It is vital to understand that Foucault argues that power is not the product of government institutions, state control mechanisms or even individuals. It is spread throughout society, and has its home in language.

It should be clear from what has been said so far that it is typical of postmodernism/poststructuralism to see truth as relative – in other words, depending on different needs, different power relationships and different perspectives, rather than being absolute, eternal and timeless. Many of Foucault's main concerns are summed up in the following passages:

> ... truth isn't outside power ... Each society has ... its régime of truth, its 'general politics' of truth: that is, the types of discourse which it accepts

and makes function as true; the mechanisms and instances which enable me to distinguish true and false statements, the means by which each is sanctioned ... by truth I do not mean 'the ensemble of truths which are to be discovered and accepted', but rather 'the ensemble of rules according to which the true and the false are separated and specific effects of power attached to the true' ... 'Truth' is linked in a circular relation with systems of power which produce and sustain it ...'[8]

I am well aware that I have never written anything but fictions.[9]

Hayden White

The American theorist and historiographer Hayden White shares standard postmodernist assumptions about the impossibility of recovering and presenting historical 'truth' and a corresponding attitude towards so-called historical objectivity. His work is more focused on the nature of historical writing than is that of Derrida and Foucault, and has therefore been the subject of particular controversy amongst historians.[10]

Georg Iggers offers a convenient summing-up of White's perspective:

a historical text is in essence nothing more than a literary text, a poetical creation as deeply involved in the imagination as the novel.[11]

White's book *Metahistory* (1973) offers an explanation of how he believes the historian puts a text together. His basic theory is that the content of the historian's work is as much invention as it is fact. White accepts that some of the raw material – the traces or original sources – may provide factual material, but such traces never provide a structure for these facts: only when the facts are given a structure by the historian do they make sense. So, there is a need for narrative – for story – to shape these traces and facts, and this is where the historian comes in. This shaping takes place firstly through the type of figurative language to be used (like irony, if the historian is disapproving). Then, he imposes on the traces of the past the type of argument which suits him (maybe Marxist style, for example). The argument is generally linked with what White calls *emplotment* – the kind of story being told: romance, tragedy, comedy or satire. These four types of story are supposedly innate to the Western literary culture with which we are all familiar, and therefore help the story/history to make sense to the reader.

There seems to me, at least, to be a somewhat different emphasis here when one compares White to Derrida. To White, the author appears to be much more present in the text than in Derrida's deconstruction. Never-theless, both clearly share the view that the past is not recoverable beyond the text, and that the text does not recover it anyway. There is no reality beyond the text to which one can appeal. As Patrick Joyce enthusiastically puts it:

> **The major advance of 'post-modernism' needs to be registered by histor-ians: namely that the events, structures and processes of the past are indistinguishable from the forms of documentary representation ... and the historical discourses that construct them.**[12]

A critique of postmodernism

It is all very well to describe the main ideas of some of the major postmod-ernist thinkers, but evaluation is a different matter. The central issue is: what impact does postmodernism have on history as a discipline, and is that impact to be welcomed?

A History and facts

There are a number of possible lines of attack on the postmodernist con-tention that the idea of the objective historian writing about the real past – and doing so in a way which is 'truthful' – is a modernist myth.

Firstly, we need to look at the view that the writings of historians are based on 'facts' or 'events'. Disagreement about this issue predates the con-tribution of postmodernism and forms a significant part of the so-called Carr-Elton debate: a controversy which most historians feel should have decomposed long ago, but which they then proceed to jolt back into life by discussing it in detail. I intend to do exactly the same. E.H. Carr's *What is History?* (first edition, 1961) took what at first sight seems like a near-post-modernist view of the relationship between history, the historian and the facts. Quite simply, Carr argued that written history is not governed and shaped by historical facts, but by the historian:

> **It used to be said that facts speak for themselves. This is, of course, untrue. The facts speak only when the historian calls on them: it is he who decides to which facts to give the floor, and in what order or context.**[15]

So, one must study the historian – his background, education, attitudes – before one can study his interaction with the facts. Carr expanded upon this point by offering a definition of historical fact. When a fact from the past is included in an historical work, it is then subjected to the scrutiny of other historians. If it is widely accepted, then – and only then – does it become an historical fact. The point is that, as soon as the historian decides to pull it out from the mere facts of the past and converts it into an historical fact, it is inevitably part of an interpretation the historian imposes on the past. Carr put it this way:

> **Its status as a historical fact will turn on a question of interpretation. This element of interpretation enters into every fact of history.**[14]

In *The Practice of History* (1969), the conservative historian G.R. Elton responded to this view by denying the interpretative element in historical facts. If, he said, an event can be known, then

> **that is all that is required to make it a 'fact of history'. Interpretation, or general acceptance of a thesis, has nothing whatsoever to do with its independent existence. The point matters so much because Mr Carr, and others who like him think that history is what historians write, not what happened, come dangerously close to suggesting either that it does not much matter what one says because (interpretation being every-thing) there are always several reasonably convincing interpretations of any given set of events, or that history is altogether unknowable, being merely what happens to be said by a given historian at a given moment.**[15]

Elton was not simply saying that the historian's role is to collect and present historical facts, although he did argue that there is a very large body of what he called 'agreed historical knowledge' on which the historian can work. But in many cases, he said, the evidence itself is not clear-cut, or there may be the need to select. Clearly the historian intervenes here, but Elton denied that the historical facts are therefore so distorted that one must accept Carr's view that studying the historian is a necessary preliminary to histor-ical inquiry. Quite simply, Elton argued that the 'cure' for the inevitable dif-ficulties of the historian over the partial nature of evidence and the allegation of subjectivity lie in the proper practice of scholarship and research.

So, Elton responded to the Carr challenge with two arguments:

1 that the methods of a trained, professional historian guard as effectively as possible against the distortions that some see as separating truth from history;

2 that the Carr approach denies the reality of historical knowledge, and therefore represents, at heart, a dangerous relativism. Relativism is to

deny that meaningful truth can be found: there are numbers of possible views, but none is demonstrably the 'right' one.

I have spent some time over a debate which some would see as rather out of date. But this is justified because many students are still presented with Carr and Elton as if they are the last word in the debate on the definition and meaning of history. This they are not, but their insights are still very much a part of the debate. As we shall see, Elton's argument – based on the skills and techniques of the historical profession – is often used to combat the claims of the postmodernists themselves.

One final point on Carr v. Elton. I suggested earlier that there were clear similarities between Carr's standpoint and that of the postmodernists. However, there is one crucial difference. Despite what he had to say about historical facts, Carr was not prepared to jettison the possibility of the historian's objectivity. Instead, he came up with a very curious argument. It seems that the objective historian is one who has the right understanding of the pattern of development of history, which includes an awareness of the likely shape of the future. This really is grim. Many would agree with John Tosh that:

> **Nothing is likely to be so subjective and value-laden as the projection of historical trends into the future, and Carr's attempt to do so with authority seems self-confident to the point of arrogance.**[16]

Quite. But what I think is happening is not so much arrogance as a rather desperate attempt to handle the danger of relativism. Carr did not want to live with the full implications of his stance on the unknowability of history as transmitted by the inevitably subjective historian, since this would mean that many interpretations of history would have equal validity. Hence his curious, rather Marxist suggestion that the future can be predicted. All one has to do is to apply Carr's own principle of 'study the historian' to see what motivated him: a belief that history did progress, and that the embodiment of progress was Soviet Russia.

The link between a denial of the possibility of historical objectivity/accuracy and relativism is one we shall need to bear in mind. For the moment, I would like to pick up on Elton's argument about the way in which the professional skills and training of the historian offer a method of recovering something close to historical truth.

B The historian as professional

In his Cook lectures of 1990 (published in 1991 as *Return to Essentials*), Elton used the model of the historian as professional-at-work against the postmodernists. He dismissed the postmodernist view of the essentially fictional nature of the historian's work by identifying the appropriate professional tools which the well-trained practitioner must use. Firstly, one must assume that the sources, traces, original documents, relics and so on do contain the truth: historians are bound by the authority of these sources. Secondly, one must approach the sources with a question in mind, but never seek a particular answer to it or distort the sources because, with the advantage of hindsight, one inevitably knows what happened next. In short, study the past on its own terms. Elton was not saying that, in an imperfect world, the historian can ever be completely objective. But he can guard himself against the dangers of reading into the past his own value-systems. Postmodernism, of course, argues that what the historian produces is inevitably present-minded (intentionally or not). Elton responded with some asperity and elegance:

> **For the historian is in the first place concerned with the people of the past – with their experiences, thoughts and actions – and not with the people of the present, least of all with himself.**[17]

What emerges from the historian's efforts will not be perfect truth, but it will have the strong flavour of it.

The stance of Arthur Marwick is very similar. In his introductory textbook *The Nature of History* (third edition, 1989), he provides a numbered list of questions the professional historian asks (instinctively or otherwise) of the primary sources, ranging from the probing of authenticity to the establishing of provenance (where the source comes from), and the viewpoint of the author. His vitriolic contribution to Kozicki's *Developments in Modern Historiography* (1993) includes a similar focus on the historian's technique. Marwick attacks the postmodernist stance of Anthony Easthope, who argues that no one can claim a knowledge of reality since that reality – and one's responses to it – are the creation of discourse. Marwick responds by asserting that reality does exist in the primary sources, and draws a significant distinction between primary and secondary sources:

> **History's critics need to appreciate that there *is* a crucial distinction between *primary* sources ... and *secondary* sources, the history which historians produce through the systematic, disciplined, study of the primary sources.**[18]

In his 1995 article for the *Journal of Contemporary History*, Marwick makes the same point about the distinction between primary and secondary sources. The explanation of why the distinction is so significant is, frankly, limited. When Marwick says of primary and secondary sources 'They are different, that is all',[19] we suspect that not a great deal is to be explained. One important issue is, however, mentioned. Marwick rightly points out that there is a danger of defining 'facts' in a narrow and mechanistic way. Historians are not just interested in events, but in states of mind, value-systems, motives.

I think we can agree with that. But have Marwick and Elton succeeded in convincing us that they are justified in their rejection of postmodernist approaches to facts, sources and the partly-recapturable reality of history? Frankly, not really. The main problem is that, when you compare them to, say, Foucault or White, they seem to be talking about different things. Essentially, the Marwick/Elton approach is technical and profession-based: their frequent complaint is that their opponents do not know what they are talking about because they are not true, practising historians. But White and company are talking about history, not as a craft or set of specific techniques, but in terms of epistemology: in other words, looking at history as a theory of knowledge and analysing its claims to provide true knowledge about the past. The Marwick/Elton critique simply whizzes over the head of its target, because it never really gets to grips with the main points of the postmodernist arguments. This is very clear when we look at Hayden White's response to Marwick's article.

White points out that he is perfectly happy to accept that events have a reality. What he is disputing is that 'facts' (which he clearly separates from 'events') are anything but a construction – either in the documents or in historians' texts. They are, he argues, 'linguistic entities' which are inevitably subject to change as our attitudes to what constitutes a 'fact' change. So, he is presumably denying that anything mentioned by an historian beyond the straightforward event and its date can be seen as 'true'. And some of those influenced by postmodernism seem unwilling to allow the possibility of knowing any past reality whatsoever.[20]

In summary, neither Elton nor Marwick have succeeded in attacking the fundamental postmodernist concepts of history as text, historical text as fiction and/or text as an expression of power. Their approach has been rather like launching a philosophical inquiry into the nature of war by explaining how one should handle weapons.

C Other objections to postmodernist approaches

So – is it possible to respond to postmodernist claims without resorting to a rather irrelevant list of the historian's techniques? I believe that it is, and on a number of levels. First of all, we need to look at the issue of the relationship between text and reality. In postmodernist terms, language creates reality: there is no distinction between historical writing and fiction. Perhaps so: but the argument depends upon the acceptance of a linguistic theory (initially, that of Saussure) which is not necessarily true and which is by no means universally accepted as such by linguists themselves. Secondly, there is a logical problem – a contradiction – in Derridean deconstruction. Remember that Derrida proclaims the undiscoverability of a single, 'true' meaning in text and denies the author's control over it. Derrida, we recall, accompanies deconstruction with an attack on the use of reason in Western philosophy. Yet, he uses reason and logic to denounce reason and logic. This hardly seems reasonable, logical or fair. Also, deconstruction rejects the standard historical technique of contextualizing a source: in other words, Derrida denies that there is any point in looking at the social, economic, political, ideological and personal background in order to understand the author's meaning. But is this really acceptable? Suppose one were studying one of the notorious anti-Semitic passages from Hitler's *Mein Kampf.* Deconstruction would have us locate the gaps, silences, metaphors and secrets within the text, but would deny that it reflects the author's meaning. It would also deny us the opportunity to help explain the text by reference to prevalent anti-Semitic ideas or Hitler's experiences in Vienna. Surely we would agree with Joyce Appleby that words are not arbitrary in origin, but result from contact with the world. And, as Richard Evans points out, words in a text 'are not, contrary to what the postmodernists suggest, capable of an infinity of meaning'.[21] In any case, just because one can detect within a text the silences, gaps and metaphors it does not mean that there is nothing else there. To say that some of an historian's work has a fictional element to it is not to deny that reasoned explanation is also there. To do so would be throwing out the baby with the bathwater.

One scholar who has gained much from postmodernism is Edward Said, but he is now keen to stress that postmodern theorists have been too squeamish about relating their findings to the world outside the text. Said's interest is in cultural imperialism, and he is concerned that some postmodernists tend to ignore the very real effect on discourse of the actual workings of imperial governments themselves. In *The World, the Text and the Critic,* Said comments:

> **My position is that texts are worldly, to some degree they are events, and, even when they appear to deny it, they are nevertheless a part of the social world, human life ... The realities of power and authority – as well as the resistances offered [to them] ... are the realities that make texts possible ...[22]**

The difficulty of separating the world from the text is clear enough when we look at Derrida's own work. In commenting on Freud's *Beyond the Pleasure Principle*, Derrida provides a biographical and psychological profile of the great psychoanalyst himself.

There are other serious objections to postmodernism. The first is that it is far too keen to see Western philosophy as all of one type. But, even at the time of the Enlightenment, there were philosophers like Rousseau whose work was anything but a hymn of praise to the Goddess Reason (see pp.90–1). Secondly, one could argue that the postmodernists themselves represent not so much a rejection of the Western philosophical tradition as a recent manifestation of a trend within it. The Greek sophists, for example, were sceptical about the possibility of discovering truth and were fond of emphasizing the existence of multiple viewpoints on any one issue. It all sounds very familiar.

Perhaps the most serious objection to postmodernism concerns its relativism. The denial that the writing of historians contains an objective reality – or that there is an objective reality one can communicate through language and which can be used to assess the quality of an historian's work – means that there is no way of judging such work as 'true' or 'untrue'. Some enthusiasts see this as a positive good. Keith Jenkins feels that those who complain about the absence of criteria of judgement are afraid of losing their élitist positions as arbiters of what 'correct' history is. According to him, the collapse of the old metanarratives and modernist certainties is liberating. Postmodernism will encourage the spread of many-voiced history, as people of all types write local, regional, and national histories – whatever, in fact, meets their needs. If it does meet their needs, all well and good. The only thing they cannot do is to claim it as 'true'.

I find this approach deeply worrying. First of all, it seems to me to be as much a reflection of free-market Western capitalism – go out and buy yourself a history – as it is a reflection of a theory of epistemology. Secondly, a small practical point. If there is no widely-held standard of good history, then how does Jenkins set and mark the essays of his students? By reference to their needs? Or to the needs of an examination system, which remains wedded to the idea of objective history? The third point is by far the most important. Denial of a 'true' history plays into the hands of those who have a vested interest in a denial of their own – namely, that the Holocaust actually happened. What postmodernism does is to accept the right of neo-Nazis and other so-called 'revisionists' to claim that the genocide of six million Jews never took place, and at the same time sabotages the right of those who oppose them to appeal to the 'truth'. Postmodernism would have us believe that countless eyewitness reports, the sufferings of survivors, the testimonies of death-camp guards and commandants, the evidence from film and the writings of historians which make use of them all are not enough to constitute the truth. This is not a train I personally care to ride, and I can only advise those who have enjoyed the postmodernist trip so far to get off now.

Richard Evans, I think, puts it well. Auschwitz, he says, is not a discourse: nor were the gas chambers a piece of rhetoric. In short, it 'trivializes mass murder to see it as a text'.[23] To his credit, White had attempted to respond to this kind of criticism in his 'Historical Emplotment and the Problem of Truth'. Evans argues that White has conceded that the real facts of the Holocaust will preclude it being described through some types of emplotment. Presenting it as a comedy would be unacceptable. He may be right, although I am not sure that White is being so clear-cut as this. White seems to argue that comedy would be acceptable if it were 'set forth in a pointedly ironic way'.[24] Alex Callinicos sees White's twists and turns in this essay as a 'hopeless muddle',[25] and I have sympathy with this view. White's position is an unenviable one, and it is doubtful whether the postmodern theorists rise to the challenge of coping with the horrors of Nazism and the Final Solution.

The moral dangers of White's relativism and the issue of Nazism are barely touched on in Jenkins. In one reference, he comments that:

> **It seems to me that whether we like it or not the kind of relativism which White articulates is a fact of life.[26]**

Well, I do not like it, and it does not seem to me to be a fact of life (whatever that means). Jenkins' curious certainties about uncertainty are hardly a substitute for argument, although they are very much part of his rhetoric. He tells us that we live in a postmodern world, we have no widely-held systems of belief or 'centres' anymore – really? Is this actually the case, or are we simply paying the price for the perverse universe Jenkins seems to inhabit?

We should conclude our critique by summarizing the impact postmodernist approaches have had on the writing of history. Whatever our stance on postmodernism, it has to be said that there are few thorough-going postmodernist works of history (as opposed to theory) on which to base comments. We can, perhaps, take Foucault as an example. But on what grounds does one evaluate his historical writing? In terms of traditional history, with its demands for proof, analysis of cause and effect, Foucault's work is a nonstarter. Simon Schama's *Dead Certainties* – set in the time of General Wolfe and in nineteenth-century America – similarly eschews the scholarly apparatus of a modern history text. His book lacks index and references and offers only the briefest of comments on sources. Instead, Schama employs the devices of fiction. The unsuspecting reader is confronted by interior monologues from historical characters, dramatic shifts in narrative style and superb building-up of tension as the details of a murder are revealed. It would be churlish to deny that the book is enjoyable, despite – rather than because of – its occasionally ironic and playful tone (as in the subtitle *Unwarranted Speculations* and equally unwarranted reference in the text to Foucault). It could be argued that it challenges the reader to consider the extent to which a traditional history book is justified in claiming to offer fact rather than fiction: on the other hand, I suspect that the reader of *Dead Certainties* is left to ponder whether the book's own classification as 'non-fiction' is justified.[27]

Postmodernism, then, is certainly no friend of traditional narrative history: event-centred, cause-and-effect, telling-the-story history. It is antagonistic, we recall, to the metanarrative, which can be seen as any history which offers an explanation of development through a wide sweep of time. And, of course, any form of narrative history is open to the inevitable challenge that it is fiction masquerading as fact. So, given the relative lack of examples of postmodern works of history, what kind of history will our postmodern historian in the future provide? This issue is tackled by Jenkins, in a chapter entitled 'Doing history in the post-modern world'. Sadly, he devotes very little space to the actual form it might take, but comes up with the following:

> **If the present can best be understood as post-modern ... then this suggests to me that the content of a preferred history should be studies of this phenomenon ... In the post-modern world, then, arguably the content and context of history should be a generous series of methodologically reflexive studies of the makings of the histories of postmodernity itself.**[28]

This means (I think) that we have before us the prospect of writing postmodern histories about postmodern histories. Not unduly enticing, perhaps. Unbelievably limiting, most certainly. The main problem with this is that it ignores completely what may well be the basic human need for historical explanation. It is an old argument (but a good one) to claim that history – particularly historical narrative – offers us the chance to locate ourselves through a sense of shared local and national identity. Historical narrative offers us a necessary help with understanding our political, economic, cultural and social present which 'methodologically reflexive studies of the makings of the histories of post-modernity itself' may not do so well (if at all). I very much like Appleby's conclusion on this point:

> **The move toward the most radically skeptical and relativist postmodern position inevitably leads us into a cul-de-sac. Dismissals of history, politics, and narrative as hopelessly modern ideas, now outmoded in the postmodern world, might seem up-to-date, but history, politics, and narrative are still the best tools available for dealing with the world and preparing for the future.**[29]

D   Politics and postmodernism

One charge against postmodernism is that it discourages political involvement and action. After all, it rejects all-embracing political theories like
Marxism as hopelessly modernist. And it cultivates a liberal, rather ironic
and perhaps mocking stance which is good at deconstruction but no help in
construction. Foucault's view of power as all-pervasive in effect makes political action difficult to contemplate because there is no obvious target for it.
If power was simply embodied in the state, or in one class, then one would
have something tangible to fight against.

Some feminist historians have criticized postmodernist/poststructuralist
approaches to language on the grounds that they block political action. They
do so by short-circuiting the writing of women's (or gender) history, which
has often been written as a political statement to stimulate opposition. After
all, it is a familiar tenet of postmodernism that power relationships are
embedded within the language and so cannot be destroyed by political
means. In any case, the words 'men' and 'women' are not to be taken as
indicating some outward, fixed reality. If feminist historians talk about
'women's experience' in history, then they are operating outside the text
and to no effect. Change has to take place at the level of language or not at
all – but it is not clear how this is to happen or what, if anything, can be
done to encourage it. Also, postmodernist history will encourage the writing
of many and varied histories: it is possible that women's history would
simply dissolve in a multiplicity of competing histories. These issues are
summarized by Joan Scott,[30] who is keen to use the insights of poststruc-
turalism/postmodernism in the service of women's history. However, it has
to be said that she fails to make it clear how the problems would be
resolved.

E   Postmodernism and time

I am afraid that I can make little sense of postmodernist perspectives on
historical time. Some theorists have argued that linear time is not a reflection of reality as such. Instead, linear time is an intellectual construct which
serves the needs of Western industrial civilization with its factory, office and
railway clocks. Were this to be true, then writing a narrative history would
be an imposture based on a fallacy, since the historian's standard discussion
of causes rests upon a sequence in time. But there is a very basic flaw in this
argument. Surely the whole concept of postmodernism itself rests on linear
time? It is itself an intellectual construct which of necessity follows the intellectual construct called modernism. It can hardly precede it. In any case,
criticism of historians for reliance on a sequence of events in time reflects
an ignorance of the variety of ways in which historians offer explanations.

In Chapter 4 is a discussion of the *Annales* school of historians, who, following the work of Braudel, have often employed a temporal model which envisages changes taking place over long, medium and short-term periods. In any case, few historians offer fundamentally chronological explanations. Every student of history knows that an essay should be thematic and not a chronological narrative.[51]

Positive postmodernism

So far, I have described the main ideas of postmodernism and postmodernists. I then pointed out what seemed to me to be the defects in postmodernist approaches to history. But I want to emphasize that, if we avoid some of the more extreme and relativistic stances, postmodernism is a healthy blast of air in the dustier environs of history. In this section, I shall concentrate on some of the more useful aspects.

A Texts and postmodernism

Although I did not accept the full rigours of the postmodernist position on textuality, this is not to dismiss the value of its insights. If we interrogate a text in a Derridean manner, then our understanding of it is significantly increased. The images chosen, the evasions dictated by social taboos, the unwitting as well as the intentional content – all these provide the historian (particularly the cultural historian, perhaps) with useful insights. If we stop short of denying that the author and reader have any control over meaning, then there is much here to be gained. Saying that, of course, is one thing – what we need are examples. I have chosen two very different works to illustrate the positive appeal of postmodernist strategies.

Firstly, I am going to look at a work edited by Averil Cameron which deals with the value of postmodernist strategies in ancient history: *History as Text: The Writing of Ancient History*. Significantly, Cameron comments that, generally, ancient historians have operated on the lines of Elton in fighting shy of postmodernism. Nevertheless, there are, it appears, things to be learned from a postmodernist approach to textuality. In her chapter 'Virginity as Metaphor: women and the rhetoric of early Christianity', Cameron explains the difficulty of trying to recapture women's experience from the early Christian texts. Close analysis of the texts shows that what we see is not only a male rhetoric presenting women as dangerous through their sexuality; we also see that the male writer's language is aimed at exerting power and control. The male-dominated Church needed discipline, authority and social respectability to survive, and so its rhetoric attacked what it saw as those who were potentially dangerous to its uniformity – and that included women. Cameron, in analysing the literary/rhetorical devices of the texts, is going beyond, not only the standard extracting of information and inference from the source, but also the traditional method of putting it into the context of contemporary theological ideas. Her method is clearly fruitful. She is able to identify the rhetoric within a well-known text on the early woman saint Perpetua which turns her into an 'honorary man ... while at the same time continuing to observe the boundaries placed on female behaviour by men.'[52] Historians treating the apparently simple and straightforward account of Perpetua's martyrdom as essentially factual (and approving of women) are therefore in danger, not only of being misled, but also of missing the way in which the text imposes power and control.

Cameron is not accepting the full weight of Derridean deconstruction here. In her Postlude, she is clearly concerned that history must not be seen only as a mode of rhetoric – a fictional text. There are, she argues, tried and tested methods of checking the truth of historical narratives, and that truth is not the 'truth' as presented in a novel. In any case, Cameron's work includes the kind of contextualizing that postmodernists would dismiss.

B Edward Said and 'orientalism'

My second example is from the work of Edward Said. Said's *Orientalism*, as suggested earlier, owes much to Foucault's power/knowledge concept. Said is looking at the links between Western theories of imperialism and the way imperialism operated in practice. The West has claimed to know what the true Orient is (and what the true Oriental is like), but this 'knowledge' simply meets the needs of power and control: it justifies colonialism. The Western imperialist claims to know the Oriental better than the latter knows himself, and can see in him an irrationality, a childishness, an untrustworthiness which need to be channelled (in his own interest, of course) by the rational, adult, trustworthy Westerner. Said opens his book with a discussion of a speech made by the former British Prime Minister A.J. Balfour to the House of Commons in 1910. Balfour is replying to a complaint from an MP about the British government's involvement in Egypt and its tone of superiority in talking about the Orient in general. Balfour replies:

> I take up no attitude of superiority. But I ask [anyone] ... who has even the most superficial knowledge of history, if they will look in the face the facts with which a British statesman has to deal when he is put in a position of supremacy over great races like the inhabitants of Egypt and countries in the East. We know the civilization of Egypt better than we know the civilization of any other country. We know it further back; we know it more intimately; we know more about it ... Western nations as

soon as they emerge into history show the beginnings of those capacities for self-government ... You may look through the whole history of the Orientals ... and you never find traces of self-government ... Is it a good thing for these great nations – I admit their greatness – that this absolute government should be exercised by us? I think it is a good thing. I think that experience shows that they have got under it far better government than in the whole history of the world they ever had before ...[33]

Said points to the obvious link being made by Balfour between knowledge of the Orient and power over it. Said is not saying anything as simplistic as 'Politicians came up with orientalism in order to justify their colonialism', because orientalism – the belief in the 'otherness' of the Orient – predated colonial and imperial expansion. In any case, as with Foucault, he is arguing that the power relationship is imbedded in language itself, and language is not the prisoner of statesmen.

It is at this point, however, that we hit a problem. Said has to admit that all knowledge, including his own academic knowledge, is distorted by this power relationship between the West and the Orient. As we saw earlier, this, in theory, makes it difficult to use the full weight of Foucault's ideas in any attempt to create political change. In 'Orientalism Reconsidered', Said admits that he has not resolved the problem of how 'knowledge that is non-dominative and non-coercive can be produced in a setting that is deeply inscribed with the politics, the considerations, the positions, and the strategies of power'.[34] In short, how can his texts, which are bound to reflect the power relationships in his own society, somehow step outside those power relationships to subvert them? As Robert Young points out, Said tries to fight against orientalism by appealing to what he calls the 'human spirit'.[35] And what is this spirit? It turns out to be little more than the best elements of the very Western culture which contains and transmits orientalism – writers like Thomas Hardy or James Joyce – who supposedly possess the ability to resist power and oppression. In arguing in this way, Said has to reject Foucault's dismissal of the importance of the effect of individuals on history.

All criticisms taken into account, *Orientalism* is a superb book: lucid, wide-ranging, immensely thought-provoking. Its use of postmodernist approaches to textuality and power/knowledge reveals the dominant colonial discourse in operation. It also exposes some of the weaknesses in postmodernism, including the failure to take account of individual impact on history and an absence of any method of encouraging change in existing power relationships. We also recall that Said, in *The World, the Text and the Critic*, was keen to emphasize that texts were a part of their social and political world and should not be deconstructed in a manner ignoring their context.

Postmodernism and the historian's objectivity

As we approach the end of the chapter, I want to look at a question which is often raised in discussions on the nature of history: how far can historians be objective? Seeking answers to this question will also provide a useful reminder of many postmodernist arguments.

In postmodernist terms, the notion of the objective historian is a) a joke and b) just the product of a modernist way of thinking. Objectivity is supposedly impossible for a number of reasons. Firstly, it presupposes that the truth about the past is recoverable. The postmodernist response is that it is not, since we are all prisoners of the fluidity of language, and we have no other way of recapturing the past save through language. Meaning is not fixed: neither we nor the authors of the texts we study are able to control meaning. Secondly, objectivity is a modernist claim which might have suited the old certainties of Western liberalism and Marxism, but is now totally outmoded (and exposed as such) in our postmodern era. Thirdly, those who claim objectivity also often claim to be letting the past speak for itself. This is rubbish. History is never neutral – it is always for someone.

Against this, we recall, Elton and Marwick set out the specific professional skills of the historian, which, in their view, effectively sift the truth and guard against his inevitable prejudices and biases. I use the word 'inevitable' advisedly, because not even Elton would argue that the historian can exclude himself totally from the sources and his work on them. But, he goes on to say, this involvement is not dominance: '... it does not mean ... that he cannot escape from his prejudices and preconceptions'.[36]

Now, I had cause to criticize both Elton and Marwick for failing to answer the philosophical arguments of the postmodernists. I then suggested that there were serious objections to postmodernist assumptions about the unknowability of the past and the lack of meaning in language. But I also suggested that historians had much to gain from postmodern insights and techniques on textuality so long as they did not accept that the author is absent. Postmodernism, in fact, helps us to identify in a sophisticated way the rhetoric in all texts, including our own. We must be prepared to accept – much more than Elton would – that the historian employs many of the devices of fiction, and be aware of it. We must be prepared to accept – much more than Elton would – that our language is often dominated by power, and that the way we discuss things may well reflect the dominant discourse and the particular type of knowledge that is accepted as 'true'.

Of course, one might argue that this is all very well for assessing the writing of historians – the secondary sources. But a good historian is going to work with – perhaps base his work on – the primary evidence (or traces),

and so all the dire warnings about textuality do not apply. But this argument (resting as it does on a Marwick-style separation of primary and secondary sources) seems quite wrong. After all, texts of all types are distorted in just the same way as the historian's own writing. However, we should be aware that historians, however traditional and dismissive of postmodernism, frequently treat their sources in a way which is not dissimilar to deconstruction. Very often, the value of a source rests in the unwitting testimony – the value-systems, the assumptions about social class or family life – that its author never bothers articulating because they are taken for granted. Historians are adept at looking for this kind of thing, and I can see no reason to argue that their efforts are going to be sabotaged by the original text or their own biases, as long as they are aware of them.

Looking back over the last two paragraphs, I notice the number of times I used the word 'aware'. This, perhaps, is the key to the question of objectivity. After all, objectivity is less a personal quality or attribute than a product of the awareness of the difficulties of being objective. If one takes those difficulties into account, then something at least approaching objectivity becomes possible. So, the historian needs to be aware of the following issues.

1 The text the historians write will be subject to their own evasions, biases, silences, relationships to power and the type of knowledge legitimized by authority. Their rhetoric may distort their text. They may, for example, portray a fake objectivity by resolutely refusing to use the word 'I'.

2 The so-called primary sources will be subject to some or all of the same distortions as the secondary sources.

3 The past may be recreated only in the mind of the historian, but its shape cannot and should not be the product of that mind. The historian, in short, has the capacity to recognize when he is shaping the past for his own purposes – largely because the traces of the past genuinely reflect its reality and its 'otherness'. Accept this, and one can guard against the distorting of the past.

4 The historian must approach the past with questions, but also be aware of the danger of dictating the answers the past gives. Against this, it is sometimes argued that the sources are mute, and what they appear to articulate is only what the historian wants them to say. This is a superficially attractive argument, but one which totally misinterprets the process of source evaluation. This is best seen as a dialogue, where the historian approaches the source with his question (which is probably part of an hypothesis). That hypothesis is measured against the evidence provided by the sources (their reply) and tentatively confirmed, modified or rejected in the light of that answer – and so the process continues. I like

E.P. Thompson's discussion of this approach, which rests on what he calls 'historical logic':

> By 'historical logic' I mean a logical method of enquiry appropriate to historical materials, designed as far as possible to test hypotheses as to structure, causation, etc., and to eliminate self-confirming procedures ('instances', 'illustrations'). The disciplined historical discourse of the proof consists in a dialogue between concept and evidence, a dialogue conducted by successive hypotheses, on the one hand, and empirical research on the other. The interrogator is historical logic ... the respondent is the evidence, with its determinate properties.[37]

Thompson's last sentence is particularly important: note his point that the evidence, in the end, determines the outcome of the dialogue. Of course, one might then argue that a further dialogue takes place – between the historian and the reader. Some historians display an acute awareness of the value of such a dialogue and appear to have sufficient control of their texts to encourage the reader to join in the creative process (see the discussion on Gibbon, pp.100–1).

5 When the cry for objectivity is yoked to a demand that the 'sources be left to speak for themselves', it may simply reflect a conservative ideological position and therefore a fear of change. This is because it may in turn reflect a denial that the present can ever use the past to help solve its own problems, on the grounds that each age is unique and should simply be allowed to speak (see p.107).

6 Objectivity is not a plant one can cultivate alone. It is encouraged by the community of scholars, where research is the subject of contentious debate.

7 The scholarly apparatus of reference and bibliography should not be dismissed as pedantry. It provides the essential means for other scholars to verify one's interpretations. This is a useful discipline and acts as a warning against the temptation to distort the history to suit a pet thesis or preferred model of the past.

8 One needs to be aware, not only of the dangers of overstating the possibilities of objectivity, but also of the dangers of denying it completely. To dismiss objectivity as hopelessly old-fashioned and modernist is to put a foot on the slippery slope of relativism. It also leads to particularism: the denial that there are universal criteria (like objectivity) for what makes 'true' history. This clearly ties in with the postmodernist notion of history always being for somebody, although particularism often predated postmodernism and stems from political consciousness rather than postmodern epistemology. Peter Novick charts the impact of particularism on

American historians, where, from the 1960s onwards, many black historians insisted that it was possible to write the history of blacks only if one
had a 'black perspective' – in other words, history was written by blacks
(in all probability) for blacks. Objectivity was an irrelevance. The same
point applies to the growing interest in women's history. Novick quotes a
comment by Joan Scott, who

> expressed astonishment that a critic of *Women, Work, and Family*,
> which she had coauthored with Louise Tilly, could imagine that
> 'somehow Tilly and I believe we are writing ... objective history'.[38]

9 It is not a good idea to assume that objectivity and neutrality are the same
thing. I have suggested that objectivity is both a necessary goal and a
demanding intellectual construct which is essential to the development of
the historian's hypotheses. Neutrality would deny the historian the right
to make judgements based upon those hypotheses. I am not suggesting
that the historian has the right to indulge in cheap name-calling, but that
there are times when judgements are necessary. I hope I have been as
objective as possible in writing this chapter, but it would have been, I
think, unhelpful to have listed arguments for and against postmodernism
without expressing a personal judgement. A strictly neutral position
would have prevented me from making that judgement, and therefore
from offering an explanation. One should not forget that something
which is neuter is, of course, sterile.

Since awareness is all, I should make it clear that I am aware that my comments on the possibility of achieving something meaningful (if imperfect) in
terms of objectivity have ended up being similar to those of Elton and
Marwick (and the left-wing historian Thompson). The difference is that I
claim to have at least considered the epistemological attack of postmodernism in a more meaningful way than Elton and Marwick, and also to have
recognized its real merits. And I do not think I lost my temper in their
manner. The late Sir Geoffrey Elton was inimitable in this, as in many other
ways. He said:

> ... we [meaning 'real' historians] are fighting for the lives of innocent
> young people beset by devilish tempters [the postmodernists] who claim
> to offer higher forms of thought and deeper truths and insights – the
> intellectual equivalent of crack, in fact.[39]

If nothing else, Elton's words certainly justify that image of battle with
which I started the chapter.

Conclusion

In his book *Re-thinking History*, Keith Jenkins bravely offers a succinct definition of history at the end of his chapter 'What history is'. This is an excellent idea, and I make no bones about doing exactly the same thing. After I have offered my definition, you may care to read what Jenkins has to say from his enthusiastically postmodern perspective. Here is my definition:

> History does not exist in the present: it cannot be recreated for us to observe or experience. It exists largely through the writings of historians, who inevitably distort it to a greater or lesser degree. The distortion takes place for some or all of the following reasons.
>
> 1 The traces from the past are never complete.
>
> 2 The historian is likely to be influenced by his academic training, the prevailing systems of power and authority in his society, his political and religious beliefs, social class, and the pressures to publish work as a criterion for success.
>
> 3 All texts, including those used by the historian and those produced by the historian, are replete with a range of complexities stemming from the nature of language. These will include elements which are rhetorical/fictional, deliberate or unintentional omissions, and unwitting testimony.
>
> Nevertheless, the competent historian who is aware of these distortions can offer an account based on the traces and historians' interpretations to satisfy the very real need of his society for an explanation of the past which is grounded in reality, even if it cannot claim to communicate the absolute truth.

And here is Jenkins' version:

> **History is a shifting, problematic discourse, ostensibly about an aspect of the world, the past, that is produced by a group of present-minded workers (overwhelmingly in our culture salaried historians) who go about their work in mutually recognisable ways that are epistemologically, methodologically, ideologically and practically positioned and whose products, once in circulation, are subject to a series of uses and abuses that are logically infinite but which in actuality generally correspond to a range of power bases that exist at any given moment and which structure and distribute the meanings of histories along a dominant-marginal spectrum.**[40]

The war over the definition of history will most definitely rumble on, thank goodness. It is a healthy sign when those involved in studying history are obliged to think about the nature of their own discipline. It is a pity when positions are defended with bile. Although most of this chapter was written before the publishing of Richard Evans' excellent *In Defence of History*, I was able to make some use of it and was pleased so to do. But I did not care for the tone of some of his criticisms.[41] They are, however, a sign of how important these debates are to all those who care for history and the uses to which it can be put. We all have to raise our heads above the parapet some time.

From the Birth of Historiography to the Renaissance

ASSESSING HISTORIANS

One of the most objectionable things we could do to the past is to assume that those living in it were stupid. There is the temptation to do so, of course. People in the past knew so little about so much, and the age of the microchip makes us arrogant and dismissive. But we have already seen in Chapter 1 that to impose the assumptions of the present day on the past is profoundly unhistorical. And yet, we cannot cut ourselves off from the mentalities and world-views of our own society anymore than we can travel in time.

Assessing historians is therefore distinctly problematic. No assessment can take place without some criteria, and the criteria cannot be derived from a fount of objectivity which flows without heeding the demands of time and place. In other words, any criteria we choose are bound to reflect our own time and the kinds of things our own society (or influential aspects of it) deem to be significant. The criteria I have selected therefore reflect my own training in the style of history taught in British universities, my experience of teaching, my reading of various works which reflect the Western liberal culture in which I live, what I think I know about the requirements of various examining systems and my acceptance of the political structures of British society. And, of course, they reflect any idiosyncrasies or simple mistakes, lack of knowledge or sheer incompetence with which I might be afflicted.

Clearly, then, there are other possible criteria for assessing historians. I would argue that the criteria I have chosen at least allow us to do the best we can to assess the historian on his own terms. They also allow us to evaluate historians in a reasonably structured and thematic way, and this makes comparison between historians much more meaningful. And so, I have outlined below in question form the criteria I want to use.

A What type of history is being written?

Is it, for example, largely narrative and event-based? Or is it heavily analytical? Is it concerned with the structures of society, like its political systems? Does it concentrate on one particular theme, such as economic history? Does the historian subscribe to a particular theory of historical change? How important is human agency in shaping the past? What kind of people are the subject of history? Does it, for example, focus on élites or on ordinary people?

B What historical techniques are employed?

What type of sources are used? Does the historian use a wide range? How does he collect them? Are they examined objectively? Does the historian discuss the sources in any way? Are they mentioned in the text or as footnotes/references? Is the reader allowed to make up his or her own mind? Is the account balanced or clearly partisan? If the historian is discussing causes, does he concentrate on one type?

C Language and style?

How readable is the historian? Are we offered a simple clarity, or are the style and language more demanding of the reader? What readership does the historian target? Are the words and phrases chosen to arouse emotion in the reader? Is the historian trying to persuade? Is the tone neutral and calm, or perhaps sarcastic and angry? Is the historian striving for a literary effect? Is he entering into a dialogue with the reader, or simply lecturing?

D What does the historian see as the purpose of history?

Might the historian be seeking to use history as a practical guide with lessons for political or military leaders, or as a call to revolution? Does he see history as an end in itself – perhaps as a stimulus to imagination or intellect? Or does the writing of history meet the social and political needs of the ordinary citizen?

E What impact has the historian had on historiography?

Did the historian inspire others to adopt a similar approach? Did he, in fact, found a school of history? If so, what developments within that school can be identified? Or was he inimitable, or perhaps the stimulus for a reaction against his approaches?

From what has already been said, I am inevitably prepared to admit that some of the above criteria are value-judgements. They might be used to label historians as 'good' or 'bad'. There is the tendency, for example, to assume that objectivity is central to the work of a good historian. This proposition is familiar enough to Western liberals of the late twentieth century (whether they agree with it or not) but that does not mean it is true. An obsession with objectivity would certainly make little sense to a Roman writer of the classical period who was wanting to use history to teach certain moral and political lessons. His intention was to teach truth on his own terms, and we must recognize what those terms were. There is also the danger of sneering at historians who do not use what twentieth-century historians regard as appropriate scholarly apparatus. To do so would be ludicrous. It is possible to complain, say, about the Greek historian Herodotus because he failed to cite his sources in footnotes. This would be rather like criticizing Julius Caesar's military strategy because he failed to use cluster-bombs and tanks. One must therefore make every effort not to use the criteria mechanically, superficially or with a smart-alec sense of the effortless superiority of the modern mind. This is why we must be careful to put the historian in the context of his own time: the time of which he was, of course, a product.

In summary, then, I have identified a set of criteria with which one can compare historians. I have accepted that the criteria are open to criticism – particularly on the grounds that they simply reflect my own present-day values, which are in turn largely a product of my own society and its education system. But they do at least make what I believe to be the necessary attempt – however flawed it might be – to evaluate historians on their own terms. Whether the attempt works or not can be judged by the following sections, in which I use the five-fold criteria in discussing, amongst others, those writers who might be seen as the founders of the discipline we call history. But I want to emphasize that the criteria are going to be used selectively and adapted appropriately. It would be absurdly mechanistic to try to force what I want to say into five paragraphs for each historian. I also want to avoid a mere survey and description of lots of historians, few of whom could be discussed in any meaningful detail. This means that I can certainly be criticized for concentrating on European (and often British) historians. There are no discussions of Byzantine historians like Procopius or Anna

Comnena, of Islamic historians like Ibn Khaldun, or of Chinese historians like Liu Chih-chi. I regret this. But I should add that providing some essential background to each of these would make the chapter even more unmanageable than – perhaps – it already is.

Herodotus of Halicarnassus (c.484–c.430BC)

The political context

The Greek town of Halicarnassus – Herodotus' probable birthplace – lay just within the borders of the great Persian empire. Herodotus was keen to emphasize that he was Greek, but in using the word he was not referring to a unified country called Greece. What he meant by 'Greek' was a people with an identifiable and shared culture, language, religious systems and customs. A Greek nation-state simply did not exist. The typical political unit in Greece was the self-governing city-state (or *polis*). Despite their obvious cultural links, the city-states were usually wont to stress their differences. In political terms, some cities were ruled by kings, some by oligarchies ('rule of the few'), some by aristocracies ('rule of the best') and some took steps towards rule by the people ('democracy'). During the so-called Archaic period (from c.700 to 500BC), the two most powerful cities, Athens and Sparta, demonstrated this diversity clearly. Sparta was ruled by kings, and most of its population were serfs ('helots'). Those with the right to be citizens of Sparta were educated and trained as warriors. Athens had the vision to adopt political and legal reforms designed by Solon in the late sixth century BC, which centred on a constitution with some democratic elements – including the innovation of a People's Council, which at least gave the better-off farmers a voice in the city. This did not lead in any seamless way to full democracy: the general Peisistratos ruled as 'tyrant' (dictator) from 546–528BC. But his successors were overthrown in about 510 and, under Kleisthenes, the political role of ordinary freemen of the city increased substantially.

The Persian Wars (490–479BC)

Athens grew in wealth and military power, with a particularly strong fleet. She had the temerity to assist Greek cities in Asia Minor in a struggle to free themselves from Persian rule in the 490s. In 490, the Persian emperor Darius I launched an attack on Athens which was defeated on the plain of Marathon. Darius' son Xerxes invaded mainland Greece in 480. Despite a brave defence by the Spartan Leonidas at Thermopylae, the Greek army retreated towards the Peloponnese. Athens was abandoned, but the Athenian fleet won the most crucial of battles near Salamis. With his fleet crippled, Xerxes retreated and crossed back into Asia. In 479, the Persians were defeated (largely by the Spartans) on land at Plataea. Xerxes' great empire had not been able to overcome the Greek city-states when they were forced into unity.

The Peloponnesian War (431–404BC)
The Greek city-states had shown what could be done through cooperation, but the rivalry between Sparta and Athens was intensified by the obvious increase in the power of Athens. Sparta decided to launch a pre-emptive strike, and even formed an alliance with the Persians in the struggle. Athens was eventually defeated, but the Spartans decided not to destroy the city itself – as a token of her efforts in the Persian Wars.

A Herodotus and his *Histories*

> Herodotus of Halicarnassus, his *Researches* are here set down to preserve the memory of the past by putting on record the astonishing achievements both of our own and of other peoples; and more particularly, to show how they came into conflict.[1]

So starts the author of the work known to us as *Histories*, which was probably written some time during or possibly just after the Peloponnesian War. His introduction seems straightforward enough, and the temptation is to assume that it is going to be easy to classify Herodotus. We appear to have here some sort of military or diplomatic history with an appropriate analysis of causes (given the reference to 'how they came into conflict'). Perhaps historians in our day might be less open about wanting to celebrate 'astonishing achievements', but it seems reassuringly familiar.

It is certainly true that Herodotus was concerned with military conflict. In particular, he looked at the fraught relationships between the Greeks and non-Greeks (particularly the Persians) from the middle years of the sixth century. He started with Croesus of Lydia on the grounds that he was 'the first foreigner so far as we know to come into direct contact with the Greeks, both in the way of conquest and alliance'.[2] Herodotus then discussed the rise of the Persian empire under Cyrus (559–529BC) and concluded with the failure of that empire (under Xerxes) to successfully invade Greece (480–479BC).

So far, so good. But we must look at some of the problematic areas which might lead the unwary to tumble into the Slough of Anachronism. The first and most fundamental is to establish what Herodotus meant when he used the word 'histories'. In fact, we have already encountered his word *historie* (or *historia*, depending on the dialect), and seen it translated as 'researches'. 'Enquiries' would be a sound alternative. The word is unlikely to have been invented by him. Its original usage by no means implied 'research into the past'. It could be used of any form of intellectual inquiry. *Histor* (the adjective) carried the meaning of 'knowledgeable', 'good judge' or 'expert'. The modern term 'history' is therefore not a direct translation of words used by Herodotus. Nevertheless, it is largely thanks to him that its meaning as 'rational enquiry into the past' was established.

But how was this enquiry to take place? How was it to be transmitted? There were, after all, no set methods of researching or communicating an enquiry of this sort. It is vital to understand that Herodotus did not have access to written archives or the works of past generations of historians: so, he had to find ways of asking questions. This means that his main sources were oral. Just how important oral tradition was in Greek culture is also reflected in the likelihood that Herodotus' *Histories* were intended to be read before an audience, not pondered by the individual reader. As we assess Herodotus' achievement, this must be borne in mind.

One final and related problem: that of translation. I made use of Aubrey de Sélincourt's very accessible and readable translation of Herodotus, but it is as well to be aware that some Greek terms do not translate readily into English. As John Gould has pointed out, Herodotus' opening words quoted above could be rendered 'What follows is a performance [literally, "display"] of the enquiries of Herodotus from Halicarnassus'.[3] This certainly empha-sizes the oral element. We might take a further example from the introduc-tion to the *Histories*. Sélincourt's translation does not include the phrase 'without renown', and yet this is potentially significant: Herodotus talked of recording the astonishing achievements so that they might not be 'without renown'.[4] This phrase ties Herodotus in with the avowed aim of Greek epic poetry: to celebrate and commemorate the renown of men. And no educated Greek would be unfamiliar with the poems whose supposed author was Homer: *The Iliad* and *The Odyssey*; tales which told of the doings of the heroes Achilles and Odysseus. So, when Herodotus set out to write an enquiry into the past, he had no models to guide him beyond epic poetry and the related tradition of oral recitation. Their influence on his histories will clearly have to be considered.

B Herodotus and his sources

The crucial questions are these: what were Herodotus' sources, and how did he use them?

I have already suggested the importance of oral tradition to Herodotus, and it is no surprise that he should, throughout his work, refer to extensive travels he had himself undertaken and to the way in which he collected data by interview. He named the places he had visited and – sometimes – referred specifically to individuals as the source of his information. Since the earlier parts of the *Histories* were dealing with the remoter past, he was of course collecting local oral tradition rather than eyewitness reports. Perhaps we should take an example at this point.

> About the oracles – that of Dodona in Greece and of Ammon in Libya – the Egyptians have the following legend: according to the priests of the Theban Zeus, two women connected with the service of the temple were carried off by the Phoenicians and sold, one in Libya and the other in Greece, and it was these women who founded the oracles in the two countries. I asked the priests at Thebes what grounds they had for being so sure about this, and they told me that careful search had been made for the women at the time, and that though it was unsuccessful, they had afterwards learned that the facts were just as they had reported them. At Dodona, however, the priestesses who deliver the oracles have a different version of the story: two black doves, they say flew away from Thebes in Egypt, and one of them alighted at Dodona, the other in Libya. The former, perched on an oak, and speaking with a human voice, told them that there, on that very spot, there should be an oracle of Zeus. Those who heard her understood the words to be a command from heaven, and at once obeyed. Similarly, the dove which flew to Libya told the Libyans to found the oracle of Ammon – which is also an oracle of Zeus. The people who gave me this information were the three priestesses at Dodona – Promeneia the eldest, Timarete the next, and Nicandra the youngest – and their account is confirmed by the other Dodonaeans connected with the temple. Personally, however, I would suggest that if the Phoenicians really carried off the women from the temple and sold them respectively in Libya and Greece, the one who was brought to Greece ... must have been sold to the Thesprotians; and later, while she was working as a slave in that part of the country, she built, under an oak that happened to be growing there, a shrine to Zeus; for she would naturally remember in her exile the god whom she had served in her native Thebes. Subsequently, when she had learned to speak Greek, she established an oracle there, and mentioned, in addition, that the same Phoenicians who had sold her, also sold her sister in Libya. The story which the people of Dodona tell about the doves came, I should say, from the fact that the women were foreigners, whose language sounded to them like the twittering of birds; later on the dove spoke with a human voice, because by that time the woman had stopped twittering and learned to talk intelligibly. That, at least, is how I should explain the obvious impossibility of a dove using the language of men. As to the bird being black, they merely signify by this that the woman was an Egyptian.[5]

On the face of it, this seems to resemble the kind of techniques one might expect an historian to use today. Herodotus had acquired some information which his sense of reality led him to question. He then sought other view-points to challenge or corroborate his information, and named precisely his sources. Next, he offered an hypothesis to account for the data. He also appears to have distinguished between myth or legend and facts about the past. Certainly, Herodotus seems to have subjected his sources to some meaningful critical scrutiny. However, it would be wise to temper our enthusiasm with a strong dose of caution. It is not an unfamiliar charge that Herodotus was frequently unscrupulous in handling sources. Detlev Fehling,[6] for example, has suggested that Herodotus appears to have tried to make his accounts seem more plausible or well-supported by simply fabricating witnesses' comments and/or the witnesses themselves. There are too many examples of convenient corroborative evidence – sometimes in cases where the content simply cannot be true. For example, there is Herodotus' discussion of a Persian attack on Delphi, where it seems that the Persians ran into some rather unusual opposition:

> ... just as the Persians came to the shrine of Athene Pronaea, thunder-bolts fell on them from the sky, and two pinnacles of rock, torn from Parnassus, came crashing and rumbling down amongst them, killing a large number, while at the same time there was a battle-cry from inside the shrine. All these things happening together caused a panic amongst the Persian troops. They fled; and the Delphians, seeing them on the run, came down upon them and attacked them with great slaughter. All who escaped with their lives made straight for Boeotia. There is a story, I am told, amongst those who got away, that there was yet another miraculous occurrence: they saw, so they said, two gigantic soldiers – taller than ever a man was – pursuing them and cutting them down. According to the Delphians, these were Phylacus and Autonous, local heroes who have enclosed plots of ground near the temple which are held sacred to them – that of Phylacus lies along the road above the temple of Pronaea, and that of Autonous is near the spring of Castalia under the peak called Hyampia.[7]

So, the account is supported by testimony from the opposing sides, and the inclusion of the apparently impressive minor detail gives it the ring of truth – until one remembers that one is being asked to swallow a very tall tale indeed (no pun intended). It is at least open to question whether Herodotus fabricated his witnesses to fit a tale he had heard and interpreted for himself. Also, scholars have identified many instances of where Herodotus' account is likely to be at odds with the truth. On the fall of Babylon, for example, Lewis concludes that Herodotus was wrong to give the Persian Zopyrus the credit for taking the city: the likely victor was his compatriot Intaphrenes.[8]

On the face of it, then, Herodotus employed a critical technique which is recognizable as part of the modern historian's armoury. And yet, when we look below the surface, it seems to be severely limited, inaccurate and, at times, perhaps a pretence. But such sweeping judgements are anachronistic: to assess Herodotus, we need to remind ourselves of the context in which he worked and not to condemn him because we work in an utterly different one. Firstly, we should recall our earlier point that his work aimed to preserve the renown of actual deeds in the past and so was unlikely to escape from the influence of the great fictional epics. Since, like Homer, they were to be read out loud, the *Histories* had to exploit the techniques appropriate to oral delivery. As John Gould eloquently puts it, 'Herodotus' world is still the world of the teller of tales'.[9] Herodotus was not averse to telling a tale for the simple reason that it would enthral the listener. Take a rather shady example: a lengthy account of a man's wonderful audacity. It seems that King Rhampsinitus of Egypt was remarkably wealthy. So, he decided to build an impregnable treasury – but reckoned without the deviousness of the builder, who designed a moveable brick and tipped off his sons accordingly. One son in particular managed to rifle the treasure and outwit the king at every turn. Rhampsinitus was filled with

> astonishment and admiration; soon after the news of it reached him, he went to every town in Egypt with a promise to the thief, should he give himself up, not only of a free pardon but of a rich reward. The thief trusted him and presented himself, and Rhampsinitus signalized his admiration for the most intelligent of all mankind by giving him his daughter in marriage.[10]

Herodotus was not exactly passing this off as fact, of course. He gave himself the opt-out clause by commenting at the end:

> Another story I heard about Rhampsinitus was ...[11]

Not all Herodotus' tales were quite so obviously included to wake up the audience. The birth of the tyrant of Corinth, Cypselus, is a case in point.[12] It is also good to listen to: it has prophecy, attempted infanticide, a baby hidden in a chest. But it is presented as part of a speech against despotism by a Corinthian representative at a conference of the allies of Sparta, and therefore serves a purpose beyond mere entertainment. Herodotus, in fact, made much use of direct speech as a narrative device. Speeches certainly added drama and pace and offered a vivid method of outlining a person's motives. Common sense, of course, tells us that they cannot be taken as literally true: neither Herodotus nor his sources were in a position to tape-record or take dictation verbatim. He did not seem to have felt the need (unlike Thucydides, see pp.47–8) to justify his use of speech.

We now need to consider further the impact of Herodotus' largely oral sources. Such sources certainly explain his constant reference to 'having heard' and his use of phrases such as 'the facts I have heard reported' or 'there is a story, I am told', as well as the numerous occasions when he spoke of things he had seen for himself. More importantly, we need to appreciate that Herodotus was writing in many cases from the oral traditions of two main groups: great families and priests of the holy places. Gould has argued that he deliberately sought out people of similar social standing to those of whom he was writing: perhaps descendants of those originally involved. This in turn may explain inaccuracies where the family had preserved a tradition which exaggerated its own role in affairs. An example of this may well be an account of Zopyrus' role in the capture of Babylon. A descendant of that family was living in Athens in Herodotus' time, and it is possible that Herodotus had made his acquaintance. It would also explain a number of references to that family, although it has to be admitted that Herodotus never actually said that he got his information from them. Also, problems of translation he experienced when using non-Greek sources may explain some of the wilder errors he fell into when discussing foreign cultures. He appears, for example, to have assumed that the Persian term 'bondsman' was little different from the Greek word for 'slave' and so presents an unlikely picture of Persian troops being forced into battle with whips.[15] And finally, the reliance on oral tradition may explain the need he felt to offer or to create rather-too-convenient corroborative evidence. If there was no written evidence available – and there rarely was – then the listener had the right to expect proof in the form of oral testimony: and so Herodotus typically remarked, 'I heard this from . . .'

What this means, of course, is that we are getting a history of Greece and its neighbours which is to a considerable extent distilled through the perspective of fifth-century Greek élites. But Herodotus was not simply repeating stories told to him by various great families or custodians of shrines. Had he done so, his work would have been more like an anthology than a narrative. After all, as we saw earlier, the local communities jealously guarded their sense of difference. In short, Herodotus transcended these differences and managed to create a reasonably unified narrative out of it all by using the Persian Wars as his central theme. It was a theme which made sense, because opposition to a common foe helped to bind the Greeks together.

C Herodotus' subject-matter and purpose

It has already been noted that Herodotus was concerned to preserve the memory of past deeds of renown. But was that all? Did Herodotus hope that people might learn in some way from his work? Did he have a lesson to teach about the causes of wars, perhaps, from which those involved in contemporary politics might gain a great deal? Were his comments aimed at a specific audience with specific concerns – perhaps the Athens of his time? The short answer is that, on the surface, he had no such aims. After all, there was no emphasis whatsoever in his own introduction on any intended message.

However, it might be that in his discussion of the causes of warfare some generalizations emerged which military and political leaders might usefully have exploited. Since his work was produced in the background of the great conflict between Athens and Sparta, it seems likely that he would have things to teach about war, or about the qualities needed for victory. Preserving deeds of renown might explicitly encourage emulation and a desire for self-sacrifice. In fact, I doubt that Herodotus had the intention of teaching specific lessons. If we argue that preserving deeds of renown is a way of glorifying war, then there are sufficient comments stressing the evil of war to counterbalance it. For example, when the Persian Cyrus captured the Lydian Greek King Croesus, he intended to burn him alive. He eventually relented, and then had a conversation (via a translator) which shows Herodotus at his most eloquent:

> 'Tell me, Croesus, who was it who persuaded you to march against my country and be my enemy rather than my friend?'
> 'My lord,' Croesus replied, 'the luck was yours when I did it, and the loss was mine. The god of the Greeks encouraged me to fight you: the blame is his. No one is fool enough to choose war instead of peace – in peace sons bury fathers, but in war fathers bury sons. It must have been heaven's will that this should happen.'[14]

Beverley Southgate has recently argued that Herodotus does seek to teach a lesson. The gods, having decreed a moral order in the universe, punish those who challenge it. The Persian king, Xerxes, was the embodiment of pride, and defeat was his fate.[15] This, perhaps, is not so much a specific lesson as a moral framework within which Herodotus operates – very much in the same manner as heroic poetry, which prompts moral reflection rather than offering precepts as a message.

Croesus' comments above are also important because they force us to consider the extent to which Herodotus believed that gods shaped events. The issue of supernatural causation is a fundamental one, because, if Herodotus believed and argued that events were entirely shaped either by the whims of gods or by a kind of predetermined fate, then it certainly short-circuits any notion of him using history to teach particular forms of political action. What would be the point, if the gods did it all? Let us say straight away that Herodotus did not state that the gods do it all, and that he was capable of a sophisticated analysis of human motives. And yet, that discussion was sometimes accompanied by what looks like an acceptance of the role of gods in human actions. For example, Herodotus discussed the reasons behind the decision of the Persian king Xerxes to attack the Greeks, and described the influence of his cousin Mardonius over the king, together with Xerxes' desire for glory and revenge. But Xerxes, it seems, changed his mind and decided that an attack would be a profoundly bad idea. No sooner was this decision made than Xerxes was visited by an exceptionally aggressive and unpleasant phantom whom he interpreted as a messenger from the gods. The phantom insisted in no uncertain terms that he should launch the attack. Xerxes then asked his counsellor Artabanus, who was against the invasion, to dress himself in the king's clothes and sleep in his bed to see if the phantom also appeared to him. And it did:

> 'Are you the man,' said the phantom, 'who in would-be concern for the king is trying to dissuade him from making war on Greece? You will not escape unpunished, either now or hereafter, for seeking to turn aside the course of destiny ...'[16]

The phantom stressed the point by preparing to burn out Artabanus' eyes. The unfortunate counsellor leapt up with a shriek and ran to tell Xerxes of the dream. Not surprisingly, the attack on the Greeks went ahead.

Now, it obviously is not easy to equate Herodotus' generally realistic psychological assessment of human motives with this kind of supernatural involvement. But the story does not suggest that the gods directly altered events; they were simply ensuring that 'destiny' was fulfilled. This means that it was essential for Herodotus to discuss human motivation: fate might dictate what was to happen, but it actually happened directly because of human actions. Nor was it clear what was going to happen: humans could and did ignore or misinterpret oracles or dreams. But whether they wished it or not, destiny was fulfilled. Peter Derow suggests that

> ... predetermination – some version of fate, or thereabouts – may be a fact, but it is not an explanation, and Herodotus knew this. The explanation of human affairs has to be done at the human level.[17]

This seems fair enough, but it has to be said that there is a problem in generalizing on Herodotus' treatment of the gods. It could be argued, for example, that he was simply repeating a story told about Xerxes rather than necessarily agreeing with it, and so was not really telling us anything about his notion of fate. It might even be said that references to 'what had to be' reflected the influence of the story-telling style of Greek epic poetry rather than a clearly thought-out concept of destiny. On the other hand, there are one or two occasions where Herodotus clearly accepted the direct intervention of the gods. He spoke of the death of the sons of Spartan ambassadors (or heralds) in the Peloponnesian War as 'clear evidence of divine intervention' and of an incident in which 'the hand of God was clearly to be seen'. He clearly was not going to dwell on the incident, though, since he added hastily:

> **This, however, took place long after Xerxes' invasion of Greece, and I must get back to my story.**[18]

Similarly, Croesus was punished for arrogant presumption by the death of his son in a hunting accident. Herodotus commented:

> **... nemesis fell upon Croesus, presumably because God was angry with him for supposing himself the happiest of men.**[19]

So, perhaps we should conclude on this rather fraught point by suggesting that it would be wrong to argue that Herodotus' work was severely distorted by supernatural causation. Most of his explanations of why things happen were rooted in human behaviour and psychology, rather than the activities of gods. We can be more precise than this, because his narrative was not simply a set of unconnected or unthematic discussions of separate sets of motives causing separate events. Instead, he saw a chain of 'obligation and revenge', to use Gould's phrase,[20] stretching through and shaping the relations between Greeks and Persians. Things happened because political leaders reacted to a desire for vengeance, to honour family ties or to repay debts of various types. It is significant that the work started with a description of charges made by Greeks and Persians against each other over the alleged abduction of women. Herodotus was not prepared to accept the truth of these allegations, but, in mentioning them, he shows what he was looking for in history: in this instance, an origin of the conflicts in a desire for revenge. This focus on personal relationships and ties fits in very well with what has already been said about Herodotus' use of family testimonies as a vital source. Of course, to root an explanation of events in an analysis of a network of personal relationships is very limiting. It means that Herodotus was ill-equipped to tackle other types of cause, such as economic rivalry or class conflict.

Despite the limitations of his analysis, Herodotus did not write a tightly-structured narrative based on those themes of obligation and revenge. He appears to have had an insatiable curiosity: one of his favourite remarks was that he was 'astonished' to learn various things. And so, we get lengthy digressions on the customs, religious practices and attitudes of non-Greeks (some better informed than others). And, of course, we have the story-teller's anecdotes. It is the earlier books of the *Histories* which contain myth or folklore: abandoned Moses-like babies, the man (Polycrates) who threw his signet-ring into the sea to try to end an unnatural run of good luck, only to find it being returned to him in the belly of a huge fish. It could be argued that these various digressions did little for the progress of the narrative, and this is true. But there are gains. Herodotus was doing more than tackling political and military action. Simon Hornblower reminds us that Herodotus gave us an 'ethnographic *logos* or account, with its four ingredients, geography, customs, marvels and political history'.[21] Herodotus' breadth of vision also gave him the opportunity to make women visible and to point to their political impact. This is anything but common in later Greek historiography.

Having discussed the nature of Herodotus' subject matter, we can now sum up on the purpose of his work. Our conclusion should be that he did not attempt to use the past to teach political lessons for his present or future. He expounded no laws of history by attempting to provide a model of change or causation. His purpose, then, was to record the memory of great deeds of renown for his and future generations. But it is not clear that he expected such deeds to be useful in any direct way. He had a story to tell, and he wanted to make it true because otherwise it would be pointless.

D The impact of Herodotus on historiography

Textbooks on historiography generally point out that Herodotus was given the title 'Father of History'. But what does it mean? The Roman writer Cicero (see p.59) appears to have been the first to award it, and did so on the basis of making a distinction between history and poetry. History, he argued, aims at truth; poetry aims at pleasure. No doubt thinking of some of Herodotus' more dubious anecdotes, he was then obliged to point out that Herodotus was actually doing both. Some of Herodotus' successors felt that his willingness to include folklore and myth made him a doubtful parent of history. Cicero himself implied that Herodotus was a liar. He was attacked in books with titles like *On Herodotus' Thefts*, *Against Herodotus* and *On Herodotus' Lies*. As we shall see, his near-contemporary Thucydides was keen to criticize the element of romance in his work. Hartog has commented on Herodotus' ambiguous position:

> In the last analysis, his position may be summed up in the following paradox: even though he is the father of history, he is not really a historian.[22]

Fehling would no doubt agree. He draws an explicit parallel between Herodotus and Homer:

> Herodotus' idea was not to research the Persian Wars; he wanted to recount them as Homer had recounted the Trojan War. For him it was a matter of staving off oblivion rather than increasing knowledge.[23]

These judgements seem a little harsh. Perhaps Herodotus' great contribution is summed up in his statement of intent after the opening of his work and its description of the mythical abductions of Io, Europa, Medea and Helen of Sparta:

> So much for what Persians and Phoenicians say; and I have no intention of passing judgement on its truth or falsity. I prefer to rely on my own knowledge, and to point out who it was in actual fact that first injured the Greeks ...[24]

In other words, he was going to research the truth. The various objections made to his technique and sometimes to his sincerity have not, in my view, exposed that claim to be a fraudulent one. Thucydides' criticism of Herodotus was not, in fact, a denial of his influence over his successors but a recognition of it. Herodotus had established that the past should not simply be treated as a quarry for stimulating fiction, but that it should be respected in its own right: one should research what actually happened. Implicitly, this would mean near-contemporary history, since the historian could investigate the sources himself. Herodotus had defined the nature of the enquiry and had attempted to realize it by (usually) distinguishing between myth and what we call history and by investigating sources. In particular, he had established that oral sources were the historian's best form of evidence, although his successors would limit that to eyewitnesses rather than oral tradition. I would also argue that Herodotus established the view that history should not be partisan, since this would obscure the truth. It has been alleged that his work favoured Athens, but there are sufficient occasions where Athens comes in for stern criticism for us to reject this view. His Greek successors, in fact, criticized what they considered to be his over-friendly treatment of the non-Greek 'barbarians'.

Having said all this, we have to accept the longer-term implications of Herodotus' bad reputation in the Greek and later the Roman world. Some – but by no means all – of his successors disliked his forays into the distant past and other cultures. They were reluctant to commit themselves to original research into remoter periods and civilizations very different from their own. As Momigliano puts it:

> They concentrated on contemporary history or summarized and reinterpreted the work of former historians.[25]

We see this emphasis on contemporary history in the work of Thucydides.

Thucydides (c.460–400BC) and *The Peloponnesian War*

Thucydides, an Athenian, wrote the history of the war between the Peloponnesians and the Athenians, beginning at the moment that it broke out, and believing that it would be a great war, and more worthy of relation than any that had preceded it. This belief was not without its grounds ...[26]

On the whole, however, the conclusions I have drawn from the proofs quoted, may, I believe, safely be relied on. Assuredly they will not be disturbed either by the lays of a poet displaying the exaggeration of his craft, or by the compositions of the chroniclers that are attractive at truth's expense ...

With reference to the speeches in this history, some were delivered before the war began, others while it was going on; some I heard myself, others I got from various quarters; it was in all cases difficult to carry them word for word in one's memory, so my habit has been to make the speakers say what was in my opinion demanded of them by the various occasions, of course adhering as closely as possible to the general sense of what they really said. And with reference to the narrative of events, far from permitting myself to derive it from the first source that came to hand, I did not even trust my own impressions, but it rests partly on what I saw myself, partly on what others saw for me, the accuracy of the reports being always tried by the most severe and detailed tests possible. My conclusions have cost me some labour from the want of coincidence between accounts of the same occurrences by different eye-witnesses, arising sometimes from imperfect memory, sometimes from undue partiality for one side or the other. The absence of romance in my history will, I fear, detract somewhat from its interest; but if it be judged useful by those enquirers who desire an exact knowledge of the past as an aid to the interpretation of the future, which in the course of human things must resemble if it does not reflect it, I shall be content. *In fine*, [in conclusion] I have written my work, not as an essay which is to win the applause of the moment, but as a possession for all time.[27]

Later in his work, Thucydides reminded us of his authorship and provided some very useful background information:

The history of this period [ten years after the start of the war] has also been written by the same Thucydides, an Athenian, in the chronological order of events by summers and winters, to the time when the Lacedaemonians and their allies put an end to the Athenian empire ... The war had then lasted for twenty-seven years in all. Only a mistaken judgement can object to including the interval of treaty in the war ... So that the first ten years' war, the treacherous armistice that followed it, and the subsequent war will, calculating by the seasons, be found to make up the number of years which I have mentioned ... and to afford an instance of faith in oracles being for once justified by the event ... I lived through the whole of it, being of an age to comprehend events, and giving my attention to them in order to know the exact truth about them. It was also my fate to be an exile from my country for twenty years after my command at Amphipolis; and being present with both parties, and more especially with the Peloponnesians by reason of my exile, I had leisure to observe affairs somewhat particularly.[28]

So, we have an Athenian military officer – a general, no less – who wrote mainly about a war with which he had been intimately involved. Remarkably, he was at least able to appreciate the Spartan viewpoint, as his exile was spent in Sparta. He was clearly, like Herodotus, making full use of eye-witnesses. His comments on his sources and the hard work he put in to discover the truth seem impressive. He claimed to have tried to evaluate his own impressions – and those of others – by a rigorous cross-checking, and also to have taken account of partiality. His reference to the lack of romance in his work might be seen as a deliberate criticism of Herodotus' inclusion of legend under the guise of 'what I was told', and his sarcasm about the truth of oracles would suggest that the supernatural was to be treated with scepticism. But what do we make of his comments about the speeches made by the people in his history? He seems candid in admitting the difficulties in remembering things *verbatim*. So, rather than claim the speeches were literally true, he decided to use them as a method of expressing what would have been said given his knowledge of the background circumstances. We might wonder, then, why bother with the speeches at all?

The point about the speeches aside, it is easy to see why Thucydides has been claimed as the father of so-called scientific history. He appears to have adopted an objective standpoint and a critical method to back it up. In practice, though, is the claim justified?

A Thucydides and his sources

We have Thucydides' word for it that he found, assessed and compared sources. Unfortunately, he very rarely demonstrated that technique in action. As we have seen, Herodotus was often prepared to provide two contrasting testimonies and to explain the inferences he made. He was also prepared, on occasion, to leave it up to the listeners or readers to make up their own minds. Thucydides claimed to have done the work, but leaves very little trace. Very occasionally, he felt the need to say a little bit more:

> That Hippias was the eldest son and succeeded to the government, is what I positively assert as a fact upon which I have had more exact accounts than others, and may also be ascertained by the following circumstance. He is the only one of the legitimate brothers that appears to have had children; as the altar shows, and the pillar placed in the Athenian Acropolis, commemorating the crime of the tyrants, which mentions no child of Thessalus or of Hipparchus, but five of Hippias ... and naturally the eldest would have married first. Again, his name comes first on the pillar after his father ...[29]

Whatever we might think of his evidence from the inscriptions, we would very much like to know who provided these particularly exact accounts. Perhaps one might think that his failure to do something reasonably obvious (and then to attempt to back it up with some largely unimpressive inscriptions) suggests that his claims to careful collection and evaluation of his oral sources are fraudulent. There is evidence to support this view – particularly Thucydides' readiness to tell us exactly what people were thinking and what their motives were. Simon Hornblower discusses the issue judiciously, and concludes that it would be unwise to accept that Thucydides invariably researched his oral sources – but it would be equally unwise to argue that he never did. Of course, trying to identify where Thucydides did investigate his oral testimony and where he made it up is fraught with difficulty. To take one specific instance: Thucydides' treatment of his opponent, the Lacedaemonian Brasidas, whose victory at Amphipolis had led to the Thucydides' exile. Brasidas is treated with scrupulous fairness. His cunning diplomacy and duplicity were not used by Thucydides as an opportunity to savage him, and he spoke appreciatively of Brasidas' moderation and gentleness. He remarked:

> ... the present valour and conduct of Brasidas ... was what mainly created in the allies of Athens a feeling for the Lacedaemonians. He was the first who went out and showed himself so good a man at all points as to leave behind him the conviction that the rest were like him.[30]

But the question then arises, from where did Thucydides get his apparent knowledge of Brasidas' intentions, strategies and motives? The short answer is that we do not know. One can point to his exile in Spartan territory, where he may have had the chance to talk to Brasidas. This can hardly explain how Thucydides knew so much about Brasidas' strategies and intentions in his later and final battle at Amphipolis, where he died. Hornblower asks the question:

> But can we really doubt that Thucydides talked to Brasidas, whom he handles sympathetically and with every appearance of possessing inside information?[31]

Given the confident detail, perhaps not. And yet, as we have seen, it is not necessarily the case that the whole of Thucydides' discussion of any one set of incidents was invariably the result of his scrupulous oral research. There must have been guesswork, and we cannot be certain how much. Maybe we can link this up with his treatment of the speeches: if necessary, making up some oral 'evidence' to fit what he genuinely thought must have been said or done.

Oral evidence and inscriptions were not the only sources used by Thucydides. In the earlier parts of his work, he provided a very long-term background to the Peloponnesian War by starting with the first nomadic Greeks. In his run-up to the War, he lifted facts (unacknowledged) from Herodotus and of course took the opportunity to distance himself from any belief in the value of oracles. He also appears to have used a history of Athens by a writer called Hellanicus, whom Thucydides disparaged – possibly because of the former's undue favouritism towards Athens itself. He was also prepared to use poetry as evidence (rather than as truth, of course). But we must emphasize that the heart of Thucydides' history – and what he saw as the heart of history itself – is the use of oral evidence from contemporary sources.

B Thucydides and the purpose of history

It seems a reasonable assumption that, if a writer sees history as having a particular purpose, then that purpose is likely to be reflected in every aspect of his work. It might affect, for example, the choice of subject matter, the selection and use of sources or the imposition of a particular standard of 'truth'. Thucydides certainly intended to tell the truth about the Peloponnesian War because it was important to do so. He did not mean that a bare accumulation of data would reflect that importance. Instead, his concentrating on finding the truth behind what happened was important because he felt that it revealed certain things about human nature which it was vital for those who wielded any form of power to know. I very much take Momigliano's point[32] that Thucydides is not making some sort of simplistic statement that history provides a set of lessons in human behaviour. In fact, anyone reading Thucydides and expecting to be provided with a convenient list of 'important things one jolly well has to know about human nature' is in for a severe disappointment. But he was very interested, as one would expect of a military commander, in such matters as human responses in times of danger. His technique was to enter into the mind of his character and to discuss his feelings and behaviour. There is an excellent example of this in Thucydides' treatment of the Athenian commander Nicias before the great defeat at the hands of Syracuse in 413BC:

> **Meanwhile Nicias, appalled by the position of affairs ... and thinking, as men are apt to think in great crises, that when all has been done they**

have still something left to do, and when all has been said they have not yet said enough, again called on the captains one by one ... and adjured them not to belie their own personal renown ...[33]

On one level, this is fraudulent. Thucydides could not have known what was going on in Nicias' mind (especially as Nicias is butchered after his surrender and therefore not in the best position to grant interviews). But, as a general himself, he presumably was able to guess his fellow commander's likely psychological state and to empathize with the situation. In short, Nicias was thinking what honourable leaders think and doing what honourable leaders do. If telling the 'truth' in this way led him beyond the mere narrative of events, then this is a price Thucydides was more than willing to pay – hence his willingness to write speeches which he could not have heard and, at times, to construct them in a dramatic and tragic style. It also explains the way in which Thucydides imposed a pattern on events, because events often follow from recurrent human behaviour. As Virginia Hunter points out,[34] Thucydides' work is a complex series of repetitive patterns, including those, not only of human behaviour, but also of character–types and sequences of events.

This suggests, of course, that there was some distortion of characterization to meet the need for a pattern from which we can learn. It also means that the generally dry and unemotional narrative of Thucydides could take on a real poetic power without ever losing its terseness. The ill-fated Nicias, for example, was given a powerful speech as he tried to rally his despairing men:

To sum up, be convinced, soldiers, that you must be brave, as there is no place near for your cowardice to take refuge in, and that if you now escape from the enemy, you may all see again what your hearts desire, while those of you who are Athenians will raise up again the great power of the state, fallen though it be. Men make the city and not walls or ships without men in them.[35]

C Thucydides' contribution to historiography

Without a doubt, it was Thucydides rather than Herodotus who had the greatest influence on successors. In place of Herodotus' oft-expressed and enthusiastic 'astonishment', we have a cool rationality. In place of Herodotean anecdote and digression, we have a clear narrative structure. In place of Herodotean credulity in the face of oracle and god, we have a dismissive scepticism. In the place of the occasional admitted uncertainty and willingness to let the reader decide, we have certainty and a judgement we are to accept as our own. In the place of a belief in the interest of the remoter past and a willingness to use oral tradition as a source, we have predominance given to eyewitness account and contemporary history. Where Herodotus invites us to an armchair for an avuncular chat about great things, Thucydides has us sitting ramrod-straight on the edge of the chair whilst he tells us things we need to know. And in place of the Herodotean breadth of interest and readiness to write about legend, customs, geography, topography, non-Greek cultural history and, of course, the Persian Wars, we have one thing: political/military history. Thucydides, it seems, wanted to distance himself so far from Herodotus that he failed to attach any importance to the Persian involvement in the Peloponnesian War. The Thucydidean concept of history triumphed over Herodotus, and, in the eyes of almost all classical historians, it was Thucydides, and not Herodotus, who wrote true history.

In the longer term, we might expect both Herodotus and Thucydides to be revered and copied by the writers of the Renaissance, to whom the rediscovered classical civilization seemed to offer an intoxicating truth and vision of the future through recovering the near-forgotten wisdom of the past (see pp.81–2). This was true only to a very limited extent. Polybius (pp.53–8) and other (arguably lesser) historians were preferred. In short, their messages appeared plainer, their purposes clearer and their uses more immediate. The father of history and the father of so-called scientific history had left some progeny of which they might not have been proud.

ROME AND THE ROMAN EMPIRE — BACKGROUND

The city of Rome came to prominence in Italy in the sixth century BC. It was a republic, governed by Senate and consuls and with a citizen army. As its power in Italy eventually grew, the city came into conflict with the great north African city of Carthage. Despite its redoubtable general Hannibal, Carthage was forced to sue for peace in 202BC after the battle of Zama. As the Roman Empire expanded into Greece, Macedonia, north Africa, Syria, Palestine and Egypt, the Romans felt able to call the Mediterranean *mare nostrum* – our sea.

Success abroad was not always reflected by peace in Rome. Power struggles developed between the Senate (dominated by the nobility) and the Assembly (representing the other citizens) from which army leaders could benefit. Triumph in the field meant riches and power at home, together with the chance of murdering ones opponents. Marius (157–86BC) is a case in point. His war against the north African king Jugurtha was accompanied by several stints as consul and – of course – those murders of opponents. Particularly successful (meaning ruthless) commanders grew to aspire higher than mere mastery of Rome. Julius Caesar's decision in 44BC to mint coins bearing his head appeared to be a clear statement of intent – he wanted to abolish the republic and rule as king. His death at the hands of senators led by Brutus and Cassius simply paved the way for more civil war. The triumph of Octavian (who adopted the name Augustus) heralded the end of the Republic and the coming of the emperor.

Polybius (c.200BC–c.118BC): background

Polybius was a Greek military leader (a cavalry commander) and statesman with no choice but to reflect on the faded power of Greece and the extra-ordinary dominance and power of the Roman Empire. This power had been brought home to him all too clearly when the Romans objected to the failure of Achaeans like Polybius to support Rome in war against Macedonia. Polybius was one of a thousand Achaeans who had been forced to live in exile in Italy from 167BC. He was, however, permitted to live in Rome, where his relationship as friend and tutor to future senator Scipio Aemilianus brought him into intimate contact with the workings of the Roman political and social élites. It was 150BC before the surviving Achaeans were allowed to return home, but Polybius was far too useful for Rome to leave him in retire-ment. He was called to assist in war with Carthage, and took the opportunity to explore the African coast on board a ship placed at his disposal by Scipio. Unsurprisingly, all these experiences left their mark on his *Histories*.

A Polybius' *Histories*

There is a problem in dating the writing of the *Histories*. The work is divided into 40 books, and Polybius probably wrote the final ten of them (which cover the period 167–146BC) towards the end of his life when he had returned from exile. So, it most certainly was not written at one time: Polybius clearly changed his mind at one point and decided to extend his work to 146BC (when he was present at the fall of Carthage). It is very possible that the books appeared in stages, which would certainly help make the work topical. Walbank[36] suggests that this would suit Polybius' purpose in writing his history – to explain to his fellow Greeks, who after all needed to understand the Romans, what made the Romans so successful. And so, what did Polybius have to say about his purpose?

I am aware that some will be at a loss to account for my interrupting the course of my narrative for the sake of entering upon the following disquisition on the Roman constitution. But I think that I have already in many passages made it fully evident that this particular branch of my work was one of the necessities imposed on me by the nature of my original design; and I pointed this out with special clearness in the preface which explained the scope of my history. I there stated that the feature of my work which was at once the best in itself, and the most instructive to the students of it, was that it would enable them to know and fully realise in what manner, and under what kind of constitution, it came about that nearly the whole world fell under the power of Rome in somewhat less than fifty-three years, – an event certainly without precedent. This being my settled purpose, I could see no more fitting period than the present for making a pause, and examining the truth of the remarks about to be made on this constitution ... What is really educational and beneficial to students of history is the clear view of the causes of events, and the consequent power of choosing the better policy in a particular case. Now in every practical undertaking by a state we must regard as the powerful agent for success or failure the form of its constitution; for from this as from a fountain-head all conceptions and plans of action not only proceed, but attain their consummation ...[37]

Now the natural laws which regulate the merging of one form of government into another are perhaps discussed with greater accuracy by Plato and some other philosophers. But their treatment, from its intricacy and exhaustiveness, is only within the capacity of a few. I will therefore endeavour to give a summary of the subject, just so far as I suppose it to fall within the scope of a practical history and the intelligence of ordinary people.[38]

So, we have here an historian who clearly wished to make history practical: pragmatic, in the particular sense of being useful in military and political affairs. There are two main elements here. First, it was vital for the readers or audience to understand causation; second, they must have the chance to study Rome to get to grips with its constitution to understand what makes it successful. And Polybius was keen to adapt the work of philosophers on this issue to make it more accessible and useful to ordinary people. By ordinary people, he meant those who actually wielded political power. The implication behind his words, of course, is that he was writing more for Greeks than for Romans.

B Polybius' subject matter and sources

Given his aims, it is hardly surprising that Polybius should have written near-contemporary and contemporary history or that he should have concentrated on diplomatic, political and military history in the manner of Thucydides. He did, however, allow himself some lengthy asides: particularly in his later books, where he was keen to exploit his seaborne adventures and display his geographical knowledge. He was also keen to remind his readers that he was a man of action and not a desk-bound scholar, and had some waspish things to say about his predecessor Timaeus for supposedly spending his time poring over written sources in a library rather than getting to grips with the most important source – the eyewitness. It is not that Polybius failed to use written sources himself, but, in the manner of Thucydides, they are not discussed or frequently identified. In Book 12, he offered something new in historiography: what Walbank calls a 'systematic exposition of the methods to be used'.[39] Specifically, Polybius commented that history has three constituent parts: the collection and study of written sources, the survey of geographical locations, and finally – and most importantly for contemporary history – political experience. By this, he meant not so much actual participation in the events described as the ability to interview eyewitnesses and to put their evidence into the appropriate political and military context. His exile in Rome gave him a wonderful opportunity to conduct probing interviews, and there is every reason to believe that he kept notes of these for future use.

His subject-matter inevitably reflected those areas where he felt he had most expertise. He offered lengthy assessments of specific campaigns, commenting knowledgeably about the personal qualities of the great general, the use of cavalry and, in particular, what one could learn from the Roman successes. There were moral lessons to be learned of how men react to challenge and adversity. But of course it was the discussion of the Roman constitution which was fundamental to his aim of accounting for the triumph of Rome:

> Now, it is undoubtedly the case that most of those who profess to give us authoritative instruction on this subject [types of constitution] distinguish three kinds of constitutions, which they designate *kingship, aristocracy, democracy* … it is plain that we must regard as the *best* constitution that which partakes of all these three elements.[40]

Polybius also identified that:

> … there is a regular cycle of constitutional revolutions, and the natural order in which the constitutions change are transformed, and return again to their original stage. If a man have a clear grasp of these

principles he may perhaps make a mistake as to the dates at which this or that will happen to a particular constitution; but he will rarely be entirely mistaken as to the stage of growth or decay at which it has arrived, or as to the point at which it will undergo some revolutionary change ...

For the present I will make brief reference to the legislation of Lycurgus ... That statesman was fully aware that all those changes which I have enumerated come about by an undeviating law of nature; and reflected that every form of government that was unmixed, and rested on one species of power, was unstable; because it was swiftly perverted into that particular form of evil peculiar to it ... in kingship it is absolutism; in aristocracy it is oligarchy; in democracy lawless ferocity and violence; and to these vicious states all these forms of government are ... inevitably transformed. Lycurgus, I say, saw all this, and accordingly combined together all the excellences and distinctive features of the best constitutions, that no part should become unduly predominant ... The result of this combination has been that the Lacedaemonians retained their freedom for the longest period of any people with which we are acquainted ... the Romans have arrived at the same result in framing their commonwealth ...[41]

This is unlike anything in Herodotus and goes far beyond any of Thucydides' comments on political forms.[42] At first sight, we have an impressive piece of political theorizing in which the author claimed to have identified from his knowledge of history, politics and philosophy a kind of natural law or pattern in the past, present and future. Clearly, Polybius expected this to be of great value to those involved in political life. His concept of the virtues of the mixed constitution perhaps sits a little uneasily with the cycle of growth and decay, although, as we have seen, he did argue that the combination of elements of the three types of political system would evade the process. What this undeniably interesting model lacks, perhaps, is a feel for the nuances of politics and the impact of individuals. Describing a constitution is one thing: understanding the people who work within it is another. Despite the time he spent in Rome, Polybius seems to have lacked the feel for the corridors of power and the less formal human interactions which shape the actual workings of government. Nor does his Greek mind-set help him much. As Momigliano points out,[43] he tended to read Rome as a Greek city-state (hence his comparison of Sparta's constitution with that of Rome) and ignored some of the vital elements in the success of the empire: namely, the way in which the aristocracy throughout Italy had been able to cooperate in imperial ventures.

Polybius' treatment of Roman religion was similar to his treatment of Roman government. We get an acute and stimulating generalization, but with something of an inconsistency at its heart and a distinct lack of any sense of an individual's beliefs. He argued that the Roman people's 'scrupulous fear of the gods'[44] was fundamentally a control mechanism for keeping the fickle multitude well-behaved for fear of punishment in the afterlife. All well and good; but why then do the very political élites who deliberately – and presumably cynically – exploit this fear apparently share it themselves?

> ... the Romans, in their magistracies and embassies ... have the handling of a great amount of money, and yet from pure respect to their oath keep their faith intact.[45]

It would seem that Polybius' stance on the gods, at least, was straightforward enough. He professed no belief in them, but calmly suggested that encouraging the belief in others is invaluable for social and political stability. There is, however, something of an ambiguity in his attitude. He had a tendency to offer a dual explanation of some events: a rational assessment of causes and then a comment which implied – rather than clearly stated – an acceptance of Fortune or Destiny. Rome's rise could be attributed to its constitution, yes; but there was also the sense in which that rise was presented as the workings of Fate. In fact, even where his analysis of causation was rational, it was often superficial. Possible underlying and long-term causes were ignored in favour of a shallow analysis of the motivation of those (usually from one side only) who were supposedly responsible for the outbreak of the conflict. Peter Derow, in his distinctly enthusiastic discussion of Polybius' qualities, admits that this kind of approach to causation is inadequate:

> Polybius is explaining ... nothing so general as why a war broke out, but more precisely why whoever began it began it ... A risk of one-sidedness, then, in the focus of the explanation ... It is inevitable ... if we agree with Polybius that the historian's task is to explain why people did things.[46]

C Polybius and speeches

Thucydides, we recall, proclaimed that the speeches in his history were written to reflect what the occasion demanded that the speaker said, with due regard (wherever possible) to the actual words spoken. This rather elastic claim to accuracy and truth was stretched beyond the breaking point by many of his successors, who, as Walbank puts it, 'dropped all pretence of giving the real words'.[47] They simply used speeches as an opportunity to display their literary style. Polybius was clearly infuriated by this, and demanded that the historian should do as he did: relay to the best of his ability the actual words spoken. Given the importance he attaches to eye-witnesses, it is hardly surprising that he should make this demand. But it would be even more surprising if he could actually adhere to it. There are occasions – particularly in times of battle – where such claims are frankly unlikely. He does admit at one point that he is following a common structure and even using the same words in some speeches. Perhaps the best assessment we can make is that he did the best he could to base his speeches on the actual recollection of eyewitnesses – particularly when the speakers were Greek.

D Polybius' contribution to historiography

Polybius acknowledged no direct debt to Thucydides, but the focus on political history remained. And it was Polybius, rather than Thucydides, who influenced the historians of Rome – Livy, Sallust and Tacitus – to write political history with appropriate political (and moral) lessons. Polybius argued that ordinary men were transformed by the study of history into leaders, natural leaders stimulated to be great by heroic examples, and the wicked deterred by the fear of being held up to ridicule and shame.

A similar pattern can be detected in the Renaissance. Polybius' story of Rome was certainly more appealing to Renaissance scholars than Thucydides on the remoter war between Athens and Sparta. The Florentine scholar and politician Leonardo Bruni, for example, did much to establish Polybius as the model for good – and politically useful – history. His concept of the mixed constitution appealed directly to writers interested in the relationship between history and political theory, like Machiavelli (see pp.84–5) and Montesquieu (see pp.91–3).

ROMAN HISTORIOGRAPHY

Roman historiography was by no means a mere imitation of a few Greek historians. It had its own native element in the terse summary of public events provided by the chief priests (the *tabulae pontificum*). Dominating it, however, were two crucial issues: the Roman sense of the political uses to which language could and should be put and the view that it was right and proper to judge political behaviour in moral terms. So, it was hardly surprising that the Romans were most influenced by the Greek historians whose work seemed to reflect those demands. Or perhaps 'influenced' is an inadequate word to use. We should say that the Romans were selectively interested in their Greek predecessors where they found their approach, subject-matter and style congenial.

Significantly, our starting point should be the work *De Oratore* (*On the Orator*) by the Roman writer Cicero (written c.55BC). It is significant because Cicero's view of the relationship between history and rhetoric was enormously influential on Roman and Renaissance historiography. He complained that Roman historians were too often merely chroniclers of facts (on the model of the *tabulae pontificum*). What was needed was the use of rhetoric to elaborate on the dry and dull skeleton of fact. Classical rhetoric was, as Roger Ray puts it, 'primarily a theory of invention ... Indeed Aristotle defined the *entire* field of rhetoric as the faculty of finding (inventing) the means of persuasion on any subject whatever'.[48] Cicero's invention (*inventio*) means the devising of material which would make a case convincing. *Inventio* and history perhaps make unlikely bedfellows if one assumes that history must present what actually happened. The rhetorical historian was interested in the pursuit of truth, but this was not the truth dictated by events or the sources: it was the moral or political truth which his history had to serve. This meant that the historian had to be judgemental. Praise, blame and a style to arouse strong feelings were vital weapons to persuade the reader to imitate or to shun the behaviour of the historian's characters. Through his mouthpiece Antonius, Cicero said:

> **And as History, which bears witness to the passing of the ages, sheds light upon reality, gives life to recollection and guidance to human existence, and brings tidings of ancient days, whose voice, but the orator's, can entrust her to immortality?**[49]

Cicero later added:

> **Do you see how great a responsibility the orator has in historical writing? ... For who does not know history's first law to be that an author must not dare to tell anything but the truth? ... The nature of the subject needs chronological arrangement and geographical representation ... it calls also ... for some intimation of what the writer approves ... and, as for the individual actors, besides an account of their exploits, it demands particulars of the lives and characters of such as are outstanding in renown and dignity.**[50]

Rhetoric was much more than a call to use emotive language to persuade and inspire. In speeches – the obvious place for the rhetorical flourish – it involved a precise and formal structure, including methods for capturing the attention and goodwill of the listener, a statement of facts, proof and conclusion.

Livy (Titus Livius) (c.64BC–c.AD17)

Rhetoric can be seen hard at work in Livy's *The History of Rome from its Foundation* (more strictly, *Ad urbe condita* or *From the Founding of the City*). It was conspicuous in the direct speeches provided by Livy in the smooth and flowing style recommended by Cicero in Book II of *De Oratore*. And Livy certainly set out to persuade:

> **The study of history is the best medicine for a sick mind; for in history you have a record of the infinite variety of human experience plainly set out for all to see; and in that record you can find for yourself and your country both examples and warnings; fine things to take as models, base things, rotten through and through, to avoid.**
>
> **I hope my passion for Rome's past has not impaired my judgment; for I do honestly believe that no country has ever been greater or purer than ours or richer in good citizens and noble deeds ...**[51]

So, we get a patriotic picture of the glory and might of Rome. Livy's reference to 'sick mind' reflected his attitude to the troubled times in which he was writing: probably the mid 30s BC, when Rome was embroiled in a civil war between Mark Antony and the future emperor Augustus. History, then, was to act as a moral and political tutor, needed more than ever when times were darkest. Livy's tales of the twins Romulus and Remus and the founding of Rome made a wonderful and intentionally inspiring story. Heroes like Hercules had their part to play in the early days of Rome, and so did the gods. Livy was prepared to accept the involvement of the gods in human affairs. The Roman king Tullus Hostilius, for example, died in his burning palace after offending Jupiter Elicius by an unintentional mistake made in performing his rites to the singularly bad-tempered and vengeful god.[52]

Livy set himself a monumental task in writing his great work. He intended to cover a period of some 800 years, and actually lived long enough to see something of the greatness of Rome revive under Augustus. Sadly, only the earlier volumes survive. Even so, we know that his undeniable skills of dramatic storytelling and unrepentant patriotism made his work extremely popular. But it seems a long way from the taut prose of the ex-soldier Thucydides to the elegance of Livy, the man of letters. Not for Livy was the Thucydidean expression of concern with the nature of historical sources: what mattered was the rhetorical impact on the reader.

Sallust (Gaius Sallustius Crispus) (86BC–35BC)

I have broken with the fundamentally chronological structure of this chapter because I wanted to trace the impact of rhetoric on history through a discussion of Livy. Sallust, writing perhaps a decade before him, was not a blind follower of smooth, Ciceronian rhetoric. He was a stark contrast to Livy in other ways too. First of all, he was very much the politician and man of action. A close associate of Julius Caesar, he commanded a legion in his service and operated as his governor in part of north Africa. He also had a turbulent political career, from which he withdrew after Caesar's murder to write history.

Although he cannot be seen as a follower of Cicero, style was of great concern to him. He wrote rather like Thucydides, but where the former was taut, Sallust was stretched to the limit; where Thucydides was terse, Sallust was abrupt. He seems to have gone out of his way to find unusual and archaic words and a peculiar sentence structure. And, as Syme[55] points out, the strange style extended itself even to the speeches of his characters.

The tension in Sallust's style mirrored the pessimism of his historical writings. In his view, the Roman Republic was in a state of irreversible decline. In *The War with Catiline*, he presented the first-century BC conspirator Catiline as a man of his time: clever, devious, corrupt. *The War with Jugurtha* looked back to the late second century BC, but the corruption was there as well.

There are clear links with Thucydides beyond the style. Both shared a scepticism towards the gods and oracles and a single-minded concentration on politics and military affairs. But the differences are as marked as the similarities. In his preface to *The War with Catiline*, Sallust offered little more than the following as his thoughts on history and the writing thereof:

> **Accordingly, when my mind found peace after many troubles and perils and I had determined that I must pass what was left of my life aloof from public affairs, it was not my intention to waste my precious leisure in indolence and sloth, nor yet by turning to farming or the chase, to lead a life devoted to slavish employments. On the contrary, I resolved to return to a cherished purpose from which ill-starred ambition had diverted me, and write a history of the Roman people, selecting such portions as seemed to me worthy of record; and I was confirmed in this resolution by the fact that my mind was free from hope, and fear, and partisanship. I shall therefore write briefly and as truthfully as possible of the conspiracy of Catiline; for I regard that event as worthy of special notice because of the extraordinary nature of the crime and of the danger arising from it.[54]**

Sallust continued with a diatribe against what he saw as the causes of strife and decline: the lust for money and, with it, power. Both were enemies of the manly qualities of boldness in warfare and justice in times of peace. So, we have no examination of the technique of the historian or references to sources in the manner of Thucydides. Instead, we have an attack on some of the pursuits of the noble classes, a profound sense of disillusion (or so it seems) and an implied desire to focus on character and personality as a means of moral teaching – largely of a negative type. *The War with Jugurtha* is little different, but its criticism of the noble class was explicitly made in the preface – along with an attack on the standards of Sallust's own times:

> ... it is the memory of great deeds that kindles in the breast of noble men this flame that cannot be quelled until they by their own prowess have equalled the fame and glory of their forefathers.
>
> But in these degenerate days, on the contrary, who is there that does not vie with his ancestors in riches and extravagance rather than in uprightness and diligence? ... But in giving expression to my sorrow and indignation at the morals of our country I have spoken too freely and wandered too far from my subject. To this I now return.
>
> I propose to write of the war which the people of Rome waged with Jugurtha, king of the Numidians: first, because it was long, sanguinary and of varying fortune; and secondly, because then for the first time resistance was offered to the insolence of the nobles ...[55]

Sallust gave Marius, the military leader and consul hostile to the nobles, a very long speech attacking their indolence, their complacency in reciting the glorious deeds of their ancestors and – significantly – their eloquence and use of rhetoric. Marius' speech is itself eloquent, but not smooth and Ciceronian.[56]

In his rapid and often bitter narrative, Sallust asks us to contemplate *virtus*: a word which translates as 'virtue', but which carried with it the meaning of manliness, love of action and sense of honour in public life. It is on this that his moral teaching was founded, but of course we are not being offered a parade of shining examples of *virtus* in action; Sallust's approach was rather to lament its absence – and particularly, of course, in his own day.

What of Sallust's impact on the writing of history? His contemporary reputation was high, despite criticisms of his style, and some saw him as the Roman Thucydides. His most direct and perhaps profound influence was on the historian Tacitus. Ronald Martin sees echoes of Sallust's *virtus* in Tacitus (whilst bearing in mind the different political circumstances under which they wrote), but his 'main indebtedness to Sallust is in style'.[57] In the longer term, Sallust's pessimistic attitude towards human nature appealed to some medieval Christian writers, but his distaste for Ciceronian rhetoric made him rather less of a model to Renaissance historians than, say, Livy. On the other hand, the writer on the lookout for a model on which to base a villain (with appropriate moral reflections) found Sallust distinctly useful. Richard of Gloucester (later Richard III) in Thomas More's *History of King Richard III* (written sometime after 1514) is a Sallustian villain and an embodiment of corruption.[58]

Cornelius Tacitus (AD56/7–?)

Tacitus was the son-in-law of Agricola, the governor of Britain. He managed to pursue a successful political career in a time fraught with danger for senators. He went on to the even higher rank of consul in AD97 and finally became proconsul of Asia in around AD113.

Political and personal experience coloured his earliest historical works. His *Agricola* (AD98) held up Agricola for imitation as a hero; his *Germania* of the same year dealt with the Germanic tribes within and outside the borders of the Roman Empire – a fascinating and elusive subject indeed, but one which Tacitus distorted by using the virile barbarians as a stick with which to beat the alleged decadence of Rome itself. It is in his two major works, *Histories* (written AD106–7) and *Annals* (written between AD109 and 120), that we see Tacitus at his best, but with plenty of axes still to grind.

Histories covered the years AD69–96, but only the first four volumes have survived intact. We have about a third of the work, in which Tacitus covered the civil war from which Vespasian emerged the victor. The *Annals* is also incomplete. It tackled the period from the death of the emperor Augustus (AD14) through successors like Tiberius, Caligula, Claudius and Nero, and so gave Tacitus plenty of opportunity for sneering and vituperation. He made the most of it. We can ignore his comment in the preface that he 'shall write without indignation or partisanship'.[59] But what we get is a vigorous and judgemental history in which the kind of tension we saw in Sallust's style is shaped into splendid drama. Whether read out loud (as he intended) or not, Tacitus' words pull the listener or reader into the scene he describes. Small details are used to bring the scenes to life. For instance, Tacitus described the toneless voice in which Tiberius recites the charges in the first of a series of show trials, the terrified defendant leaning on his brother's arm as he hears the accusations read out.[60]

Tacitus, then, was more than happy to write history to suit his purposes. Much of what he wrote attacked the role of emperor, but he had little better to say of the republic. So – was he a born critic with more than a dash of cynicism? Against this view, we should accept that he could present a character to be admired where he saw fit – Germanicus, the adopted son of Tiberius, is a case in point. But even Germanicus was flawed: he made misjudgments, he could be devious at times. Tacitus, it seems, was happier when condemning, and he did it very well.

A Tacitus and his sources

Unfortunately, we cannot comment on what use Tacitus made of his own experiences and possible contacts from the time of his participation in political life because the relevant books of the *Histories* have been lost.

As we might expect, Tacitus followed the usual pattern of classical historiography and almost never mentioned specifically the sources of his information. For example, in the *Histories* only two authorities were named. He did use general expressions like 'many have recorded' or – as in his discussion of the controversial death of the emperor Claudius – 'contemporary writers stated'.[61]

There are occasions where he implied that his practice was to derive his account from the comparison of a number of historians and what we would call archival evidence. Ronald Martin, for example, points to the instance where Tacitus admitted that he could not uncover the truth on the way consular elections were conducted in the reign of Tiberius due to inconsistencies within Tiberius' speeches which were, in turn, compounded by the lack of agreement between the accounts of historians. He would certainly have had access to public records of the workings of the senate (*acta senatus*), to a kind of daily update of things citizens should be aware of (*acta diurna*) and possibly to a separate publication of the emperor's speeches. Syme argues that significant parts of the *Annals* were based on conscientious archival research.[62] It would, however, be dangerous to generalize on Tacitus' historical technique from this kind of example; it is all too tempting to read twentieth-century style source-analysis into a writer whose processes are usually concealed from us. Martin's careful analysis suggests that there are occasions where Tacitus was over-dependent on the writings of earlier historians or annalists – sometimes to the extent of relying heavily on one source. In fact, Tacitus' approach is not one which fits well with disinterested source evaluation. Apart from the grinding of his axes, his love of character analysis means that he 'proves' a point by reference to his view of a person's psychology and not the weight of evidence. Martin offers a conclusion which recognizes both Tacitus' limitations and his qualities:

> **Tacitus operates within the canons of ancient historiography. It is enough that he does so with a penetration that rivals Thucydides and a pungency unequalled by any writer, Greek or Roman.[63]**

Conclusions on classical historiography

Denys Hay rounds off a brief chapter on Greek and Roman historians in his book *Annalists and Historians* with a timely reminder which he then, it seems, proceeds to ignore:

> ... a word of warning should be addressed to those who did not heed the initial remark that classical historians were not trying to do what modern historians aim for.[64]

But he adds:

> ... it is salutary to remember how feeble was the tradition of ancient historiography. The three Greek authors mentioned [Herodotus, Thucydides and Polybius] had considerable merit. The Latins were a poor lot and it was the Latin writers rather than the Greeks who were to have the largest influence in the centuries ahead, indeed almost to our own day.[65]

In my introduction, I suggested a set of criteria to help us to identify the aims and characteristics of historians. I wanted as far as possible to avoid the kind of judgement Hay appears to be making. Criticism can avoid anachronism if every attempt is made to assess the historians on their own terms. It is impossible to imagine an historian winning much credibility today if he or she attempted to employ rhetoric to teach a moral or political lesson, or perhaps made up speeches to encompass those aims. By the same token, our objections would make little sense to Livy or Polybius. Nor would a modern definition of historical truth which emphasizes objectivity and impartiality impress an historian for whom history was to serve truth, rather than claim it for itself. To most classical historians, a work of history was a fusion between the real and what could be passed off as real – all in the service of truth. We cannot complain because this is not 'history as it really happened', which is the tradition many of today's historians were taught to accept as truth (along with the heroic study of the archive sources which gave history its voice). But what we can do is to identify if and when a Greek or Roman historian failed to match his own claims. We certainly had our suspicions that Herodotus was a little too inclined to come up with convenient corroboration, and that Polybius' speeches were unlikely to be as accurate as he claimed.

The general themes of classical historiography are these. Herodotus made inquiry into the past a valid enterprise and stimulated his successors to react to his approaches. Thucydides replaced the Herodotean sense of wonder, excitement and acceptance of the supernatural in history with a cooler rationality which focused more narrowly on military and political history. Polybius in turn saw the value of history as a tool for statesmen and used it to elucidate a political theory explaining change through the identification of a pattern in history.

The assumption that history taught and should be used to teach moral and political lessons was treated to the intoxicating allure of rhetoric. Cicero offered to Roman historians the technique to convince and persuade. Livy in particular made full use of it as he sought to inspire the reader to shun or to emulate the actions of the villains and heroes of his beloved Rome. Equally judgemental but writing in a darker mood and with fewer heroes was Sallust. He too was out to persuade and to teach, but his style is the antithesis of the smooth and flowing Ciceronian approach. In Tacitus we see a writer who could add a gift for dramatic writing to the pessimism of Sallust. Common to all was the view that the mentalities and world-view of individuals – and human nature itself – changed little throughout history. This is why the past could be used to teach by means of an analysis of a man's actions.

To say that the classical historians lacked a developed sense of technique for tackling and evaluating a range of historical sources is true enough. The emphasis placed on oral tradition or more particularly on oral contemporary history is entirely understandable – especially when we consider that the majority were political and military leaders themselves, and with valuable contacts to exploit. To blame or mock them for apparent limitations is another matter. We have no right to take them out of their time.

THE FALL OF THE ROMAN EMPIRE AND THE GROWTH OF CHRISTIAN HISTORIOGRAPHY

It was very tempting for a contemporary writer contemplating the might of Rome to assume that its empire was eternal. It was, of course, no such thing. In the later fourth century AD, the Empire was battered by the movement of Germanic tribes, themselves being forced from their traditional lands by pressure from the east in the form of the nomadic Huns. Franks, Alemanni, Vandals, Visigoths and Ostrogoths broke down the imperial borders. In AD410, the Visigoth king Alaric took Rome itself. In AD451, the Huns themselves were in Italy. The last emperor in Rome, Romulus Augustulus, was dethroned by Odoacer in AD476. This was the end of the western empire based on Rome, but the eastern empire based on Byzantium (created a capital by the emperor Constantine in AD325) survived for another thousand years. Britain, that far-flung outpost of the Empire, was similarly under threat, not only from the Germanic tribes, but also from its traditional enemies such as the Picts. Following the withdrawal of Roman military assistance, there seems to have been a gradual deterioration of Roman-style civil and military institutions and (as far as we can tell from archaeological evidence) in economic life as well. The situation was further complicated by accusations of heresy amongst British Christians under the influence of Pelagius, which led to the despatch of the bishop of Auxerre, Germanus, and the bishop of Troyes, Lupus, to Britain in 429 with orders to quell it. Significantly, Germanus did not only provide religious assistance: as a former Roman general, he also found himself leading British forces to victory over an army of the old and new enemies – Picts and Saxons. But the future lay with the pagan Saxons. In fact, Germanic tribes had already established areas of settlement in Britain before the collapse of Roman authority, but invitations – probably from Vortigern, a dominant figure in Britain from c.425–450 and an opponent both of Rome and Germanus – brought in many more. By 500, Saxons and others were in control of areas of the eastern and south-eastern coasts: Kent, Sussex, Essex, East Anglia and east Yorkshire. By the middle of the seventh century, great Anglo-Saxon kingdoms had been established over much of England.

This brief summary at least provides us with two main themes for examination: the collapse of the Roman Empire and the development of Christianity. What effect did these have on historiography?

Firstly, Christian historians found aspects of classical historiography impossible to accept. God, they argued, had a design for the world which was expressed through linear time – there was nothing cyclical about the Christian vision. History began with the creation of Adam and would come to an end with Christ's Second Coming. And, since history contained the divine plan, it should be universal: a work of history should locate its particular subject in the history of the whole world through time. As Smalley puts it, 'Jewish, Gentile and Christian history must be included, since God embraced all three in his plan.'[66] This explains why medieval writers frequently felt the need to start their works with summaries of the main events – usually in the pattern of six ages identified by St Augustine in the early fifth century. The six ages corresponded with the account in the first chapters of Genesis of God's creation of the world in six days. To Augustine, the world had entered its sixth age with the coming of Christ. And then, when Christ returned – the Second Coming – this seventh age would herald the end of the world and, as we have seen, of recorded time.

Secondly, there was the problem of the Christian's attitude to the Roman Empire to consider. It was difficult to see it in a positive way when its emperors like Nero and Diocletian persecuted Christians. But then, when the emperor Constantine in 313 allowed Christians freedom of worship and subsequently gave Christianity the status of the official religion of the Empire, it became possible to see Rome as part of the divine plan. This attitude is at the heart of the *Ecclesiastical History* of Eusebius, bishop of Caesarea and adviser to Constantine. Eusebius came to believe that the church and the Empire were tied together in the most intimate of relationships. This belief, of course, was difficult to sustain when the Empire fell in ruins. St Augustine, for example, in his *City of God* (written between 413 and 426) drew a distinction between the City of God and any earthly institution. It was therefore dangerous to ascribe a divine purpose to any empire or kingdom. Even so, some historians found it difficult to let the eternal Empire go. Augustine's follower Orosius, in his work *The Seven Books of the History against the Pagans*, saw the Empire as sanctified by its adoption of Christianity. He also took the opportunity to attack the pagans who argued that the Empire was collapsing as a result of becoming Christian.

Christian history was inevitably propagandist. We can take this word both in the modern sense of 'trying to persuade, usually by appealing to emotions and instincts' and in its original meaning of 'propagating the truth of faith'. In the centuries where Christianity had to oppose paganism, history was an important weapon. After all, it could be used to demonstrate the workings of that truth through time. Events themselves had a different meaning and a different set of fundamental causes. The indiscriminate nature of the wheel of fortune was replaced by the divine plan: the arbitrary behaviour of gods or fate by the justice of God. Sin – often the sins of an entire people – therefore became an explanation of great events.

And finally, classical historians, as we have seen, generally preferred oral tradition or eyewitness account to the written source. This was an uncomfortable approach for a Christian historian, since his faith was fed, not by oral sources, but by a work of written history – the Old and New Testaments of the Bible. It is significant that Eusebius, for example, should halt his narrative with copious extracts from documents to 'prove' his argument.

The Venerable Bede (c.672–735)

I decided to discuss the Anglo-Saxon writer Bede for a number of reasons. In the first place, as I remarked in the introduction to the chapter, I think it preferable to focus in some detail on particular historians rather than offer a bland survey of several with whom the reader would then make only a fleeting acquaintance. In Bede's case, he gives us the chance to follow up on the problems and issues facing the Christian historian writing in the post-Roman world. He also offers a fixed point from which to make more general comments on so-called 'Dark Age' or early medieval historiography and so point forward to later medieval historiography. The final reason – and the reader will have to take my word that this is not uppermost in my mind – is because I find Bede and his age fascinating in their own right. As we shall see, he wrote with a splendid clarity and vigour which carry their own appeal.

Bede was a monk of the twin Northumbrian abbeys of Monkwearmouth and Jarrow. It is all too easy to imagine his home as isolated and bereft of cultural (or any other) life, but this would be quite wrong. The seven Anglo-Saxon kingdoms of England had close contacts with the Continent, and it was the Anglo-Saxon Church which sent missionaries to Europe in the late seventh century in an attempt to convert the many remaining pagans amongst the Saxons. The Church in Northumbria itself owed much to the Irish missionaries from Iona, and Bede's own monastery had a superb library courtesy of its founder in c.681, Benedict Biscop. The works by Eusebius and Orosius were amongst many available to Bede.

The European cultural links were reflected in Bede's contemporary popularity in Christian Europe. He was not seen primarily as an historian, but more as a scholar whose biblical commentaries were the most popular of his many works.

Bede's considerable output also included chronicles of the world (in the sense of lists of dated events, based on Eusebius and his continuators). These lists were part of two works on chronology, *De Temporibus* (*Time*) and *De Tempore Ratione* (*The Reckoning of Time*) which, together with his historical writing, represent the first consistent attempt to date events using the Incarnation of Christ as the focal point. The dating systems used by classical historians were confusing and imprecise, and some Christian writers had attempted to introduce a system of dating by reference to Diocletian, the great persecutor of Christians. Bede's work spread the AD/BC system throughout Europe. He also wrote on the geography of the Holy Land and saints' lives (hagiography). His summarizing of saints' lives in the order in which they appeared in the Church's calendar was highly influential. He wrote lives of individual saints and works of science derived from classical writers like Pliny the Elder. There is a central theme running through this impressive list, and that is Bede's view of himself as a teacher; or, more precisely, as a propagandist for his version of orthodox Christianity in a society which was by no means fully converted. This role was clearly important to him. Even as he lay dying, he struggled to finish a work of biblical translation. The future abbot of Wearmouth and Jarrow, Cuthbert, reported:

> **There was one of us with him who said: 'Beloved master, there is still one chapter missing from the book you were dictating, but it seems to me difficult to ask you for more.' But he answered: 'It is easy. Take your pen and prepare it and write quickly.' And this he did.**[67]

A Bede's use of sources and his purpose

Historians who have little good to say of the classical historians or the Christian historians of the so-called Dark Ages generally raise their hats to Bede. It is easy to see why. His *Historia Ecclesiastica Gentis Anglorum* (*Ecclesiastical History of the English People*) – completed in c.732 – had some things to say about methodology which sound sweet to modern ears. In his preface, Bede addressed King Ceolwulf of Northumbria, to whom the work is dedicated:

> But in order to avoid any doubts in the mind of yourself, or of any who may listen to or read this history, as to the accuracy of what I have written, allow me briefly to state the authorities upon whom I chiefly depend.
>
> My principal authority and adviser in this work has been the most reverend Abbot Albinus, an eminent scholar educated in the church of Canterbury by Archbishop Theodore and Abbot Hadrian, both of them respected and learned men. He carefully transmitted to me verbally or in writing through Nothelm, a priest of the church of London, anything he considered worthy of mention that had been done by disciples of the blessed Pope Gregory in the province of Kent or the surrounding regions. Such facts he ascertained either from records or from the recollection of older men. Nothelm himself later visited Rome, and obtained permission from the present Pope Gregory to examine the archives of the holy Roman Church ... Also the most reverend Bishop Daniel of the West Saxons, who is still alive, sent to me in writing certain facts about the history of the Church in his province ... I have learnt by careful enquiry from the brethren of Lastingham monastery how by the ministration of the holy priests Cedd and Chad, their founders, the faith of Christ came to the province of the Mercians ... With regard to events in the various districts of the province of the Northumbrians, from the time that it received the Faith of Christ up to the present day, I am not dependent on any one author, but on countless faithful witnesses who either know or remember the facts, apart from what I know myself.[68]

Goffart enthusiastically comments:

> ... a mastery of historical technique incomparable for its time ... and, not least, an author whose qualities of life and spirit set a model of dedicated scholarship.[69]

We can see what Goffart means. Bede is naming many of his sources and types of information and not simply paying lip-service to the process.

Antonia Gransden[70] points out that he even instructed scribes to name authorities in the margins of his biblical commentaries. Like Eusebius, he copied documents directly into his text (many of which, of course, would have come from Nothelm's work in the Roman archives). We have, for example, a number of papal letters. In Book I is the correspondence surrounding the decision by Pope Gregory I to send Augustine as a missionary to England in 596; in Book II, Pope Boniface's letters to King Edwin attempting to persuade him to adopt Christianity. Where Bede's sources were oral, he often named the informant. In Book V, for instance, he talked of miracles performed by John of Beverley and cited as his main source Berthun:

> ... a most reverend and truthful man, formerly John's deacon and now abbot of the monastery known as In-Derawuda ...[71]

So, we are not only given the name and a comment on his likely veracity, but also the relationship between the informant and the person who was the subject of his information. We also discover the informant's whereabouts. It was by no means unknown for medieval writers to come up with a fictitious informant, but the detail here is too extensive (and verifiable by Bede's readership) for it to be likely in this case.

Despite – or rather because of – these laudable and rigorous attempts to uncover the truth, Bede was, it seems, only too willing to admit his fallibility:

> Should the reader discover any inaccuracies in what I have written, I humbly beg that he will not impute them to me, because, as a true law of history requires, I have laboured honestly to transmit whatever I could ascertain from common report for the instruction of posterity.
>
> I earnestly request all who may hear or read this history of our nation to ask God's mercy on my many failings of mind and body.[72]

Dahmus comments that this statement marks Bede as a 'true historian'.[73]

On the other hand, lovers of dramatic contrast will like the next quotation (from Higham's *An English Empire*):

> Bede could be, and often was, mischievous. He was also writing within a particular literary and intellectual environment so far distant from our own that it is a risky business to describe him by such words as 'historian' at all.[74]

Given what I have already said about the dangers of anachronistic judgement, then I am likely to welcome Higham's reminder about the need to root an evaluation of Bede in his own time. This does not mean, of course, that Higham's interpretation itself is right. His charge is that Bede was not a detached scholar, remote from the world, seeking to employ a methodology which allowed him to recover the past without the distortion of his own political circumstances. Much of this charge, I believe, sticks.

Let us take a small point to start with – Bede's apparent humility. This, Higham sees as an essentially literary device known as *sermo humilis* rather than something personal to Bede. And secondly, we have to consider Bede's purpose. As we have already seen, he spoke of his work as being written for the 'instruction of posterity'. This sounds like many a classical historian, but Bede was not writing an overtly political manual. His work had an evangelical purpose – to spread the correct teaching of Christ's gospel, as distilled by the Roman Church and the contemporary needs of his own Northumbrian Church. Nor is this all. I do not accept that Bede was somehow detached in a political sense from that time. He was a Northumbrian, proud of his Northumbrian kingdom of Bernicia; and this, too, distorted his work.

It is hardly surprising that Bede should have a polemical purpose in his history. We recall that he saw himself primarily as a teacher with the most important message of all: the true faith of Christ. This evangelism similarly shaped the work of the earlier historians Eusebius (as translated into Latin and extended by Rufinus), Orosius and Gildas, whose mid sixth-century work *De Excidio Britanniae* (*The Ruin of Britain*) dealt with the end of Roman Britain and the Anglo-Saxon invasions by blaming them largely on the sins of the Britons. With all these authors, Bede shared the view that God's providence was working through history.

The workings of God were charted by Bede in a number of ways. The most obvious is the frequent references to miracles – a superb teaching aid, of course, to reveal to the pagan and faithful alike the power of God. Some of the miracles are particularly dramatic and defy every natural law. In Book IV, we have a wonderful (in every sense) tale of a young thegn, Imma, who was wounded in battle and imprisoned. But no fetters could be made to stay on him, and this was because his brother, thinking him dead, was having prayers said for his soul.[75] Similarly, when pagan Old Saxons in Germany martyred two English missionaries, the Hewald brothers, and threw them into the Rhine, their bodies were carried *upstream* nearly forty miles with appropriate lighting effects courtesy of a spectacular thunderstorm.[76] Nor should we forget the tale of the eyes of St Alban's executioner, which dropped out as he struck the fatal blow.[77] This is not to say that the *Ecclesiastical History* is little more than a list of the spectacular results of equally spectacular piety, related with maximum credulity. Some of the miracles seem a little more mundane, in that God did not always suspend the workings of nature. Dangerous fires are blown out through prayer, but also through a relatively natural occurrence: a change in wind-direction, or a sudden calm. And Bede did make some effort to name his witnesses for the miracles where possible. The hermit Ethelwald's miraculous calming of a storm is attested to by

> **one of the brethren among whom and for whose benefit it was per-**
> **formed; this was the venerable priest and servant of Christ Guthfrid,**
> **who afterwards presided as abbot over the brethren of the church of**
> **Lindisfarne where he had been brought up.**[78]

Miracles of whatever type have the necessary persuasive power, and Bede was keen to make the point that God intervened directly in the world to reward virtue and to punish sin. Bede stressed the workings of the hand of God in the affairs of kings, whose role was to serve and protect the Church. Gransden sums this up conveniently:

> **... God rewarded good kings with victory and prosperity, and punished**
> **bad ones with earthly calamities.**[79]

There is nothing very subtle about Bede's approach here. Take his comments on King Edwin of Northumbria:

> **As a sign that he would come to the Faith and the heavenly kingdom,**
> **King Edwin received wide additions to his earthly realm.**[80]

This highly propagandist style of history is bound to lead to distortion. It would, for example, be very difficult for Bede to admit to the successes of pagan kings. In Book II, we have a list of kings with lordship (known later as Britain-rulers or 'Bretwaldas') over much of England – and he missed out two who just happened to be pagans. Similarly, he took from Gildas the view that the Anglo-Saxon invasions had been a punishment from God on the sins of the Britons. His attitude to the Britons was also unreasonably harsh for religious reasons.

Bede's deeply-felt loyalty to the Pope meant that he was angrily unfair to the Church of the Britons – particularly those Christians in Wales who would accept by the time he was writing neither the authority of English bishops nor Roman practices, such as the method of dating Easter. In Book II, he described the attempts made by Augustine to persuade them to conform. They remained obdurate, despite a miracle performed by him for their benefit. Augustine offered a compromise: if they would abide by the dating of Easter, conduct the sacrament of baptism properly and – signifi-cantly – preach the gospel to the English, then their other unique practices could be maintained. Still they refused, and Bede had the monks of Bangor put to the sword by the pagan king Ethelfrid as punishment from God.[81] It may have helped Bede in his apparent preference for pagans over

Christians that Ethelfrid was king of Bernicia. Bede maintained his bitterness into his final chapter, where he complained once again about their un-Catholic customs and their hatred of the English.[82]

There is the hint here that we would be wrong to see Bede's distortions as purely religious. In an era where Church and state were bound up in the most intimate of ties, Bede was in no position, even if he had wanted to, to isolate himself from secular considerations. There is no sign that he wanted to. Bede was every inch a Northumbrian, and every millimetre a Bernician. With Bernicia he identified, and this meant that he wrote his history with the contemporary political situation very much in mind. Higham's discussion of this issue is most helpful. He argues – to my mind, convincingly – that Bede responded to the contemporary dominance of Mercia over the Anglo-Saxon kingdoms – a dominance fought over with Bernicia for a century – by downplaying the importance of Mercia and exaggerating the power of Bernicia. The rightful claim to *imperium* – to the inheritance of the Roman domination of much of Britain – is handed over to Bernicia and denied to Mercia in a way which flies in the face of historical fact. When Bede felt obliged to praise a Mercian king, he made sure that the Bernician perspective remained paramount. In Book V, for example, we have the example of Coenred, king of Mercia, who resigned his throne and left for Rome to become a monk. His departure is dated not according to his own years on the throne, but according to the fourth year of the *imperium* of the eight-year-old King of Northumbria. We are then treated not to an account of his stay in Rome, but to a very lengthy description of the death and career of the Northumbrian bishop Wilfrid.[83] It is not that Bede failed to praise Coenred, but that his attention was rather blatantly and deliberately elsewhere. Even the Mercian Church got scant mention. We recall that, in the preface, Bede cited his source for information on that church – the monastery of Lastingham. All well and good, one might think. But Lastingham was not in Mercia. It was – naturally – in Northumbria.

There are other distortions caused by the Bernician bias. Bede was full of praise for Northumbrian missionaries to Germany. But Boniface, from Wessex, was unheralded despite his great contribution in the same area – a contribution greatly appreciated by Pope Gregory III, who made him an archbishop and head of the German province of the Church in 732. Even the Northumbrian bishop Wilfrid suffers from Bede's partisanship. There were two main problems with Wilfrid. Firstly, he was probably Deiran (i.e. south Northumbrian) rather than Bernician. Secondly, he appears to have been presented as the great victor at the Synod of Whitby in 664, where the Roman system of dating Easter – which he advocated – clashed with the Celtic system (defended by Irish representatives). One might expect Bede to applaud this, but the writer of the *Life of Wilfrid*, Eddius Stephanus, had the audacity to criticize the Irish savagely and to suggest that Wilfrid was obliged to rescue the cause of Rome after the comparative failure of Pope Gregory the Great's initiative. This offended both Bede's respect for that Pope and also his genuine gratitude for the part played by the Irish in guiding the fledgling Bernician Church. Goffart argues that the result of all this is that Wilfrid does not receive the recognition he deserved in the *Ecclesiastical History*.

So, the picture we are getting of Bede is not that of the unworldly scholar, unaffected and uninterested by the secular world lapping at the doors of his haven. Instead, we have a realistic picture of a man of his time. His evangelical zeal and his love for Bernicia were hardly likely to be cast aside when he picked up his pen. In fact, they complemented each other. As Gransden points out, Bede looked at the reign of King Edwin (616–32) as a golden age for Northumbria in both secular and spiritual terms. He wanted that age to come again, and wrote his history with that aim in mind. One can see his priorities very clearly in his dedication of the *Ecclesiastical History*, not to a bishop or abbot, but to the Northumbrian king, Ceolwulf. And his deep pastoral concerns are equally as clear in his letter to Egbert, Bishop of York, in 734. He lamented the state of the Northumbrian Church, but suggested that reform could be made through cooperation with Ceolwulf:

> **who through his innate love of religion will take care constantly and firmly to help forward whatever belongs to the rule of justice ...**[84]

B Bede's style and rhetoric

It is a commonplace – but none the less true for that – that Bede was an excellent stylist. He wrote with exemplary clarity, and could describe with admirable vigour and without pretension. But what really matters is the question of whether Bede sought to use the tools of classical rhetoric in his desire to evangelize and persuade. According to Roger Ray,[85] he did. After all, Bede made use of writers like Orosius and Eusebius who were certainly familiar with rhetoric. Ray believes that Bede knew something of Cicero's work. The strongest part of Ray's case is when he looks in detail at what Bede had to say. He stresses a telling quotation from the preface, in which Bede describes the purpose of his history:

> **For if history records good things of good men, the thoughtful hearer is encouraged to imitate what is good: or if it records evil of wicked men, the devout, religious listener or reader is encouraged to avoid all that is sinful and perverse and to follow what he knows to be good and pleasing to God.**[86]

Much of this could have come from the pen of Livy himself. Ray also believes that the geographical and ethnographical introduction after the preface bears the hallmarks of the rhetorical historian. But when we get to the debate at the Synod of Whitby, we see Bede adopting not only the technical terminology of rhetoric, but also a pattern of paired speeches:

> a favourite form of Roman deliberative oratory and a preferred device of rhetorical historians.[87]

This is not to suggest that Bede invented speeches with the profusion of Livy. But one has to say that there are times when the sheer quality of his writing betokens his desire to persuade more than it betokens his concern for strict accuracy. Take this wonderful speech by a member of King Edwin's council as it deliberated the value of adopting the Christian faith:

> Your Majesty, when we compare the present life of man on earth with that time of which we have no knowledge, it seems to me like the swift flight of a single sparrow through the banqueting-hall where you are sitting at dinner on a winter's day with your thegns and counsellors. In the midst there is a comforting fire to warm the hall; outside, the storms of winter rain or snow are raging. This sparrow flies swiftly in through one door of the hall, and out through another. While he is inside, he is safe from the winter storms; but after a few moments of comfort, he vanishes from sight into the wintry world from which he came. Even so, man appears on earth for a little while; but of what went before this life or of what follows, we know nothing. Therefore, if this new teaching has brought any more certain knowledge, it seems only right that we should follow it.[88]

It comes as no surprise to the reader that, following such eloquence, the chief priest should rush off to smash his pagan idols.

C   A conclusion on Bede

Antonia Gransden offers a suitably upbeat assessment of Bede which is well worth quoting at some length:

> ... the *Ecclesiastical History* owes its lasting reputation to Bede's ability as an historian. His grasp of historical method was unique in the middle ages. It appears in his chronology and in the competence with which he collected data ... Bede exploited all resources. He ransacked the library and archives at Wearmouth/Jarrow, asked his friends to search for documents, and questioned people he met. Unlike most medieval writers he meticulously named most of his sources of information, literary, documentary and oral.[89]

It was clearly important for Bede to name his authorities, and one can see why. His history was propagandist: like Eusebius and Orosius, he was out to persuade the pagan or to cement the faith of the Christian. To do so, he sought to convince in a number of ways. Citing sources was one, but so was – if we accept Ray's argument – the use of rhetoric. And so was the use of miracles, and the distortions whereby he aimed to convince listeners (or readers) that Christians succeed both in this life and in the life to come. The truth for Bede was not some sort of neutrality marked by objectivity; nor was history a method of letting the past speak for itself. It was the Christian truth, and in the truth of history was God's plan revealed. Even then, Bede's particular version of Christian historical truth was further coloured by his love for the Church of Rome, Bernicia, Northumbria and Anglo-Saxon England – very much in that order. He was not in a position to ignore secular matters given the way in which Church and state were intertwined in his society, and it is odd that Smalley seems to think that he made the attempt to so.[90]

Because Bede is something of a jewel among medieval historians, it is sometimes tempting to set him apart as if he was untouched by the historiographical context. The influence of Orosius we detected in his geographical introduction, and his chronologies reflect the work of Eusebius. The influence of Cicero was more problematic, but we pointed to rhetorical flourishes in his work.

Finally, we should also consider the relationship between the so-called annal and Bede. Annals were essentially lists of events, generally without a connecting narrative. The *tabulae pontificum* (see p.58) can be seen as a type of annal. The Christian version of annals grew out of the Easter tables, which were drawn up in monastic and other great churches to calculate the date of Easter – a moveable feast and the greatest of the Christian festivals. From this date, one could calculate the Paschal Term (the date of Passover) and write in the other important days in the Church year. And, in the gaps, one could write down news of any important events which the computist (the calculator of the tables) thought of interest. Given that the computist was almost always a monk, the events were often of significance to his own monastery, but references to national happenings were rarely politically astute. Storms and sheep, yes – political analysis, absolutely not. What Bede was doing in the *Ecclesiastical History* was, of course, far more sophisticated than this. The closest he gets to the annal is Chapter 24 of Book V, where he offers a year-by-year chronological summary of his work. Perhaps because Bede is so relatively sophisticated, the standard form of medieval historiography – the medieval chronicle – developed more out of the annals than it did out of Bede. There are other possible reasons. Bede's miracle stories were much appreciated and enjoyed but, as society became more exclusively Christian, the evangelical purpose of Bede's anti-pagan stance became less appropriate. Against this, there are some medieval historians who clearly appreciated and sought to copy Bede's methods. The best examples are the twelfth-century chroniclers of England, Orderic Vitalis and William of Malmesbury.

Medieval historiography

Denys Hay points to the *Anglo-Saxon Chronicle* (or chronicles, as there are several versions reflecting different local interests) as typical of the way in which the annal developed into the chronicle, even though it was most unusual in being written in the vernacular rather than Latin. The *Chronicle* began with the Creation, offering brief factual statements year by year. It was probably first started sometime in the reign of Alfred (871–99), using earlier Latin annals and probably oral epic poems to fill in the earlier Saxon years. Detail certainly increased from Alfred's reign onwards, but with little or nothing by way of a linked narrative. We can take an example to illustrate this from the entry for 891:

> In this year, the host went east; and king Arnulf fought against the mounted host, before the ships came, with the East Franks and the Saxons and the Bavarians, and put it to flight.
>
> And three Irishmen came to king Alfred in a boat without any oars ... and Suibhne, the best teacher among the Scots, died ... And the same year after Easter ... appeared the star which in Latin is called 'cometa' ...[91]

The standard of explanation is clearly poor, and information which is neither connected nor differentiated is thrown together. Even the chronology was sometimes unreliable – partly because of copyists' mistakes, partly because it is not always clear on which day the particular chronicler started the new year.

The *Anglo-Saxon Chronicle* started to offer more by way of a linked narrative with the tenth-century Danish invasions, but the annalistic format inevitably hindered an effective analysis of causes. After all, how does one explore longer or medium-term causes when tied to a one-thing-after-another, year-by-year approach? And it was this framework that the *Chronicle* (which lasted into the twelfth century) bequeathed to subsequent chroniclers, in England at least. As we have seen, William of Malmesbury, for instance, was unusual in recognizing and attempting to imitate the qualities of Bede, speaking of his predecessor as a 'man of singular learning and modesty',[92] but even he wandered into the snares of the annal at times.

Difficulty with handling sophisticated causation was not a characteristic of English medieval historiography alone. Throughout Christian Europe was the tendency to ascribe causes either to God's will or to a rather superficial account of personal motives. In any case, since many of the chroniclers were monks, their awareness of secular affairs was generally limited. There was little false modesty about the comments of Orderic Vitalis:

> **Skilful historians could write a memorable history of these great men and women ... We, however, who have no experience of the courts of the world, but spend our lives in the daily rounds of the cloisters where we live, will briefly note what is relevant to our purpose.**[95]

It was a characteristic of medieval society that change was so slow to be almost undetectable. This meant that there were few examples where historians could actually see clear breaks between times in the past. The trap of anachronism therefore lay gaping, and most fell straight in without noticing the thud. The medieval writer (like his Greek predecessor) simply assumed that the structures of society and human behaviour were unchanging, and therefore foisted on the past his own attitudes and experience. This partly explains the prevalence and success of what we would call forgeries. Perhaps the best-known example is the spurious *Donation of Constantine* in which that emperor is supposed to have granted Italy to the Pope as his own territory. As Peter Burke says:

> **To be a historical 'forger', as we now understand the term, is impossible without a sense of historical perspective. It is necessary to realise the difference between past and present ... if the authors [of the *Donation*] lacked a sense of change, it is likely that they really thought that Constantine must have made the pope his heir ...**[94]

The frequent use of forgery – and many monasteries forged land deeds for property they genuinely felt but could not prove was theirs – is suggestive of a cavalier approach to historical evidence. It is unusual to find a medieval historian who balanced different types of evidence to make a judgement, and very usual to find him simply lifting evidence from other writers without any form of assessment or evaluation. Bede stands out as an historian who was, on occasion, prepared to compare and evaluate; but then some of his miracle stories were imported wholesale from other, much less critical sources.

By the late thirteenth century, the monastic chronicle appeared to be on the wane. I am reluctant to use an unhelpful phrase like 'the spirit of the age was changing', so perhaps I can suggest that the monastic life, with its assumption that the attitude of *contemptu mundi* – avoiding the snares of wordly life – was the best route to salvation, found itself increasingly challenged by the activities of the new orders of friars who worked with and in the secular world. Towns and universities were growing, and, with an increasing lay readership, urban chronicles started to develop which were as interested in the doings of burghers and mayors as they were in the deeds of saints, bishops and kings.

Renaissance historiography

It is very tempting to avoid defining as slippery a term as 'Renaissance', but I shall do so with a certain superficial confidence and inner misgivings. The word is, of course, an historian's construct, so it might be best to start with the Swiss scholar Jacob Burckhardt whose book (he called it an 'essay') *Die Kultur der Renaissance in Italien* (1860) (*The Civilization of the Renaissance in Italy*) established a definition which has endured, even if only as a target at which modern historians can aim. The Renaissance, said Burckhardt, was indeed a 'new birth', represented by the

> ... **great and general enthusiasm of the Italians for classical antiquity [which] really begins in the fourteenth century. For this a development of civic life was required, which took place only in Italy, and there not till then: that noble and burgher live together on equal terms, but a society arise which felt the need for culture, and had the leisure and the means to obtain it. But culture, as soon as it freed itself from the reverie of the Middle Ages, could not at once and without help find its way to understanding the physical and intellectual world. It needed a guide, and found one in the ancient civilization, with its wealth of truth and knowledge in every spiritual interest. Both the form and the substance of this civilization were adopted with admiring gratitude; it became the chief part of the culture of the age.**[95]

Most of Burckhardt's arguments have been exposed as over-generalizations, exaggerations or both. Medieval attitudes and traditions survived into the so-called Renaissance period; Burckhardt's dramatic contrast between Italy and the rest of Europe is similarly overplayed. There was more adaptation and less slavish imitation of classical models than he thought. As Burke[96] points out, Burckhardt found Switzerland dull and stuffy and read into some of his Renaissance heroes his desire to break with the past.

Even so, the Renaissance remains a meaningful label – in part because those involved in its wide-ranging cultural life believed that they were shaping something new. And there are other labels. We also have German historians of the nineteenth century to thank for 'humanism', although they in turn were adapting the fifteenth-century word *humanistae*, referring to teachers of *studia humanitatis*: grammar, rhetoric, poetry, ethics and history. For our purposes, the meaning of humanism is really twofold: in its wider sense, it is 'associated with the belief in the dignity of man';[97] in its narrower sense, it means 'an interest in Latin and Greek literature which sets a high value on the lessons to be drawn from it'.[98] The two meanings can be combined, because the assumption behind much Greek and Latin literature was that humankind could progress, and that there were vital lessons to be learned – in which process, of course, history played a significant part.

A sense of progress demands an awareness of change, and this represents one of the most important characteristics of Renaissance thought. The founding father of Renaissance humanism is traditionally seen as the Florentine scholar and poet Petrarch (1304–74), whose researches and antiquarian interests led him to an awareness of the distinction between the classical period and his more recent past. In one sonnet, he significantly referred to the glories of the past and the middle age in which he lived:

> **Living, I despise what melancholy fate**
> **has brought us wretches in these evil years.**
> **Long before my birth time smiled and may again,**
> **for once there was, and yet will be, more joyful days.**
> **But in this middle age time's dregs**
> **sweep around us, and we bend beneath a heavy**
> **load of vice. Genius, virtue, glory now**
> **have gone, leaving chance and sloth to rule.**
> **Shameful vision this! We must awake or die.**[99]

The sense of the essential difference of the past – so foreign to the medieval chronicler – was subsequently reflected in many aspects of Renaissance culture. In painting and architecture, artists were castigated for anachronism. The architect Antonio Filarete insisted:

> **If you have to do a thing that represents the present time, do not dress your figures in the antique fashion. In the same way, if you have to represent antiquity, do not dress them in modern dress.**[100]

This awareness of difference enabled scholars of philology (the study of language) to exploit a parallel awareness of style and the development of language to evaluate the authenticity of documents. The most celebrated example is the devastating (and bad-tempered) critique by Lorenzo Valla of the fake *Donation of Constantine* in 1440 (see p.79). Valla pointed to the clear failures of the forger to understand the contemporary meaning of words like 'diadem'; in Constantine's day diadems were made of cloth and were not, therefore, anything like the gold and bejewelled crown described in the *Donation*:

> **I know that for a long time now men's ears are waiting to hear the offence with which I charge the Roman pontiffs ... For during some centuries now, either they have not known that the Donation of Constantine is spurious and forged, or else they themselves forged it ... Which shall I censure the more, the stupidity of the ideas, or of the words?**[101]

The humanist call, then, was for a return *ad fontes* – to the well-spring or sources of knowledge; in other words, to the shapers and recorders of the ancient world. In his enthusiasm, Petrarch wrote letters to his long-dead heroes Cicero and Livy, calling the latter 'thou matchless historian'.[102]

It is hardly surprising that Renaissance historians should seek to model their history on their classical predecessors. One mark of this was the desire to write the history of one's city-state in the manner of Livy. A good example is Leonardo Bruni (c.1374–1444), whose *History of the Florentine People* offers the typical classical justification for the study of history: it was to encourage virtue by offering examples to emulate or to shun. Bruni charted the rise of Florence, drawing parallels with that of ancient Rome, and invoked republican liberty as the great cause of Florence's eminence. He followed his masters in making up speeches, and wrote a Latin which was classical rather than late medieval. Bruni admitted that his desire to write in the appropriate manner nearly led him to abandon writing about Florence, given 'the sheer clumsiness of the names, scarcely capable of being rendered into elegant Latin'.[103] Nevertheless, Bruni, as we shall see, stands out amongst a rather less worthy group of emulators of Livy and Sallust, who, overdosing on Ciceronian rhetoric, produced slavish imitations which distorted the history of their chosen cities. Felix Gilbert[104] charts the failings of Bernardo Rucellai, who tackled the Florence dominated by the charismatic friar and preacher Savonarola by ignoring Savonarola whenever possible, on the grounds that he did not fit conveniently the classical models. Or, we have the official Venetian historian Pietro Bembo, who praised Venice as a state which, he claimed, craved the well-being and freedom of its citizens. He performed this civic duty in the accepted rhetorical manner but blithely ignored the possibilities afforded by the wealth of written sources available to him.

It is a sign of the importance attached to humanist scholarship in the Italian city-states that good scholars could hope for influential political posts without necessarily having undergone an apprenticeship in administration or diplomacy. And the experience of the hazardous world of fifteenth and sixteenth-century Italian politics was in turn likely to exert a marked influence on those who subsequently wrote history. The best example is Niccolò Machiavelli (1469–1527), who was made second chancellor of the Florentine Republic in 1498 largely on the strength of his preparation in the *studia humanitatis*. His education and his diplomatic missions to France, where he met the ruthless and audacious Cesare Borgia, Duke of Romagna, and to the papal court, where he met the equally ruthless and audacious Pope Julius II, shaped his important works of history and politics: namely, the *Discourses on Livy* (1513–21), the *Florentine Histories* (c.1525, published posthumously in 1532) and *The Prince* (1516). The work on Livy reflected his acceptance of the standard classical assumption that the study of history was of inestimable value to statesmen. He therefore attempted to explore the history of Rome and to make use of Polybius' cyclical pattern of historical change to provide lessons for Florence itself. His *Florentine Histories* also made use of his observation of Borgia and Julius II in action. He came to admire their capacity for decisiveness, for quick thinking, for ruthlessness and for sheer dissembling and hypocrisy in the interests of political gain. Fortune, in Machiavelli's terms, clearly favoured the brave, and the man of virtue who was to be emulated was more Cesare than Christ. Writing up this kind of insight in the political manual *The Prince* meant that Machiavelli was distancing himself even from Roman moralists,for whom princely virtue (*virtu* in Italian, *virtus* in Latin) (see p.62) meant honesty, wisdom and justice. He was also creating an unenviable reputation for himself as an amoral political thinker: hence the origin of the term 'Machiavellian', which means crafty, cunning and – of course – ruthless.

The overwhelmingly secular spirit of his work is ably revealed in the *Discourses on Livy*. *Virtu* is explored in the context of an analysis of how Rome became great: there were, Machiavelli felt, direct lessons to be learned if Florence itself was to echo that greatness. It was vital, he argued, that the citizens of a city should possess *virtu*: only then might the cycle of decay be arrested. In this context, *virtu* meant a willingness to respond quickly to the needs of the city and to do whatever was necessary to uphold or further its interests. Christian ethics were irrelevant. If it would serve the city to lie, cheat or murder, then so be it. It was, argued Machiavelli, acceptable for the alleged joint founder of Rome, Romulus, to murder his brother because he did so to serve the needs of the city:

> **That Romulus was among those who deserve to be excused for the death of his brother ... and that what he did was for the common good and not for private ambition, is shown by the fact that he immediately established a senate with which he consulted and according to whose opinions he made decisions.**[105]

Some of Machiavelli's ideas for instilling *virtu* can be seen in these comments on Romulus. The establishing of the senate to work with Romulus reflects Machiavelli's belief in the importance of the mixed constitution, established by a law-giver. This idea – familiar from Polybius, of course – was a commonplace in humanist thought. But what separated Machiavelli from his contemporaries was a refusal to place it, implicitly or explicitly, in the context of a Christian world-view. Machiavelli's constitution was to thrive, not on Christian cooperation, but by a creative but very real tension between the social classes – a tension which would be set in place by the law-giver, who would make sure that the various groups were obliged to be on the alert for any attempt by one group to dominate the other (see p.199). Establishing a new government would require the ruthless elimination of those associated with the former régime:

> **every prince should be warned that he will never live in security in his principality as long as those whom he deprived of it are alive.**[106]

Equally remarkable was Machiavelli's view of the value of religion to the establishment of civic virtue. Religion was presented as a mechanism to encourage the development of *virtu*, but Machiavelli clearly found aspects of Christianity distinctly inappropriate. In praising humility, self-abnegation and other-worldliness, it failed to serve the needs of the city or principality. Machiavelli's examples are revealing. He described approvingly the use by Roman nobles of religion to secure their own election as tribunes by convincing the plebeians that the gods were angry with the policies of the former tribunes – who just happened to be plebeian.[107] Similarly, he praised the perspicuity of the army commanders who were prepared to manipulate their soldiers' belief in soothsayers and auspices to send them confidently into battle.[108]

The *Florentine Histories* has some of the characteristics of a typical humanist history, but distorted and even satirized as a result of Machiavelli's singular views and constant politicizing. His secular definition of *virtu* is again greatly in evidence, and its absence in the Florence of his own day is much bemoaned. His belief in the existence of political laws – the importance of the mixed constitution, the dangers of tyranny – led him to dwell on some events which illustrated his ideas, and to skim over whole decades where no lessons could be discerned. Book II ends with a lengthy discussion of the overthrow of the tyranny of the Duke of Athens and the attempts and failures to balance the constitution.[109] At the start of Book III, Machiavelli offered a comparison between ancient Rome and contemporary Florence in which he made clear the difference between creative tension and resultant law-making in Rome and disastrous disunity in Florence:

> The grave and natural enmities that exist between the men of the
> people and the nobles, caused by the wish of the latter to command and
> the former not to obey, are the cause of all evils that arise in cities ...
> Those [enmities] in Rome ended with a law, those in Florence with the
> exile and the death of many citizens; those in Rome always increased
> military virtue, those in Florence eliminated it altogether ...[110]

His attitude to the corruption of Florentine political life is ably revealed in
the way in which he parodied the great set-piece battles beloved of the classical historians and humanist imitators. The famous battle of Anghiari
(1440) – a Florentine victory – was described in detail (including the sketch
of the topography of the battlefield derived from classical models); but
Machiavelli was at pains to emphasize how little glory was won in a virtually bloodless, day-long slog between forces whose *virtu* was never tested by
any real risk of death:

> In such a defeat and in so long a battle that lasted from twenty to
> twenty-four hours, only one man died, and he not from wounds or any
> other virtuous blow, but, falling off his horse, he was trampled on and
> expired.[111]

Machiavelli's work, then, illuminates humanist historiography as much by
his departure from its assumptions as by his use of its standard techniques.
In common with his contemporaries was his view that history taught by
examples, but the examples in Machiavelli were not intended as illustra-
tions of moral behaviour to emulate or immoral behaviour to shun: they
were intended to illustrate the workings of political principles and laws. The
events he described and the characters he drew were therefore distorted to
meet these objectives. He provided set speeches in the usual humanist
manner, but in his case his purpose was to illustrate those political principles, rather than to provide examples which the historian could exploit to
make – and encourage the reader to make – the necessary moral judgements.

Humanist historians had to bear in mind the need for patrons, and, in Florence itself, the chancellor was expected to write a history of the city.[112]
Machiavelli himself wrote the *Florentine Histories* at the behest of the
Medici family, whose influence over Florence he deplored. Unsurprisingly,
there are instances of mealy-mouthed praise of the Medici,[113] but his dislike
surfaced when describing the régime of Lorenzo de' Medici. There is an
uneasy tension between the final sentence of his work, which laments the
ruin of Italy, and the praise of Lorenzo ('loved by fortune and by God').[114]

It is surely significant that Machiavelli should have chosen to write in
Italian rather than in Latin. This reflects the way in which he adapted,

rather than imitated unthinkingly, the tenets of classical historiography. His younger contemporary, Francesco Guicciardini (1483–1540), similarly wrote in Italian, also had a political career which fell short of his hopes and expectations, and shared with Machiavelli a pessimism and understanding of *realpolitik* which carried him beyond the essential optimism of humanist exemplifications of moral virtue. His *History of Italy* (1561–4) offered a distinctly sophisticated analysis of causation which, although it concentrated on individual motives, also allowed for the influence of political concepts such as the search for a balance of power. The extract below also demonstrates that Guicciardini – most unusually for an historian of this period – recognized the uncertainty involved in making judgements on human motivation:

> **Lorenzo [de' Medici] had lately allied himself through marriage to Pope Innocent VIII (who listened readily to his counsels); his name was respected throughout Italy and his authority was great in all discussions on matters of common interest. Knowing that it would be very dangerous to himself and to the Florentine Republic if any of the larger states increased their power, he diligently sought to maintain the affairs of Italy in such a balance that they might not favour one side more than another ... Ferdinand of Aragon, King of Naples, shared his desire for universal peace ... Perhaps because a few years earlier he had experienced, with the gravest danger, the hatred of his barons and of his common subjects ... Or perhaps he realised that to balance the power of the Venetians, which was then a threat to the whole of Italy, he must remain allied with the other states ...[115]**

In any conclusion on Renaissance historians, it is important to remember that Machiavelli and Guicciardini have been used to help identify characteristics of humanist historiography from which they departed rather than slavishly followed themselves. It is tempting to see most historians of the period as pale imitators of their classical heroes. As we have seen, some did distort everything they wrote to fit the antique model. Most were influenced by the Roman historians rather than Herodotus and Thucydides, and this was perhaps unfortunate. Ciceronian rhetoric lured the historian into writing set pieces which not only allowed him to demonstrate his rhetorical skill, but also gave him the chance to ignore the inconvenience of lack of sources or any need to explore the detailed psychology of a particular individual. What mattered was the general truth about leaders, or about the conduct of battles. To communicate this general truth, inventing a speech (or perhaps even distorting a personality) was not a misfortune – it was a necessity. The Renaissance historians were confident that rhetoric could change minds, overturn corrupt régimes and inspire the winning of military glory.[116]

On the other hand, there were clear restrictions on invention. Since history did teach lessons of political and other morality, it was important to recover facts as far as possible: to know how men actually conducted themselves. Rhetoric filled in the gaps and underlined the lessons. However, the historians' methods for recovering the true facts almost always involved a search for the one narrative account on which the historian could base his work and to which he could subsequently apply the techniques of rhetoric for the elucidation of lessons. Generally speaking, this would mean finding a narrative history close to the time of the events themselves. There was rarely any attempt to synthesize different sources, and no development of a technique to evaluate them. City archives existed, but were tapped equally rarely; Bruni's *History of the Florentine People* is a notable exception, in this as in other ways. For example, unusually for a humanist, he recognized the extent to which economic factors influenced decision making. Even so, his account was unashamedly narrative and focused on personalities: he never stopped the flow to offer a real analysis of economic structures or trends (see pp.197–8). In any case, it is probably fair to argue that Bruni mined the archives only when he could find little chronicle evidence.[117]

One should, perhaps, conclude with a reminder of the great contribution of the Renaissance to the understanding of history: that vital sense of anachronism and therefore of change. The humanist historians did not, perhaps, take it to its logical conclusion – namely, to a questioning of the assumptions that human behaviour was constant through time and that the past could meet the needs of the present.

Conclusion

I can pick up the theme of anachronism by recalling my introduction to the chapter. There I suggested that to impose any modern standard of judging historians would be deeply anachronistic. It would also lead us to a failure in contextualizing the writers and, in so doing, to ignore their aims. On the other hand, we had to have some sort of criteria to identify the characteristics of the historians and to compare them. Bearing in mind our discussion of the nature of history in Chapter 1, I recognized that the criteria cannot be timeless and therefore universally valid, and that, to some extent at least, they reflect my own education, historical training and system of values. Even the attempt to be determinedly objective and apparently non-judgemental is itself subjective and judgemental, because I believe that making the attempt itself is the *right thing to do*. Others might see it as wishy-washy Western liberalism. But the criteria do at least reflect what virtually every writer of history would recognize as being part of his discipline: using sources, writing to convey meaning effectively and in what is seen as a suitable style, focusing on particular aspects of the past (such as military or political history), formulating a view of the purposes of one's discipline and responding to the work of predecessors.

Importantly, the criteria do not demand an assessment in terms of 'good' and 'bad', except where the historian fails to meet his own claims. Nor do they assume that historiography somehow improves through time. This is just as well, since, as we have seen, it was not possible to trace anything so facile as a line of development from Herodotus to Machiavelli. I certainly do not intend to conclude with a superficial overview, but with the thought that studying Herodotus is as demanding and rewarding as studying any modern historian, and that the questions his work poses about the nature of history, its value and the method of transmitting it are as pertinent now as they were in his time, when the discipline called history did not exist.

From the Enlightenment of the Eighteenth Century to von Ranke and the Rankean Tradition

THE ENLIGHTENMENT

When I was at school in the sixth form, I can remember being enlightened thanks to the Enlightenment. My history teachers never bothered to explain what a decent A level essay was or how one should write it, and so my fellow sixth-formers and I floundered around mightily and to little effect. And then, we were set a question along the lines of 'How much of an enlightened despot was Frederick the Great?'. It occurred to me that I should do something mind-numbingly straightforward and mechanical: simply extract from our one textbook the so-called 'principles of the Enlightenment' and assess how far Frederick – or was it Maria Theresa? – followed these. My teacher showed his approbation (and, I suspect, his surprise) by asking me to read it out as an example of how a decentish essay should be approached. Of course, he never bothered to point out what it was that made the essay decentish, but the incident stuck in my mind – and so did the principles of the Enlightenment. These, it seemed, included a rabid distrust of organized religion, a belief in the necessity of education as a key to human progress and a concomitant belief in the power of human reason to measure, to experiment and to establish laws which would allow mankind to control his world.

Since then, I have learned to be chary of laying down any such set of principles. The danger is twofold. Firstly, in doing so, we inevitably over-generalize. Were the enlightened ones – whoever they might be – really subscribers to a distinct, precise and uniform list of ideas? And secondly, there is the tendency to divorce a set of ideas from the society which produced them, as if they emerged from the teeming brains of certain thinkers who were remote from the social, cultural, political and economic realities. This means that my very necessary definition of the Enlightenment will be less convenient, but hopefully rather more historical, than that offered in the decentish essay of the seventeen-year-old.

The eighteenth-century Enlightenment in Europe followed on the heels of the major religious conflicts of the seventeenth century. The evils of wars of religion offered object lessons to the increasingly affluent secular intelligentsia of the time, whose ideas could flourish in a period of rapid, cheap printing and increasing literacy. For the first time, it seemed, men of ideas were not clerics, and they did not scruple to attack the Church – particularly the Catholic Church – for allegedly holding in thrall the intellect of mankind, for attempting to hold back progress and for weaving webs of superstition which served to maintain the power of the clergy at the cost of the suffering and deaths of untold thousands in conflicts which should never have happened.

The 'man of sense' of the Enlightenment was therefore no friend to established religion. He applauded the way in which the thinkers of his day interpreted the world in a critical, enquiring, rational, but above all, *secular* spirit. God's revelation or providential action was not an adequate explanation for the world as it was. In particular, the 'man of sense' turned to the writings of the *philosophes* for instruction. The English translation 'philosophers' will hardly suffice; the German version *Aufklärer* or 'enlighteners' is better. From writers such as Voltaire or from the *Encyclopédie* edited by Diderot and d'Alembert, he would be encouraged to visualize a society based on an understanding of human nature and the laws governing human behaviour. He would learn that it was not enough to dream: that the man of sense was a propagandist and an activist whose aim must be to improve education, the legal system and administration and to encourage religious toleration and the freedom of the intellect.

This is not to say that the *philosophes* spoke with one voice. The Genevan Jean-Jacques Rousseau might write at one time for Diderot's *Encyclopédie*, but he did not share the assumption of many of his fellow contributors that science and intellectual freedom would lead to progress. Mankind, Rousseau felt, needed to be led into virtue: no society could be virtuous without an organized religious faith. And, in his treatise *The Social Contract* (1762), he argued that liberty does not stem from individual freedom but from subservience, not to a monarch or any other single person, but to an impersonal state which gives voice to the so-called General Will of the People. But, despite his distance from other *philosophes*, there are key elements in common. Rousseau's approach rested upon his observation and experience, his refusal to argue by quoting dogmatic religion, his dissatisfaction with the old systems of government in the European monarchies – the *ancien régime* – and on his willingness to use his reason to evaluate systems of government and to point to a better future. This willingness is ably revealed in his statement of purpose in Book 1 of *The Social Contract*:

> **My purpose is to consider if, in political society, there can be any legitimate and sure principle of government, taking men as they are and laws as they might be.**[1]

Enlightenment historiography

It is hardly surprising that *philosophes* should write history. After all, history offered examples of behaviour which might be used to illustrate or support generalizations or laws about human nature. This is different in kind from the examples used by Renaissance historians, who, as we saw in Chapter 2, brought a Christian world-view to bear on the moral and political lessons beloved of their classical masters. As Roy Porter puts it, they united 'the good man and the good Christian'.[2] Most *philosophes* felt that the good man and the good Christian were mutually exclusive. Enlightenment historiography was also different in kind from the writings of many seventeenth and early eighteenth-century historians who, enthused by the antiquarian spirit, produced massively detailed factual works which were replete with references but weak in narrative thrust. Voltaire called them *érudits* (the 'learned ones') with more than a tinge of sarcasm. In his view, they were pursuing mouldy futilities in dark corners with stuttering candles; the philosophic historian would light up the entire room, even if that meant ignoring the nooks and crannies of mere detail. History could be used to identify the development of 'civilization' – a term coined in the eighteenth century. This meant that history should be about the development of manners, customs, legal and political institutions, rather than an obsessive recounting of military and political matters. The tracing of that development rested upon the assumption that human nature and behaviour were constant through time, and therefore dependent on the discernible laws referred to above. In his work of 1734, *Considerations on the Greatness and Decadence of the Romans*, Montesquieu argued that:

> ...because men have had the same passions throughout time, the occasions which produce the great changes might be different, but the causes are always the same.[3] [author's translation]

Similarly, the Scots philosopher and historian David Hume (1711–76) argued that the chief use of history

> **is only to discover the constant and universal principles of human nature, by shewing men in all varieties of circumstances and situations.[4]**

As Womersley has argued,[5] in practice Hume followed the standard and rather circular method of the philosophic historian. One's knowledge of human nature must precede the history, which then allegedly confirms it. In other words, the *philosophes* tended to select a (by no means exhaustive) number of facts to fit their preconceived theories, without bothering to offer any balanced assessment of detailed evidence. In a letter to a friend, Hume displayed his lack of interest in research from original sources, claimed that he tried to weigh printed authorities without prejudice but added that he based his

> **probable conclusion which the *nature of man* [author's italics], the experience of ages, and the conduct of political men during those ages warranted his drawing.[6]**

And, of course, their writings are extremely judgemental. Voltaire's anti-clericalism permeated his work and encouraged him to exercise his considerable capacity for invective. Phillipson offers a very enthusiastic defence of Hume as an historian, arguing that 'no one could have pleaded less dogmatically than Hume'[7] and that his *History of England* encouraged readers to exercise their own judgement. But Hume's *History* – not to mention his early essay *Of Superstition and Enthusiasm* – resound with claims that priests thrived on superstition, turned themselves and their princely masters into tyrants and revelled in persecution.

One last point needs to be made about the *philosophes* and their writing of history. All were keen popularizers, in the sense that they wanted their works to be accessible to polite society throughout Europe. But they were not intended to be rallying cries for the masses, even though later enemies claimed that the writings of Rousseau and Voltaire led directly to the excesses of the French Revolution.

Edward Gibbon (1737–94)

Perhaps the greatest historian in the disparate group of *philosophes* was the Englishman Edward Gibbon, but it could be argued that his positive qualities as an historian lay precisely in those areas where he differed from

Voltaire and Montesquieu. Before I provide a brief biography of Gibbon and then assess his work, I want to include a number of extracts from his great work, *The History of the Decline and Fall of the Roman Empire* (1776–88). The extracts are, of course, intended to make some important points about Gibbon as an historian. But it is as well to admit that just one or two have also been chosen because they make me laugh – a very rare pleasure in a history book.

At the risk of making it all sound like a seminar, perhaps I could suggest that the reader should consider how far the extracts fit the model of the philosophic historian, and what characteristics of Gibbon as an historian may be inferred from them.

> **(i) In the second century of the Christian era, the empire of Rome comprehended the fairest part of the earth, and the most civilised portion of mankind ... The gentle but powerful influence of laws and manners had gradually cemented the union of the provinces. The peaceful inhabitants enjoyed and abused the advantages of wealth and luxury. The image of a free constitution was preserved with decent reverence: the Roman senate appeared to possess the sovereign authority, and devolved on the emperors all the executive powers of government.[8]**
>
> **(ii) [footnote]**
> **Arrian's *Tactics*. With the true partiality of a Greek, Arrian rather chose to describe the phalanx, of which he had read, than the legions which he had commanded. [9]**
>
> **(iii) [footnote]**
> **M. de Voltaire, unsupported by either fact or probability, has generously bestowed the Canary Islands on the Roman Empire.[10]**
>
> **(iv) (footnote)**
> **See an excellent dissertation on the origin and migrations of nations, in the *Memoires de l'Académie des Inscriptions*, tom. xviii. p.48–71. It is seldom that the antiquarian and the philosopher are so happily blended.[11]**
>
> **(v) [footnote]**
> **Spartianus, in his undigested collections, mixes up all the virtues and all the vices that enter into the human composition, and bestows them on the same object. Such, indeed, are many of the characters in the Augustan History.[12]**
>
> **(vi) [footnote]**
> **The president de Montesquieu (in his dialogue between Sylla and Eucrates) expresses the sentiments of the dictator, in a spirited and even a sublime manner.[13]**

(vii) [footnote]
Sir William Temple and Montesquieu have indulged ... the usual liveliness of their fancy.[14]

(viii) [footnote]
May we not suspect that superstition was the parent of despotism?[15]

(ix) The condemnation of the wisest and most virtuous of the Pagans, on account of their ignorance or disbelief of the divine truth, seems to offend the reason and the humanity of the present age. But the primitive church, whose faith was of a much firmer consistence, delivered over, without hesitation, to eternal torture the far greater part of the human species.[16]

(x) ... the resurrection of the dead was very far from being esteemed an uncommon event; that the miracle was frequently performed on necessary occasions, by great fasting and the joint supplication of the church of the place, and that the persons thus restored to their prayers had lived afterwards among them many years. At such a period, when faith could boast of so many wonderful victories over death, it seems difficult to account for the scepticism of those philosophers who still rejected and derided the doctrine of the resurrection. A noble Grecian had ... promised Theophilus, bishop of Antioch, that, if he could be gratified with the sight of a single person who had been actually raised from the dead, he would immediately embrace the Christian religion. It is somewhat remarkable that the prelate of the first eastern church, however anxious for the conversion of his friend, thought proper to decline this fair and reasonable challenge.[17]

(xi) The acquisition of knowledge, the exercise of our reason or fancy, and the cheerful flow of unguarded conversation, may employ the leisure of a liberal mind. Such amusements, however, were rejected with abhorrence, or admitted with the utmost caution, by the severity of the fathers [i.e. the earliest authoritative Christian writers], who despised all knowledge that was not useful to salvation ...[18]

(xii) ... the primitive church was filled with a great number of persons of either sex who had devoted themselves to the profession of perpetual chastity. A few of these, among whom we may reckon the learned Origen, judged it the most prudent to disarm the tempter.

The footnote reads:

Before the fame of Origen had excited envy and persecution, this extraordinary action was rather admired than censured. As it was his general practice to allegorise Scripture, it seems unfortunate that, in this instance only, he should have adopted the literal sense.[19]

(xiii) ... as the timid are always cruel, the mind of Constantinus was inaccessible to mercy.[20]

(xiv) [footnote]
Augustin composed the two-and-twenty books *de Civitate Dei* in the space of thirteen years, AD413–426. His learning is too often borrowed, and his arguments are too often his own; but the whole work claims the merit of a magnificent design, vigorously, and not unskilfully, executed.[21]

(xv) Orosius, piously inhuman, sacrifices the king and people ... without a symptom of compassion. The bloody actor is less detestable than the cool, unfeeling historian.[22]

(xvi) [The emperor] Justinian was so profuse that he could not be liberal.[23]

(xvii) [Of Pope John XII] we read with some surprise ... that the Lateran palace was turned into a school for prostitution; and that his rapes of virgins and widows had deterred the female pilgrims from visiting the tomb of St Peter, lest, in the devout act, they should be violated by his successor. The Protestants have dwelt with malicious pleasure on these characters of antichrist; but to a philosophic eye the vices of the clergy are far less dangerous than their virtues.[24]

(xviii) Besieging Rome by land and water, he [Ladislaus, King of Naples] thrice entered the gates as a barbarian conqueror; profaned the altars, violated the virgins, pillaged the merchants, performed his devotions at St Peter's, and left a garrison in the castle of St Angelo.[25]

(xix) [footnote]
[Henry I took for his wife a Scythian of Russia, daughter of king Jeroslaus]. Voltaire might wonder at this alliance; but he should not have owned his ignorance of the country, religion, etc., of Jeroslaus – a name so conspicuous in the Russian annals.[26]

Some brief biographical points will also help our assessment of Gibbon as an historian. A sickly child, Gibbon took the opportunity of a fragmentary formal education to read voraciously. Sent to Magdalen College, Oxford just before his sixteenth birthday, he was horrified by the lack of scholarship and supine venality of the tutors. His anger persisted into his unfinished memoirs, where he wrote:

From the toil of reading or thinking or writing they had absolved their conscience, and the first shoots of learning and ingenuity withered on the ground ...[27]

Short of murdering the entire college hierarchy, Gibbon came up with the best possible way of showing how much he despised Oxford: he converted to Catholicism. His horrified father despatched him to the care of Daniel Pavilliard, a Protestant pastor in Lausanne, Switzerland. Pavilliard recognized the intellectual capacity of his charge and encouraged him to read the works of the *philosophes*. Sure enough, the five-year stay in Lausanne stripped Gibbon of his Catholicism, but it stripped him of his Christianity too. His French was now sufficiently fluent for his first published work to appear in that language: *Essai sur l'étude de la Littérature* (1761). He was to make the acquaintance of Diderot, d'Alembert and Voltaire. The first volume of *The History of the Decline and Fall of the Roman Empire* was published in 1776; the final volume appeared in 1788. After a period as a remarkably silent MP in Britain, he decided to settle in Lausanne. The last year of his life was spent in England, and he died in 1794.

A Gibbon as a philosophic historian

Decline and Fall owed a great deal to Voltaire and Montesquieu, who pioneered a fundamentally secular approach to history. As Momigliano puts it, 'Gibbon followed Voltaire in boldly sweeping away every barrier between sacred history and profane history'.[28] And, in his *Memoirs*, Gibbon commented:

> **I had likewise flattered myself that an age of light and liberty would receive without scandal an enquiry into the *human* [his stress] causes of the progress and establishment of Christianity.**[29]

It is quite clear from the above extracts that Gibbon was judging from a secular perspective. His dismissive comments on Augustine's *City of God* (xiv above) are a case in point. That great work had had an influence over Christian thought which can hardly be overstated. It met head-on the crisis facing Christianity after the sack of Rome in AD410 and tackled the issues of the fate of Christian society, its relationship with God and the course of the past, present and future. But this was of little concern to Gibbon, who weighed Augustine in the scales of eighteenth-century scholarship and found him wanting. Gibbon's opening paragraphs (i above) also reflect the *philosophe's* concern with civilization, since he chose to use the term to identify what he saw as the most important feature of the Roman Empire: not its military conquests for their own sake, but its impact on laws and manners. Voltaire, we should note, wrote an *Essay on Customs* in 1756.

Gibbon's stance on the early (and medieval) Christian Church was little different to that of Voltaire. I want to examine his use of irony later, but several extracts have shown that he regarded Christianity of the time with considerable contempt. Gibbon treated Jesus himself with much respect, but theologians, priests and particularly monks or hermits (whose spirituality was world-denying) are presented as hypocritical, superstitious, obscurantist, fanatical, bigoted and nonsensical. In fact, Gibbon clearly saw Christianity as one of the main reasons why the Roman Empire fell apart (see my comments below on Gibbon and causation); an argument familiar enough from the *Encyclopédie* and Voltaire's *Essay on Customs*. One can trace many similarities in world-view between Gibbon and the French *philosophes*. Assumptions he made about the decadence of the Orient and its allegedly enervating effect on the emperors are reminiscent of Montesquieu's comments on the effect of warm climates in *Spirit of the Laws* (1748). His belief that great empires tend inevitably to their own dissolution is an echo of a number of writers, including Montesquieu (in his essay *Considerations on the Greatness and Decadence of the Romans* of 1734) and the Scot William Robertson. In his 'General Observations on the Fall of the Roman Empire in the West', Gibbon commented '... the decline of Rome was the natural and inevitable effect of immoderate greatness'.[30]

And so, the intellectual climate of the *philosophes* is very much the climate of Gibbon. But, when it came to the writing of a work of history, clear differences emerge. Here, Gibbon demonstrated his respect for the disciplined scholarship of the seventeenth-century *érudits* through his frequent complaints about the failure of his fellow *philosophes* to respect the vital importance of factual evidence and the need to cite it as proof of one's contentions. In other words, he disliked the quasi-sociological system-building of his peers for the simple reason that it seemed to him to be fundamentally unhistorical, since it was not derived from fact. This, of course, explains his criticisms of Voltaire in the above extracts. Neither did Montesquieu escape unscathed. There was plenty of praise for him, but he was also variously accused of 'strange', 'whimsical' and 'inexcusable' errors of interpretation and fact. There was, no doubt, the element of enjoyment here in ticking off one's peers, but I would argue that Gibbon was inclined to find factual errors inexcusable because it was, he believed, on fact that his own explanations were based. This is not to say that Gibbon felt that the correct writing of history was that of the *érudits*. Such antiquarianism on its own was as bad as unrestrained philosophic theorizing. Ironically, none other than Montesquieu was ticked off on one occasion for overdoing detail and losing sight of the shape of his work:

Montesquieu ... has condescended to explain and excuse *'la manière de penser de nos pères'* ('the way our forefathers thought') on the subject of judicial combats. He follows this strange institution from the age of Gundobald to that of St Lewis; and the philosopher is sometimes lost in the legal antiquarian.[31]

Gibbon saw the good historian as a combination of the *érudit* and the *philosophe*, and also saw just such a combination in himself. Momigliano put it with characteristic elegance:

> **I submit that Gibbon broke new ground ... by offering the treasures of erudition to the contemplation of the philosophic historian.**[32]

My example (iv) above would seem to confirm Momigliano's contention. His thesis explains not only Gibbon's strictures on his fellow *philosophes*, but also the careful footnoting and comments on his sources we noted in the extracts. There are over 8,000 footnotes in *Decline and Fall*. If Gibbon's referencing and love of detail are his inheritance from the *érudits*, his tone of magisterial self-confidence and the willingness to make Olympian judgements are his inheritance from the *philosophes*. So, too, is his tendency to assume that human nature is fundamentally unchanging; after all, his comment on the personality of Constantinus (xiii) makes no sense unless he believed that the human personality is constant throughout history. However, there is a fundamental difference between Gibbon and other *philosophes* in the way in which human nature is exploited in the writing of history. Hume and others were inclined to look at the inevitable gaps in the historical record and, rather than try to resolve them as far as possible by historical means, simply plaster over the whole issue with generalizations based on their supposed understanding of behaviour. Gibbon was much more prepared to wrestle with the gaps in the record and use his understanding of human nature to resolve them as far as possible – and without attempting to ignore them. In other words, Gibbon felt that the past merited due consideration and sympathetic treatment, rather than a cavalier disregard for its inevitable deficiencies. In his relationship with history, Gibbon had some of the patience of a lover. Most *philosophes* treated the past like a prostitute.

B Gibbon and causation

Gibbon's treatment of causation has been much criticized by modern historians, not only on the grounds of obvious bias against Christianity, but also because he failed to offer an in-depth analysis of causes of various types (political, economic, class conflict) and a clear indication of their relative importance. The near-absence of any such analysis does seem surprising, but the ogre of anachronistic judgement looms. Just because we expect causal analysis nowadays, we have no right to demand it of Gibbon unless he set out to provide it. The short answer is that he did not. After all, his book is not titled *The Causes of the Decline and Fall of the Roman Empire*.

Gibbon wrote a narrative history in which the characteristics of Roman civilization were more worthy of attention than an account of causes. This is not to say that causes are completely ignored. In his 'General Observations on the Fall of the Roman Empire in the West', Gibbon offered a rather hasty summary:

> The rise of a city, which swelled into an empire, may deserve, as a singular prodigy, the reflection of a philosophic mind. But the decline of Rome was the natural and inevitable effect of immoderate greatness. Prosperity ripened the principle of decay; the causes of destruction multiplied with the extent of conquest; and as soon as time or accident had removed the artificial supports, the stupendous fabric yielded to the pressure of its own weight. The story of its ruin is simple and obvious; and instead of inquiring *why* the Roman Empire was destroyed, we should rather be surprised that it had subsisted for so long. The victorious legions, who, in distant wars, acquired the vices of strangers and mercenaries, first oppressed the freedom of the republic, and afterwards violated the majesty of the purple. The emperors, anxious for their personal safety and the public peace, were reduced to the base expedient of corrupting the discipline which rendered them alike formidable to their sovereign and to the enemy; the vigour of the military government was relaxed and finally dissolved by the partial institutions of Constantine; and the Roman world was overwhelmed by a deluge of barbarians ...
>
> The decay of Rome has been frequently ascribed to the translation of the seat of empire; but this history has already shown that the powers of government were *divided* rather than *removed* ... This dangerous novelty impaired the strength and fomented the vices of a double reign: the instruments of an oppressive and arbitrary system were multiplied; and a vain emulation of luxury, not of merit, was introduced ...
>
> As the happiness of a *future* life is the great object of religion, we may hear without surprise or scandal that the introduction, or at least the abuse of Christianity, had some influence on the decline and fall of the Roman Empire ... The sacred indolence of the monks was devoutly embraced by a servile and effeminate age ... If the decline of the Roman Empire was hastened by the conversion of Constantine, his victorious religion broke the violence of the fall, and mollified the ferocious temper of the conquerors.[35]

This is a reasonable summary of the points made *en passant* by Gibbon, although the balanced and rather cautious references to the link between Christianity and the fall of empire are a little surprising in their moderation. It is interesting to note that, when Gibbon discussed the writing of *Decline and Fall* in his *Memoirs*, the only cause of decline referred to is the growth of Christianity:

> ...I believed, and as I still believe, that the propagation of the gospel and the triumph of the Church are inseparably connected with the decline of the Roman monarchy ...[34]

C Gibbon's style

There are those who would argue – Elton being a case in point – that the only sound reason for reading Gibbon nowadays is to enjoy his style. I do not agree, and intend to use this section to explore how Gibbon's style is not simply a bolt-on extra which is more attractive than the history beneath. Instead, I think we should see it as a reflection of the mind of an historian who had important things to say about the writing of history, and who said much of it through his style.

Having said this, perhaps we should at least appreciate the way Gibbon's irony works first of all. In my example (xvii) above, we have the irony of understatement. The reader is invited to consider an utterly appalling list of papal crimes, with Gibbon suggesting that it comes as 'some surprise' to us. Indeed! And then, in the same example, we enjoy an ironic reversal as Gibbon asks us to consider that such vices are less dangerous than clerical virtues. In example xviii, the irony works through incongruity. Ladislaus performs his devotions in the midst of a list of barbaric savageries. This is an irony familiar to readers of Alexander Pope's poetry. In *The Rape of the Lock* (1712), Pope listed the objects to be found on the fashionable young lady's dressing table, and slyly introduced a most inappropriate book:

> **Puffs, powders, patches, Bibles, billet-doux ...[35]**

There is also the irony of apparent approval or approbation. The truly gruesome self-castration performed by Origen (example xii above) is introduced from Origen's point of view as a prudent action. The irony is effective because it makes his behaviour seem even more unspeakably fanatical and ludicrous than any simple statement of the writer's opinion possibly could.

All I have done so far, of course, is to suggest that Gibbon was very good at irony. But does his style – ironic or otherwise – serve any other purpose? I very much agree with Roy Porter[36] that Gibbon is seeking first and foremost to engage his readers and to challenge them by putting himself before them with the invitation to consider the workings of his mind and his imagination as, together, they tackle historical fact. In so doing, the readers must use their own intellect and imagination, and in this way, history comes alive. It cannot do so through the antiquarian's obsessive failure to narrate; nor can

it do so through the fundamentally unhistorical theorizing of the *philosophes*. In his *Memoirs*, Gibbon revealed very clearly the purpose behind his style:

> **The style of an author should be the image of his mind; but the choice and command of language is the fruit of exercise. Many experiments were made before I could hit the middle tone between a dull chronicle and a rhetorical declamation ...[37]**

I do believe that Gibbon does engage the reader, does appeal to his intelligence through the style and so does pull him into the story he tells – almost in the sense of a dramatist inviting the audience to share in his play. Take the very opening of *Decline and Fall* (example i above). The introduction of the word 'abused' into the sentence 'The peaceful inhabitants enjoyed and abused the advantages of wealth and luxury' is something of a shock after the initially positive opening, and carries with it an interpretation that the reader must now note and await its further development. In fact, Gibbon was fond of challenging the reader with two adjectives in close proximity which carry different and strikingly disparate meanings.[38] We then note that the apparent freedom of the constitution and power of the senate are circumscribed by the introduction of the words 'image' and 'appeared'.

This is not to suggest that Gibbon's irony or style as a whole is never self-indulgent, or that his many judgements are always the product of his desire to engage the reader in intellectual and imaginative gymnastics. No doubt there are times when he said things because they were clever, funny or both. Womersley is perhaps a little kind to Gibbon in suggesting that his irony is 'delicate' and that he is 'unmatched as an ironist because he so rarely surrenders his intelligence to the mode, thereby reducing irony to a gloat'.[39] I think he did gloat more than rarely, and that his comments on Orosius or John XII are cases in point.

D Gibbon's purpose

There is nothing facile about Gibbon, and therefore one should not expect him to have written a history claiming to teach straightforward political or moral lessons. Some historians have argued that Gibbon was keen to use *Decline and Fall* as an opportunity to reflect on the British Empire and its struggle with its American colonies between 1775–83 – the American War of Independence (or American Revolution). But beyond some rather teasing references to the revolt of the Armorican (echo of 'American', of course) provinces of the Roman Empire (northern France), no analogies were made. Of course, as the whole work was imbued with Gibbon's personality and philosophic ideals, his opinions and arguments reflected

eighteenth-century concerns. This is why his comments on Christianity aroused considerable controversy, and, as he remarked, gave those clerical opponents who rushed into print the chance to earn some preferment in the Church. Gibbon's various comments on civic virtue and his preferences for a 'mixed constitution', where political power was not restricted to one man or one group, were no doubt interesting enough to MPs in a constitutional monarchy. But we recall that Gibbon aimed to enter into a dialogue with his readers: to challenge, to provoke, to engage and to encourage them to consider his views on the nature of civilization and how it could and should progress through the curbing of priestcraft and superstition. All this would stimulate the intellect and arouse the imagination. He neither wanted nor expected readers to draw simplistic lessons as if history somehow repeated itself. It clearly did not.

E Gibbon – a conclusion

> To the literary mind, the great English historians may be Clarendon, Gibbon and Macaulay, even though hardly anyone reads them any longer and their readability is their main claim to fame. Surely, they are worth reading and wrote splendid books, but they wrote in the prehistoric age ...[40]

So said Geoffrey Elton, and his rather dismissive comments need to be considered carefully. By 'prehistoric age', Elton was referring to the periods before the professionalization of history, when, stimulated by the work of Leopold von Ranke, history developed a methodology which rested upon the canons of objectivity and 'scientific' source evaluation (see pp.104–13). By these criteria, Gibbon is clearly found wanting. Although he stressed the virtues of impartiality, Gibbon did not claim that the historian could or should distance himself from his writing. One should have respect for the facts – hence the need for impartiality – but history was given shape by the dialogue between historian and reader. In terms of source evaluation, Gibbon is indeed open to criticism. He fully accepted the Enlightenment spirit of rational inquiry and questioned his sources shrewdly and critically but without a systematic technique. He had no firm and consistent method for assessing reliability, and failed to allow for the way in which the nature of the source related to the author's purpose and so affected its value. And, as Momigliano put it, Gibbon 'never went beyond a superficial impression of the comparative value of his sources'.[41] On the other hand, he was adept at identifying bias and in sifting a source to exploit its value and discard its irrelevancies.

No one would deny that Gibbon used a considerable quantity of sources,

but did he use a full range? He was not entirely restricted to literary sources, as he was interested in and made some use of inscriptions, medals, coins and architecture. But he relied on published sources – in the main, the contents of his own, well-stocked library. He never mastered palaeography (the study of ancient handwriting) or diplomatic (the analysis of the forms of documents) and so could not make use of original documents. Nor did his understanding of German allow him to exploit the relevant researches of German scholars.

On one level, then, Elton's criticisms seem well-founded. But there are major objections to be made to them. Firstly, we should never forget to praise Gibbon for the extraordinary range, erudition and fundamental accuracy of his monumental work. After all, he covered the history of the Empire both east and west (based in Rome and Byzantium/Constantinople) from the second century AD through to the fall of Constantinople in the fifteenth century. He discussed the rise, not only of Christianity, but also of Islam and was interested in the Persian Empire as well. Burrow reminds us that a work on this scale which supersedes Gibbon has yet to be written.[42] And, when one assesses Gibbon's scholarship by the Rankean standards (as Bury did in his edition of *Decline and Fall* in 1912), then his factual accuracy is nothing less than astonishing. Secondly, as we saw in Chapter 1, we cannot afford to accept without question (as Elton appears to do) that correct, objective history is attainable and can be communicated without recourse to literary techniques which would cloud objectivity. In a way, Gibbon's habit of directly addressing the reader and inviting him to enter into the mind of the historian is more up to date than the denial that this should or does happen. Of course, there is a price to pay for writing a work like *Decline and Fall* which is so clearly individualistic, idiosyncratic and personal. It is literally inimitable, and so Gibbon founded no school of historians. But he has nonetheless left an invaluable legacy. He pioneered the secular treatment of religious history. He reminds us that, in the end, history must engage the reader. This was brought home to me when I was selecting the extracts for the start of this section: there were so many I wanted to include because they were genuinely memorable and because they were so downright enjoyable. Gibbon's irony pulls us into his writing, makes us want to understand, invites us to use our intellect and leaves us with the feeling that human nature is itself ironical in its complexity. The excellent book by John Clive, *Not by Fact Alone*,[43] reminds us that Gibbon and other great historians were able to make the reader feel a sense of personal involvement in the events being described and that amusement and instruction complemented each other very well. I think I can justify a little self-indulgence at this point by including perhaps my favourite Gibbonism. Talking about St Simeon Stylites, who subsisted for years in contemplation of God from the vantage point of a pillar, Gibbon says:

Among these heroes of the monastic life, the name and genius of Simeon Stylites have been immortalised by the singular invention of an aerial penance.[44]

Leopold von Ranke (1795–1886) and the professionalization of history

Leopold von Ranke is a favourite with students answering examination questions on the methodology and nature of history. It is easy to understand why. On the face of it, Ranke had a near-revolutionary impact on historiography. Reacting against the system-building and generalizations of the Enlightenment, he allegedly claimed that one should study the past for its own sake and respect the uniqueness of each age: a viewpoint to which the label 'historicism' might be attached. In the search for history 'as it actually happened', he seems not only to have come up with a new historical technique based on rigid objectivity, but also to have single-handedly created the historical profession – complete with professors of history of repute, seminars, and a stress on original documentary research as the mark of the real historian. The student who remembers to evaluate as well as to describe often points out that Ranke has been criticized for overstating the possibility of objectivity, and that his own objectivity can be called into question, since he wrote from a conservative and indeed pro-Prussian viewpoint. It might also be pointed out that Ranke focused purely on the history of the élites and on diplomatic and political history. And so, although his emphasis on rigorous scholarship remains to this day, history has expanded into a much fuller and broader concern with the totality of human experience.

The least sophisticated reader will have noticed that my summary of the 'standard answer' is peppered with phrases like 'allegedly' and 'seems'. It would therefore seem that I am inclined to dismiss that picture of Ranke as an alleged caricature. Perhaps. There is certainly caricature – or over-simplification – in it, but then caricature can hardly work without some element of truth. The task will be to assess how much. But there is an additional complication in that, although it is important to try to establish what Ranke actually represented and what his ideas were, it is also important to establish what those he influenced *thought* his ideas were. As we shall see, there were those who claimed inspiration from Ranke for positions he would not have recognized as his own.

A Ranke's background and Enlightenment historiography

Ranke was born in the small town of Wiehe in Thuringia, Germany. Germany, of course, was not a nation-state in the late eighteenth century, but a loose grouping – alliance is far too strong a term – of over 300 separate states owing paper allegiance to that relic of medievalism, the elected Holy Roman Emperor (in practice, one of the Habsburg family, with a power-base in Austria). Habsburg predominance (such as it was) within Germany was potentially challenged by the kings of Prussia (the Hohenzollern dynasty). More to the point, German nationalism (fanned by the experience of, and opposition to, the expansion of France in the revolutionary and Napoleonic eras) was increasingly significant as the nineteenth century progressed. There were a number of possible routes to a German nation-state, but one which earned the support of those who preferred time-honoured systems of government was through the expansion of the kingdom of Prussia. It was indeed through this route that the Empire of Germany was established by 1871. Ranke's birthplace had been part of the independent Electorate of Saxony, but the area was annexed by Prussia in 1815. Iggers and Moltke[45] rightly point out that Ranke was therefore by no means emotionally committed to Prussia itself, and that the image of a more federal Germany was a potent one for him.

Of even greater importance in the making of Ranke the historian were his deeply-felt Lutheran religious beliefs. Ranke's father was a lawyer, but regretted not following in the family tradition of entering the Lutheran ministry. Ranke entered the University of Leipzig in 1814 to study theology and philology. Significantly, he never completed his theological studies because he objected to the university faculty's cool, rationalistic approach to faith. Ranke's God was not to be pigeon-holed or labelled in any such atmosphere of calm deduction; His presence was reflected in past and present events, but, because of the distance between God and humanity, one should not presume to reveal or uncover him fully or simplistically. This religious belief coalesced with strands in German idealist philosophy – particularly the work of Fichte – which Ranke found appealing (or so his early notes and correspondence suggest). In particular, he sympathized with Fichte's concept of the sanctified role of the scholar in uncovering something of the 'divine idea' from the world as we perceive it.

Clearly there were aspects of Enlightenment thought which were unlikely to impress Ranke. He could only abhor the impiety of Voltaire, and rational systematizing would fit uneasily with his concept of the relationship between what the human mind could do and its limits in uncovering the ultimate truth which was God. On the other hand, since God lay behind the unfolding of human history, there ought to be some sort of meaning or discernible purpose therein, even though it would be wrong and presumptuous to identify a precise pattern. With this in mind, Ranke found the thought of the philosopher Herder congenial. Herder argued that there is not some sort of Enlightenment-style progress to rationality throughout history, but a God-given flowering of separate national cultures. There is therefore no way of judging a period in history by its contribution to linear progress. Instead, one must seek to understand that period on its own terms, by studying its own unique set of values and without assuming that it was essentially no different from the present day – an approach which has sometimes been labelled 'historicism'.[46] This approach was, of course, diametrically opposed to Enlightenment historiography, which, as we have seen, treated the past with the condescension of the present.

At least it would seem that my caricature of Ranke's thought was accurate on his rejection of all that the Enlightenment stood for. This is basically true, but we need to interject a word of warning. As I suggested earlier, it would be dangerous to assume that the Enlightenment was a fully unified movement with a clearly-defined programme. The work of Peter Reill reveals that the *Aufklärer* of Germany were at odds with French *philosophes* in retaining a strong religious conviction, which in turn led them to argue that spirituality could not be explained by the same natural laws as applied in the material world. Some *Aufklärer* also took the view that historical understanding itself changed as society changed; history could not be understood through timeless laws of human nature. Small wonder, then, that Reill should argue that one might 'locate the origins of historicism within the mainstream of the German Enlightenment'.[47] Elsewhere, Reill states:

> **It is my contention that the basic postulates of Rankean historiography were established during the Enlightenment by Enlightened thinkers in Germany.[48]**

The picture beginning to emerge of Ranke is therefore a more sophisticated one than was offered tongue-in-cheek in my caricature. In particular, putting Ranke into his cultural context has helped to explain the origin of some of his ideas.

B Ranke and *'Wie es eigentlich gewesen'*

Ranke's first published work was *Histories of the Latin and Germanic Peoples* (1824), written when he was a schoolteacher of history and classics. In his preface, Ranke wrote:

> **To history has been given the function of judging the past, of instructing men for the profit of future years. The present attempt does not aspire to such a lofty undertaking. It merely wants to show how, essentially, things happened.[49]**

'How, essentially, things happened.' *'Wie es eigentlich gewesen.'* Now, this phrase is usually translated 'how things really (or actually) happened'. Iggers points out that, in the nineteenth century, the term *eigentlich* meant, not only 'actually', but also 'essentially' or 'characteristically'.[50] Iggers believes that Ranke's meaning was closer to 'essentially' than 'actually', and that his famous phrase is not simply the endorsement of history as the recovery of facts that historians then and since have believed it to be. Given Ranke's religious views and his belief that God's presence in history could be glimpsed – perhaps the essence of history – then this argument is indeed plausible. However, there are occasions when Ranke's commitment to uncovering facts is stated with less ambiguity:

> **Strict presentation of facts, no matter how conditional and unattractive they might be, is undoubtedly the supreme law.**[51]

But what did Ranke mean by 'facts'? It is important to appreciate that Ranke's work was not restricted to the recovery of factual information about events. To him, the feelings or ideas of those who produced the sources were as meaningful and true – or more meaningful and more true – than a date and the course of a battle or terms of a treaty. I very much agree with Krieger's comment that Ranke's principle was:

> **... that all historical statements are true in the ideas and feelings they express and in the circumstances that they reflect, over and above the truthfulness of the facts that they purport to convey.**[52]

It is clear, at least, that Ranke expressed an historicist distaste for judging the past or trying to make use of it for present ends. The past was to be studied on its own terms, with appropriate recognition of the value systems unique to each age. But how was this to be done? Writing about his *English History, Principally in the Seventeenth Century* (1859–68), he said that he had tried to 'extinguish my own self, as it were, to let the things speak ...'[53] In other words, he claimed to let the past speak for itself through deliberately recognizing and then setting aside his own prejudices, aims and values. And with what was the past to speak? In Ranke's view, the past spoke through original documentary sources, as long as they were appropriately evaluated by the objective historian employing systematic techniques of archival research. In the memorable phrase of Lord Acton, Regius Professor of Modern History at Cambridge at the end of the nineteenth century, Ranke was the 'real originator of the heroic study of records'.[54]

Having said this, Ranke was not the first to rely heavily on original sources or to develop an appropriate research technique for so doing. German philologists of the late eighteenth and early nineteenth centuries had evaluated the documents of classical literature using a method readily transferable to archival sources. Ranke's philological training clearly helped him in textual analysis. And the historian Niebuhr's 1810 lectures at the University of Berlin, published as *History of Rome*, dissected the fictional elements in the historical accounts of writers like Livy and so provided a framework for the critical evaluation of sources (including such issues as a discussion of their provenance and purpose). Nor did Ranke write a manual or guide to historical research techniques. But, on the strength of his first published book, Ranke was appointed to the University of Berlin in 1824 and swiftly instituted a seminar system of instruction which enabled him to pass on his methods of source evaluation (*Quellenkritik*) – and so to shape the coming generation of scholars.

This may seem straightforward enough so far, but we are in danger of oversimplifying Ranke's position. After all, discussions in Chapter 1 left us wary of accepting at face value any historian's claims to pure objectivity. Might we not need to take into account Ranke's strong Lutheran beliefs? Did they not affect his approach to history and the way in which he wrote it? In his preface to the *Histories of the Latin and Germanic Peoples*, Ranke duly concluded with an invitation to the reader to put aside his present values, to avoid judging, in the effort to grasp the events of the past. And yet he added that, at some point, the reader should also be able to detect (albeit through a glass darkly) the intentions of God. One is tempted to suggest that doing so may in practice mean imposing a value-system on the past. Ranke is demanding an objectivity from the historian, but at the same time suggesting what that objectivity should lead to. This is, perhaps, an uncomfortable approach. On the other hand, one should see it as a two-stage process in which the first stage is more certain than the second. The historian starts with his objective analysis to uncover facts about the past. Having done so, and without imposing any theory of his own, he should then be able to move from the particular to the general. In this second stage, his generalizations may hint at the vaguest of outlines of God's intentions. In contemplating such possibilities, Ranke's prose takes on a religious tone:

> **A lofty ideal does exist: to grasp the event itself in its human comprehensiveness, its unity, and its fullness. It should be possible to attain this goal. I know how far I am from having achieved it. One tries, one strives, but in the end one has not reached the goal. Only let no one become impatient about this failure ... our subject is mankind as it is, explicable or inexplicable, the life of the individual, of the generations, of the peoples, and at times the hand of God over them.**[55]

We should, perhaps, at this point consider both how effectively Ranke maintained his objectivity and also how well his techniques of source analysis worked. We might at least start with the working hypothesis that complete objectivity is inhuman. We can hardly expect Ranke to choose to research and write about issues which, given his background and beliefs, were of no interest to him purely to preserve that total objectivity. To criticize him for wanting to write about peoples, nations and the interface between politics and religion would be unfair. It would be another matter if his treatment of nations was exclusive, perhaps in upholding Prussia or Germany as a whole as somehow 'the best' or most deserving. This does not happen. As we have seen, Ranke is keen to explore links between different peoples, and, in any case, was no supine supporter of Prussian control of a new Germany. His preferences appear to have been in the direction of a more federal Germany. Another good testing ground of his objectivity should be his *History of the Popes* (1834). As a Lutheran and a German, he might be expected to take every opportunity to attack the institution of the Roman Catholic Church. In fact, Ranke emerges from the test rather well. For example, his criticisms of the Church at the time of the Reformation are generally more measured than vitriolic; witness his comments on the Pope who excommunicated Luther:

> ... in the court of Leo X there were few things deserving blame in them-selves, although we cannot but perceive that his pursuits might have been more strictly in accordance with his position as supreme head of the Church.[56]

On the other hand, in the 1871 edition of his papal history, Ranke tackled the defeat of Catholic France by Prussia in that year. He clearly found it difficult to preserve his objectivity, and so sheltered (not very successfully) behind what a 'convinced Protestant' might think:

> A state [Prussia] prevailed which had risen in antagonism to the exclusive rule of the papacy, and which now had also become the champion of the German cause. It attained a position which guaranteed an important part in the universal political and religious movements of the world. A convinced Protestant would say this was the divine decision against the pretensions of the Pope who claimed that he was the sole interpreter of the faith and of the divine mysteries on earth.[57]

Despite the occasional lapse of this type, Iggers concludes that 'Ranke achieves a remarkable degree of impartiality'.[58] His technique of scrupulously allowing the facts to emerge from the sources before considering the general issues must have contributed to this success.

In analysing Ranke's technique of source evaluation, I want to make use of an assessment by Gino Benzoni[59] of Ranke's work on what was undoubtedly his favourite source: the Venetian *relazioni,* or reports made by the Venetian ambassadors to various countries and to the papal court after the completion of their missions. Benzoni describes Ranke's excitement in discovering the potential of these sources, offering as they did a superb insight by intelligent practitioners into the great events of the time (and also into the characteristics of the states with which they were familiar). So Ranke's enthusiasm is understandable, and also reflects his view that first-hand information was inevitably better than contemporary or subsequent narratives (or literary evidence, for that matter). But herein lies Ranke's problem, because the *relazioni* were treated by him far too incautiously. He neglected to consider how far they were distorted by literary elements such as conventions of style or the need to persuade the reader of the writer's intelligence, efficiency and accuracy. They were also distorted by the ambassadors' inevitable assumptions of prior knowledge amongst the recipients and by their outlook – that of the Venetian upper-class.

Ranke was making every effort to free original sources from their past neglect, but, as we have seen, there was a sense in which he became their prisoner. As with the *relazioni,* he was so excited by what they had to offer that his critical technique failed to exploit them. Also, as a pioneer in the field of archival research, he was not always able to gain access to collections which would have made his research far more valuable. The Vatican archives were closed to him, and the Venetian authorities were often obstructive. As Ugo Tucci has suggested,[60] Ranke was often obliged to buy his sources on the private document market; hardly the best way to ensure a thorough and representative assessment. This means that Ranke's work itself has long been superseded.

C Ranke's subject matter and style

One might expect that Ranke's books would be detailed and narrow in compass – precursors of the earnest modern PhD thesis, perhaps. This would seem to follow from his insistence on thorough research and evaluation. In fact, we get sweeping narrative histories written – and this again is a surprise – with considerable flair for dramatic possibilities. How can we account for subject matter and style?

Firstly, we should recall Ranke's interest in some aspects of the thought of Herder and Fichte. The latter's precept that a love for the life of the past could lead to God clearly complements Ranke's view that the proper study of history was a contribution to knowing what we could of God. The philosopher of nationality, Herder offered the spirit of the *Volk* – an almost untranslatable word, with meanings including a people, a sense of nationhood and shared culture – as the motive force of history, because within the *Volk* is the divine spirit. Herder was adamant that *Völker* (in the plural) arising through history were to be studied on their own terms and without any attempt to judge. It is significant that so much of Ranke's work should focus on the history of peoples, and that he should speak of nations being 'spiritual substances ... even one might say thoughts of God'.[61] Here we see again the spirituality which appears to call Ranke to identify God's will in history – to trace patterns, in fact. But, once again, Ranke will not fall into what he sees as the trap: to systematize, to force history into a particular mould, to have the arrogance to claim to know God's purposes, for that would mean knowing God – the ultimate hubris. In the 1830s, Ranke jotted down comments on the relationship between history and philosophy. He wrote:

> **Two qualities are necessary to form a true historian. The first is a feeling for and a joy in the particular in and by itself. He will try to comprehend all ... without any purpose other than joy in the individual life ... without thinking how the whole appears in the particular. This, however, is not all. It is necessary that the historian keep his eyes open for the general. He will not have preconceived ideas as does the philosopher, but rather while he observes the particular, the course which the development of the world in general has taken will be revealed to him ...[62]**

This would seem to be a difficult balancing act. On the one hand, the historian must objectively, and without a head full of theories, allow the sources to speak to him – the joy of the particular. On the other hand, there comes a point in the course of this study of the particular that significant connections are somehow made. Ranke sees in this the hand of God, leading peoples into power on the world stage; for, he says, 'no state has ever existed without a spiritual basis and a spiritual content. In power itself a spiritual essence manifests itself'.[63] And so, Ranke writes the histories of peoples who are significant in world history (by which he means European history), hence: *Histories of the Latin and Germanic Peoples; Princes and Peoples of Southern Europe: The Ottomans and the Spanish Monarchy; German History, 1555–1618*; and *German History in the Age of the Reformation*. The *History of the Popes* fits the pattern because the power of the Roman Catholic Church made it a great player on the European/world stage. An historian who sees in the history of the peoples a spiritual dimension will hanker after writing a world history, and it is no coincidence that, near the end of his long life, Ranke should write his *Universal History* (1880). In his preface, Ranke said:

> **... it was impossible to remain content with the history of individual nations. A collection of national histories, whether on a larger or smaller**

scale, is not what we mean by Universal History, for in such a work the general connection of things is liable to be obscured. To recognise this connection, to trace the sequence of those great events which link all nations together and control their destinies, is a task which the science of Universal History undertakes.[64]

With his interest in the relationships between nations and the spirit of God lying behind them, one might expect Ranke to write cultural history. He did not do so. Given the breadth of his themes – and particularly the stress he placed on the relationship between church and state – it is perhaps inevitable that Ranke should have concentrated on political history throughout his work. Specifically, much of what he wrote focused on monarchs and statesmen as they dealt with international affairs. His desire to recognize the connections between great events meant that he had to make a judgement on which were most significant and which could be left out. In his *Civil Wars and Monarchy in France in the Sixteenth and Seventeenth Centuries*, he commented:

I have not devoted much space to less significant events; but this has enabled me to pay the greater attention to those of world-historical importance.[65]

Ranke's version of what was 'world-historical' was heavily eurocentric. He left out the Orient on the grounds that it was and would be unchanging. But what did Ranke see as a significant event? In part, it was whatever was presented as such by the sources to which he had access – diplomats' reports, letters, diaries; in other words, mainly records of the élites, by the élites about the élites. These were almost always couched in personal terms, and so implicitly stressed the impact of the individual on history. And, of course, he felt that significance lay in certain events which encapsulated the spirit or the moral energy of a nation and which helped it to grow.

The style of Ranke is something of a surprise. Some of Ranke's admirers like the American Herbert Baxter Adams (1850–1901) – founder of the American Historical Association – claimed him as the father of scientific history and hailed his objectivity as a crucial element in the necessary professionalization of history. One might reasonably expect to see the father of scientific history eschewing as far as possible all literary devices in his narrative. In fact, as Peter Gay argues, Ranke

displayed the gifts we normally associate with storytellers or playwrights: speed, colour, variety, freshness of diction, and superb control ... he establishes his characters with the precision of a novelist.[66]

There are numerous examples of Ranke's sense of drama. Sometimes it can appear as the tautest of taut sentences. Discussing the assassination of the French King Henry IV in 1610 – a figure who Ranke clearly saw as one of the great personages of world history – he says bluntly: 'There was one man less in the world'.[67] In a strict historical sense, this comment is entirely super-fluous. Dramatically, it is tremendously effective because the reader knows that Ranke saw the murder as a great loss and is therefore startled by his blunt and bitter remark. Other examples of the storyteller's art are the numerous anecdotes which appear to obstruct the flow of the narrative in, say, the *History of the Popes.* So, why is Ranke writing like this? Iggers suggests that the anecdote is used to reveal the essence of a situation better than a mere factual description could. Perhaps so, but a more straight-forward explanation would be because Ranke's stylistic devices and anec-dotes encourage an empathetic response. To see the past as it actually was is more than a merely intellectual exercise; it is an emotional and spiritual one as well. In the *History of France*, Ranke argued that the historian's task was both science and art: it had to fulfil the scientific demands of a philolog-ical work, and yet, at the same time, had to offer the joys of imaginative literature to the educated mind.

D Ranke's contribution to historiography

I have suggested that Ranke's writing of history is far more complex than our original picture of him as the would-be scientific/impartial prober of archives and historical technician. However, what we are now concerned with is the reception of Ranke – a reception which frequently misunderstood and simplified his position.

Without a doubt, Ranke's influence was profound. Historians in Europe and North America, hungry for academic respectability, seized on those aspects of his thought which appeared to give history a 'scientific' status – namely, the demands for research into original documents and the need for objectivity. In this way, Ranke did much to elevate the status of history as a discipline at university level. Many a history professor owed his new chair to the sudden professionalization of the subject.

Of course, this meant that less clear or more inconvenient aspects were missed, distorted, ignored or criticized. German historians of the so-called Prussian school disliked Ranke's lack of enthusiasm for the unification of Germany through Prussian expansion, but they respected much of his methodology. Others – the so-called Neo-Rankeans – tried to adapt (i.e. distort) his ideas on relations between nations to justify the expansion of Imperial Germany at the end of the nineteenth century. But they too respected his methodology.

From the British perspective, Lord Acton's response to Ranke is instructive. He recognized Ranke as his master and claimed that he

> ... is the representative of the age which instituted the modern study of
> History. He taught it to be critical, to be colourless, and to be new. We
> meet him at every step, and he has done more for us than any other
> man ... He decided effectually to repress the poet, the patriot, the reli-
> gious or political partisan, to sustain no cause, to banish himself from
> his books ...[68]

Colourless? Unpoetic? To banish himself from his books? Surely Acton is wrong – and yet we can learn from his misinterpretations by suggesting that he saw in Ranke what he wanted to see, and in Ranke something of the history he wanted to write himself. Acton wrote to his friend and fellow polymath Richard Simpson that, when studying history or theology, 'our studies ought to be all but purposeless. They want to be pursued with chastity, like Mathematics'.[69] Famously, in his editor's prospectus for the Cambridge Modern History, he made his aim clear: he expected such detachment from his contributors that the account of the Battle of Waterloo would be acceptable to English, French, Germans or Dutch alike. This is not to say that Acton was a clone of Ranke. He was no Lutheran, but a Liberal Catholic. He was anything but a productive historian – publishing no works of history whatsoever, in part because his quest for yet more sources to establish the definitive truth was never-ending. And, unlike Ranke, he was ready and willing – once he had that supposedly definitive truth – to use history to judge. But what Ranke was able to offer Acton and others like him was a 'scientific' method that did not involve the kind of theorizing which explained the past through mechanistic laws which excluded God.

Similarly, those who objected to history being used to buttress contemporary opinions – 'present-minded' history – had the tradition of Rankean-style historicism for support. A good example would be the British historian Herbert Butterfield (1900–79), whose short work *The Whig Interpretation of History* (1931) attacked those who wrote history through the distorting glass of their political views. So-called Whig historians were accused of making assumptions about the direction history had taken: namely, towards a political system (British parliamentary democracy) of which they fully approved. Whig history was therefore nationalistic, liberal, optimistic, judgemental and teleological (written with a goal or ideal in mind).

The Whig Interpretation of History is an odd book. In the first place, it is surprisingly limited in scope. Astonishingly few historical themes are brought in to elucidate arguments, and Luther and the Reformation appear with a regularity which becomes truly irksome. And astonishingly few historians are mentioned by name; only one – Acton, no less – is discussed in any detail. In Lord Acton, it seems, the Whig historian 'reached his highest consciousness'[70] not only because he made moral judgements in his historical writing, but also because he made morality the judge of good and bad historical writing. More obvious targets, perhaps, were historians like Thomas Babington Macaulay (1800–59) and his great-nephew George Macaulay Trevelyan (1876–1962), whose work did indeed trace the development of liberty in a suitably Whiggish manner. Macaulay, for instance, started his monumental *The History of England from the Accession of James II* (4 volumes initially, published 1848–55) with a paean of praise to progress:

> ...unless I greatly deceive myself, the general effect of this chequered narrative will be to excite thankfulness in all religious minds, and hope in the breasts of all patriots. For the history of our country during the last hundred and sixty years is eminently the history of physical, of moral, and of intellectual improvement.[71]

He traced the origins of the English nation in the signing of the Magna Carta, which he saw as limiting the tyrannical power of the foreign, Norman kings. Further limits were placed on kingly despotism by the developing powers of parliament, and alongside these powers came prosperity. Liberty and prosperity both benefited from the individualism encouraged by Luther and the Protestant Reformation. In the time of Charles I, an attempt was made to sabotage such progress. After the execution of the king, extremism flourished under the mercifully-brief Cromwellian republic before the Stuarts had a second chance to show that they could respect the constitution of England with the coronation of Charles II in 1660. Under his brother James II, the new king's backward-looking Catholicism inevitably coalesced with a renewed despotism which was smashed by the Glorious Revolution of 1688, where the Whigs called upon William of Orange (as King William III) to rescue the traditional liberties of England.

This kind of Whiggish history is an easy enough target. It was, of course, deeply anachronistic. Macaulay was fond of referring to the English of the past as 'we', so assuming that their thought processes were earlier versions of those of the nineteenth-century liberal gentleman. He meted out praise to those on the side of progress and blame to those on the side of reaction. Setting out to persuade, he employed the most effective literary devices to convince the reader. Having decided (quite erroneously) that the Quaker William Penn was a reactionary hypocrite and traitor to William III, he made full use of emotive language and sarcasm (and untrustworthy sources) to blacken his name:

> After about three years of wandering and lurking he [Penn], by the mediation of some eminent men … made his peace with the government [of William III], and again ventured to resume his ministrations. The return which he made for the lenity with which he had been treated does not much raise his character. Scarcely had he begun to harangue in public about the unlawfulness of war, when he sent a message earnestly exhorting James to make an immediate descent on England with thirty thousand men.[72]

Macaulay very much enjoyed using the type of ironic contrast we see in the last sentence of his remarks on Penn. A look at his comments on John Churchill, Duke of Marlborough, will provide us with further insight into Macaulay's style and its effect on his writing of history:

> His stature was commanding, his face handsome, his address singularly winning … He was not loquacious: but, when he was forced to speak in public, his natural eloquence moved the envy of practised rhetoricians. His courage was singularly cool and imperturbable … Unhappily the splendid qualities of John Churchill were mingled with alloy of the most sordid kind … He was thrifty in his very vices, and levied ample contributions on ladies enriched by the spoils of more liberal lovers. He was, during a short time, the object of the violent but fickle fondness of the Duchess of Cleveland. On one occasion he was caught with her by the King, and was forced to leap out of the window. She rewarded this hazardous feat of gallantry with a present of five thousand pounds. With this sum the prudent young hero instantly bought an annuity of five hundred a year …[73]

Macaulay's delight in dramatic contrast is again evident. Churchill's laudable qualities are more than matched by the bad ones. We have an initial sketch of an impressive, manly and brave character – but the description then turns to farce as his gallantry takes a very different form. Macaulay clearly enjoyed both the sarcastic use of the word 'hero' and also the ironic comment on Churchill's prudence (in the course of describing an affair in which prudence was conspicuous by its absence). Of course, one might doubt whether a credible picture of Churchill emerges from this device of engaging the attention by contrast. The same might be said of Macaulay's use of caricature. His portrait of Titus Oates, an admittedly sinister figure who falsely claimed to have uncovered a Popish plot to murder Charles II, takes caricature to the outer limits. Oates is a villain in the manner of Sallust or the humanist historians; a Thomas More's Richard III minus a hunchback but plus a jaw:

> ... his short neck, his legs uneven, the vulgar said, as those of a badger, his forehead low as that of a baboon, his purple cheeks, and his monstrous length of chin ... those hideous features on which villainy seemed to be written by the hand of God.[74]

In short, Macaulay's *History of England* made deliberate use of the techniques of imaginative literature because its author believed that the link between history and literature was an intimate one. In an early essay (1828) for the Whig periodical the *Edinburgh Review*, he argued that the perfect historian must strive to authenticate all facts, but also that '... by judicious selection, rejection, and arrangement, he gives to truth those attractions which have been usurped by fiction'.[75] It is, as we have seen, unlikely that a strict attachment to fact will survive an attachment to the techniques of fiction. Macaulay used direct speech for its vividness, but did not restrict himself to what he could claim as authentic from the written record. I very much like Owen Dudley Edward's comment (which also suggests the distance between Ranke and Macaulay):

> The idea of making the past speak for itself became the practice of making it speak through him.[76]

Allied to this was Macaulay's oft-quoted remark on his hope that his *History of England* would 'for a few days supersede the last fashionable novel on the tables of young ladies'.[77] Macaulay was, of course, being a little disingenuous. His ambition was not only to write a genuinely popular work, but also one which would stand the test of time and be genuinely instructive. His readers were to appreciate the glories of the English brand of freedom and to accept that there was progress still to come as the parliamentary franchise was extended in the nineteenth century. But that progress should not be rushed. Did not his *History* warn of the dangers of extremism?

Herbert Butterfield's objections to this form of historical writing were not limited to its 'present-mindedness' and other distortions. He was obsessed with the evils of what he calls 'abridged' history, commenting 'indeed all history must tend to become more whig in proportion as it becomes more abridged'.[78] This, it seems, comes about the further one removes oneself from the painstaking work of the research student. In fact, Butterfield argued that the danger of studying the past for the sake of the present 'is one that is really introduced for the purpose of facilitating the abridgement of history'.[79] A typical abridgement, of course, is the wide-ranging, narrative, explanatory and popularized 'general history' in the manner of Macaulay. Small wonder that historians have seen Butterfield as one of the chief inspirations behind the post-war tendency for British historians to dislike the broader canvas and prefer the detailed monograph. J.H. Plumb, himself a believer in the importance of making history accessible to a wide audience, commented in 1969 that he felt the need to toll the bell for the passing of the great narrative histories, and that Butterfield's work opened the 'fusillade' of 'technical history' against them.[80] Similar points are made by R.H.C. Davies, who comments:

> **Butterfield himself had never intended that his work should cause historians to stop trying to explain history. But because he had demonstrated that the Whig historians had read their own ideas into historical events, lesser historians have felt timid of expressing any ideas at all.[81]**

It would therefore be a mistake to see in Butterfield nothing more than an advocate of the narrow scholarly monograph, written by the painstaking efforts of an historian who deliberately distanced himself from all the concerns of his own times. In *The Englishman and His History* (1944), Butterfield responded to the demands of the Second World War by accepting that the Whig version of history at least offered a shared set of values and a belief in liberty which had helped to unite the nation in opposition to Nazism. And, like Ranke, his deep Christian beliefs informed his whole conception of what history was and what historiography should be. In his view, Christianity, based on the historical Jesus, had the most intimate of relationships with history. Like Ranke, he would not presume to identify what God's intentions were, but was adamant that God did work in history and that, in the links between events, some awareness of his work was possible. To deny that God was at work within the world was, at the very best, to make him an absentee God. In *God in History* (1958), Butterfield complained that belief in an absentee God led to an enervating optimism about the workings of the universe which made a personal religion unnecessary:

> **And if God cannot play a part in life, that is to say, in history, then neither can human beings have very much concern about him or very real relationships with him.[82]**

One can, perhaps, link this with Butterfield's exasperation at the complacency of Whig history. Indeed, he had a very strong sense of the essential sinfulness of human nature which made optimism and complacency doubly difficult to accept. Sin – and God's judgement on sin – fatally compromised all human system-building and institutions. In *Christianity and History* (1949), he complained of those who saw merely human political structures and organizations as being 'the actual end of life, the ultimate purpose of history' and proclaimed:

> Though the judgment is always upon us – upon man's universal sin – the sentence falls on great human systems, on nations, civilisations, institutions; indeed on all the schematised patterns into which human life ranges itself in various periods ... The very things which provide the neat developing patterns in our history books – provide the supra-personal edifices like state, culture, capitalism, liberalism – and which are associated with the idea of progress, are the things which are shattered when the judgment falls on men.[83]

For Butterfield, therefore, as for Ranke, it was vital for historians to study the past on its own terms without distorting it through their own present-day concerns and imposing on it their own pet models and theories. For those without religious beliefs, this was sufficient providing they did not attempt to find therein a meaning for life itself:

> Those who complain that technical history does not provide people with the meaning of life are asking from an academic science more than it can give...[84]

For the Christian, the task was to engage in objective research and to make the past intelligible to the present day:

> having in his religion the key to his conception of the whole human drama, he can safely embark on a detailed study of mundane events, if only to learn through their inter-connections the ways of Providence.[85]

It is clear that Butterfield's attitude towards historical writing was largely informed by his Christian beliefs, but it would be ill-advised to ignore the influence of the political upheavals through which he lived. The shock of the First World War and the economic crises of the Depression made a simplistic belief in progress hard to sustain. The Second World War, the Holocaust, the dangers of atomic warfare and the growing tensions of the cold war had a similar effect. *Christianity and History* is replete with references to the challenge of Marxism.

There is clearly something problematic in Butterfield's concept of what made good historical writing. In particular, we see a tension between his dismissal of 'present-minded' history and the fact that his vision of history was itself historically determined – namely, the product of his own religious beliefs and the sense of crisis within his own society. Claims that historical writing should in essence be timeless (albeit made meaningful to the present day) do not accord well with such a recognition. In any case, some of Butterfield's comments betray an inconsistency. He could even sound like Macaulay at times:

> As far as I am concerned, the point of teaching history to undergradu-
> ates is to turn them into public servants and statesmen, in which case
> they had better believe in ideals, and not shrink from having ideas and
> policies and from carrying their policies through ... I know it sounds
> priggish – but I happen to think history is a school of wisdom and
> statesmanship.[86]

Not so much priggish, perhaps, as Whiggish. It is, however, important to
take into account the context of Butterfield's words. He was keen to distance
himself from the highly influential work of his contemporary Lewis Bernstein Namier (1888–1960) on the grounds that Namier was inclined to
dismiss the impact of ideas on human conduct (a contention difficult for a
Christian of the Butterfield mould to stomach). Nevertheless, there were
clear links between Butterfield and Namier. A discussion of these links and
the work of Namier himself will help to illuminate further the responses of
historians within the British historical tradition to the example of – and
issues associated with – Rankean historiography.

Sir Lewis Namier's immense influence on the British historical profession
of the 1950s and 1960s stemmed from the way in which his approaches
appeared to coincide with the methodological, social and political stances
prevalent within that profession. His meticulous and minute scholarship
and heroic archival research appealed to historians who increasingly
accepted that such apparent Rankeanism was the basis of true historical
writing. His work ran virtually parallel with that of Butterfield, and can also
be seen as an attack on the confident, sweeping narratives of the Whigs. His
distaste for theories (Whig or Marxist) which imposed patterns of progress
on the past suited the conservative-minded historian shaken by the collapse
of liberal optimism and the threat of Communism. In the years after the
Second World War, Namier's élitism and obsession with the landed aristocracy offered an appealing alternative to those who were antagonistic
towards the increasing egalitarianism of Labour-led Britain.

Namier's main contribution to the development of British historiography
was to eschew the standard narrative of the actions of an institution like the
British parliament. Instead, his 'structural analysis', as it came to be called,
uncovered its actual workings through his use of prosopography (collective
biography). Avoiding the Whiggish assumption that the ideals and policies
of Whig and Tory parties shaped political behaviour, his researches into the
backgrounds and aims of eighteenth-century MPs led him to argue that
their main motivations were essentially personal. Political behaviour, then,
was the result of self-interest, ambition and local rivalries rather than
adherence to principle. In *The Structure of Politics at the Accession of George
III* (1929) and *England in the Age of the American Revolution* (1930) he
demolished other Whig convictions. George III was generally seen as the

foe to democratic progress and a king whose autocratic ways led directly to the loss of the American colonies in the American War of Independence (or American Revolution) of 1775–83. Namier attempted with some, albeit partial, success to rehabilitate the king by examining his personal papers and so arguing that there was no evidence of a desire to increase his own power at the expense of parliament. His opening chapter of *England in the Age of the American Revolution* made the case:

> ... George III never left the safe ground of Parliamentary government, and merely acted as *primus inter pares* [first among equals], the first among the borough-mongering, electioneering gentlemen of England. While the Stuarts tried to browbeat the House and circumscribe the range of its action, George III fully accepted its constitution and recognised its powers ...[87]

In Namier's view, the so-called Whig politicians were not to be seen as the defenders of British liberties against a Stuart-like would-be tyrant, but as self-seeking politicians who played the 'Constitution in danger!' card as a useful weapon in factional intrigue. And, in any case, the terms 'Whig' and 'Tory' were not party labels attached to opponents and supporters of the king respectively. Some of George III's ministers had called themselves Whigs. The words were more like the 'left-wing' and 'right-wing' as used today – and, of course, the words tell us more about the standpoints of people who apply them than they do about the people to whom they are applied.

There is no denying that Namier's approach involved minute and painstaking, card-index style, research. One can certainly see why he was hailed as 'Britain's answer to Leopold von Ranke'. And, as Linda Colley points out,[88] he sometimes saw himself in the mould of the objective researcher into the documents of past politics. The word 'Namierization' was coined – and indeed entered the Oxford English Dictionary – to refer to exact and detailed scholarship. But, as with Ranke himself, the truth is more complex. We need to look very carefully at the type of source habitually used by Namier to understand his approach. Faced with letters and memoirs, Namier was in his element. The more personal the source, the better he liked it and the more exhaustively he used it. The link with prosopography is clear. But the question is, why this interest in this type of source? In short, he was fascinated by the individual in history because he was obsessed by his own psyche, scarred as it was by the many contradictions of his life. Born Ludwik Bernsztajn vel Niemirowski in Galicia, eastern Poland, his parents were Jews, but did not practise their religion. His native tongue should have been Ukrainian, but his parents tried to stop him from speaking it on the grounds that it was inappropriate for those who wished truly to belong to the landed élites of Poland. He stood to inherit his father's lands and had the tastes and outlook of a patrician, but was disinherited. He became a British subject in 1913, having emerged from Balliol College, Oxford with a first-class degree and a profound, quasi-mystical belief in the values and outlook of the British aristocracy. But he was too strident, too sharp, too arrogant, too self-tormented and – given an atmosphere of latent anti-Semitism – too Jewish, to be accepted into the ranks of the élites. Despite his evident abilities and his burgeoning academic reputation, he failed to secure fellowships or chairs at either Oxford or Cambridge. His attempts to come to terms with his Jewishness led him to work with zeal for the Zionist Organization whose aim was to establish a Jewish homeland in Palestine. His craving for acceptance into the world of the British establishment led him to hope (against all reason) that such a state would be part of the British Empire. He then proceeded to alienate his Jewish friends by converting to Anglicanism in 1947. Namier, then, was the quintessential outsider whose quest for self-identity led him to sink himself into obsessive work and onto the couches of the psychoanalysts.

Namier approached the writing of history with a belief that what shaped the past was political behaviour, and that what shaped political behaviour was human nature. Ideas were a potent force, but ideas were adopted not because human beings calmly and rationally selected the ones appropriate to their needs; they were adopted at an instinctive and emotional level. It was this level, he felt, which must concern the historian. This meant that an ideology such as Communism could hold few attractions for him, even beyond his landowner's distaste for the urban masses. He denied the truth of any system based on an appeal to reason and a promise of progress, since, in so doing, it failed to take into account the troubled human psyche. The one intellectual system which did allegedly base itself on the workings of the psyche was Freudian psychoanalysis – of which Namier had personal experience. It not only explained for Namier his own personality – in particular, his conflict with his father – but also gave him the approach he needed to study history; namely, at the level of the individual and the group. In effect, he was being offered the chance of writing himself into his history and history into himself, and who could resist such a temptation? Namier recognized this relationship between an historian and his work:

> A great history work becomes, and indeed has to be, part of the life of its author ... An intimate knowledge of a past period and the author's own life experience ... must blend, grow and develop (not mingle) together.[89]

The flaws in Namier's work are a reflection of his virtues. As John Cannon has pointed out,[90] Namier's books are ill-structured – minute analysis of archival material and prosopography are hard to integrate into any form of narrative. Namier was a fine stylist, and found his inability to make his work flow for the reader deeply frustrating. His Freudianism led to often illumin-ating discussions of the background and motivations of his characters, but also to a tendency to concentrate on those who were clearly neurotic; or, if they were not so clearly neurotic, then Namier found a suitable neurosis for them. It was helpful to be reminded of the extent to which human behaviour was affected by impulse and emotion, but less helpful to be informed that impulse and emotion are virtually all there is. In a lecture to the British Academy in 1944, Namier commented on the contribution of the German populace in the revolution of 1848:

> **The mob had come out in revolt, moved by passions and distress rather than ideas: they had no articulate aims, and no one will ever be able to supply a rational explanation of what it was they fought for, or what made them fight.**[91]

To dismiss the influence of ideas on human conduct in this way is simplistic and scarcely reflects Namier's own experience. His attachment to his particular brand of Zionism was surely more than the product of his own psyche.

And finally, there is something contradictory in what Namier was doing. He was refusing to accept the validity of patterns, theories and models in history, and yet was imposing on history his own understanding of Freud, whose writings he treated as if they had established incontrovertible laws. To do so meant that he was projecting onto history the view that human nature was unchanging at the level of emotions, instincts and feelings – a procedure which at least lays itself open to the danger of anachronism. Like Butterfield, Namier had not left the Whigs behind in his own work.

Namier's impact on the writing of history outside Britain was negligible, but inside the country, immense. Richard Evans comments:

> **When I was an undergraduate in the 1960s, Namier's *Structure of Politics* was considered by history tutors to have been the greatest work ever penned about English history, and Namier was a god.**[92]

He was a god because he was, it seemed, providing a technique which raised historical scholarship to new levels. Such precision, such detail, such exactitude, such relentless dismissing of over-arching theories about progress; Namier was supposedly offering to his followers the mantle of true objectivity and a recognition of the value of the individual. This mantle was well worth having as a protection against the claims of one's Marxist oppo-nents across the cold war divide. And yet, as we have seen, using Namier in this way is to distort him, just as Ranke was distorted by his followers. The extent to which his work was the product of his own tortured life and obsession with Freud was all but ignored.

The impact of both Butterfield and Namier was to confirm the pre-existing tendencies of British historiography towards the Rankean empiricist (roughly, one who works not on the basis of theory but through observation and evidence). It is scarcely to be denied that a kind of bastardized Rankeanism dominated – perhaps still dominates – academic history in Europe and North America. Assumptions about what makes a good historian are very often based on methodology derived ultimately from Ranke. In his book on the Cambridge legal historian F.W. Maitland (1850–1906) – one of the great communicators of the Rankean tradition to the English historical establishment – G.R. Elton commented not only on Maitland, but also on what Elton himself saw as the goal of historical writing:

> ... Maitland tackled the task of writing real history. Reading the sources properly and solving their problems may seem so obvious a preparatory stage that it hardly deserves so much comment. It is nothing of the sort: great reputations have been made ... by men who fudged both the reading and the analysis of their sources.[93]

That supposed mark of entry into the profession of history, the PhD, generally remains a heavily detailed and narrow discussion based largely on original sources. On a stylistic level, the use of the first person singular is often deprecated. As for *The Past and its Presenters*, I have made a conscious decision to use it in what is, after all, a somewhat opinionated book, rather than pretend that its absence indicated objectivity. But I defy anyone unlucky enough to come across my PhD thesis to spot it there.

It is also scarcely to be denied that bastardized Rankeanism led to a restricted subject-matter for history. Peter Burke points out[94] that the Rankean approach brought the shutters down on the very Enlightenment historiography which was expanding the concerns of the historian into the areas of social history (particularly, as we have seen, customs and manners) and economic history. We recall that it was not as if Ranke was uninterested in these areas, but rather that his sources and his views on the God-given national spirit led him into political and military history. Many of his successors lacked even that interest.

The Rankean, anti-Whig style of history can be criticized because it fights shy of evaluating development through time. Studying development need not necessarily be judgemental, and, even when there appears to be a definite line of progress from past towards the present (as in the history of science), the good historian can still evaluate those who did not contribute towards progress in the context of their own times and with fairness. This point is well made by Ernst Mayr, who argues that what he calls 'horizontal historiography', which dwells in loving detail on one moment of time, is inadequate in presenting the constant searching and experimenting which make up the spirit of scientific enquiry. Mayr is right to resent the attaching of the label 'Whiggish' to any form of developmental historiography.[95]

To deny to history the right to study development causes other potential problems. As we shall see in Chapter 5, the fundamental human need to understand the present requires an understanding of the past and how the past shaped the present. If historians refuse to help provide it, then others who are less qualified will. The dangers of allowing them to do so are legion (see pp.163–5). There are certainly those who would argue that to deny a link between historical study and present politics and society is, ultimately, a dangerous dereliction of duty. Memorably, Pieter Geyl, writing in the aftermath of his experiences at the hands of Nazis in his native Holland, commented in his *Debates with Historians* that:

> **Historicism, in the sense of an interpretation of history which acknowl-
> edges no standards outside the object, is abhorrent to me ... a disinter-
> ested understanding of what is alien to you – this is not the function of
> the mind which will supply the most trenchant weapons for the political
> rough-and-tumble.[96]**

And yet, Geyl also offers an eloquent testimony to the abiding appeal of impartiality and objectivity, although it should be pointed out that, strictly speaking, objectivity is possible without impartiality. After all, one could search for the truth objectively, but, having supposedly found it, one could then throw aside impartiality and make a value judgement. Be that as it may, Geyl argues that, as they are intrinsic parts of liberal culture – an academic version of fair play – their seductiveness is very real. After all, the opposite could easily be seen as chauvinistic bigotry or arrogance. This is why Geyl suddenly stops dead in his tracks:

> **Yet how admirable, nevertheless, is that serene matter-of-factness, that
> striving after comprehension, that openmindedness ... qualities which
> have had a broadening effect on nineteenth-century civilization and
> which (need I remind you?) are the complete opposite of the revolution-
> ary fanaticism and doctrinairism of the men who half a century after his
> [Ranke's] death threw Germany and the world into the catastrophe ...
> To understand is a function of the mind that not only enriches the life
> of the individual but is the very breath of the civilization we are called
> to defend.[97]**

4

Historiography from Marx to the *Annales* School

KARL MARX AND MARXISM

■

Karl Marx (1818–83) was a contemporary of Ranke, also had a lawyer for a father and was nurtured, like Ranke, in German culture at a German university. He too had a major impact on historiography in his own country and beyond which very much persists to this day. But there the similarities end. Marx was not an historian as such, detested German nationalism, saw religion as a cause of man's alienation from himself and his society and spent a considerable part of his adult life an exile from his own country. To Marx, the great shaping force of the nineteenth century was not the Rankean mix of nationalism, the power of the state, the politics of the élites and behind them all the barely-detectable workings of God; it was the bitter drama of industrialization and the dominance of capitalism. And finally, Marx wanted and expected his ideas to change the world (and they did); to Ranke, this would seem to be sacrilegious presumption.

In 1843, after concluding his doctoral thesis at the University of Berlin and working as a journalist, Marx moved to Paris, where he found himself in the congenial – if quarrelsome – company of progressive thinkers. By 1844, he had met Friedrich Engels who, despite (or because of) being the son of an industrialist, was a revolutionary socialist. Both Marx and Engels were more than happy to be labelled Communists and got themselves commissioned by the congress (in London) of a new organization called the Communist League to publish a pamphlet explaining the League's stance in a straightforward form. And so, Marx and Engels' *The Communist Manifesto* was published in February 1848. According to Engels' preface to the English edition of 1888, its nucleus and fundamental proposition originated from Marx: namely, that the whole history of mankind was a history of struggles between classes in societies which were shaped by the 'prevailing mode of economic production'.[1] The publication of the *Manifesto* had nothing to do with the outburst of revolutions in a number of European countries later that year, but the failure of those revolutions meant that Marx fled to London in August 1849. There, he spent the rest of his life, partly supported by Engels, partly by journalism and partly due to fortunate legacies to his wife, Jenny. In 1867, he completed the first volume of his massive work *Capital*, but his work *The Civil War in France* (1871) (about the contemporary and abortive workers' uprising, the Paris Commune) brought him more immediate recognition as a Communist thinker. His personal political influence over such Communist organizations as the First International was, however, limited. His last major work, the *Critique of the Gotha Programme*, reflected his distaste for an 1875 programme drawn up, without his participation, to try to unite German socialist parties. It was left to Engels to fan the flame of Marx's ideas, and the twentieth century, particularly through the Communist revolutions in Russia in 1917 and in Mao's China after 1949, to claim them as inspiration for a new world order.

And yet, how times change. As the twentieth century draws to a close, we see Communism apparently in retreat across the world. States officially subscribing to the ideas of Marx are increasingly few and far between. Of course, this may seem to be irrelevant to a book on historiography. Perhaps so, but, since Marx's ideas on the nature of history were part and parcel of his revolutionary teachings and vision of progress through time, no critique of his thought can afford to ignore modern political events which might be seen as evidence of the accuracy – or otherwise – of those ideas.

Marx and history: historical determinism

Many millions of words have been spilled on Marx's ideas, but before I spill a few more it is best, in the standard historian's manner, to recognize the pitfalls and limitations. First of all, there is simply no single, indisputable Marxist canon which allows us to say 'Yes, this is what Marx meant about history'. There are, as we shall see, possible inconsistencies and gaps in his thought as revealed in his published and unpublished writings. For example, to explore the link between Marx's philosophical methods and his ideas on economics, scholars since the 1970s have felt obliged to make considerable use of an uncorrected manuscript called the *Grundrisse* (containing preliminary ideas, some but not all of which appeared in *Capital*).

In fact, some of his most significant arguments are susceptible to different interpretations; so much so that Engels, after Marx's death, felt obliged to comment on what Marx – in Engels' opinion – *really* meant. We shall be able to trace the varied interpretations of Marx in the differing use to which his ideas were put by historians. Perhaps, after all, it is the explaining of this non-uniform legacy which is the most important task for this chapter, at least.

We should start by taking a key passage from *A Contribution to the Critique of Political Economy* (1859) in which Marx explained the genesis of his ideas:

> **The general conclusion at which I arrived and which, once reached, continued to serve as the leading thread in my studies may be briefly summed up as follows: in the social production which men carry on they enter into definite relations that are indispensable and independent of their will; these relations of production correspond to a definite stage of development of their material powers of production. The sum total of these relations of production constitute the economic structure of society – the real foundation, on which rise legal and political superstructures and to which correspond definite forms of social consciousness. The mode of production in material life determines the general character of the social, political, and spiritual processes of life. It is not the consciousness of men that determines their existence, but, on the contrary, their social existence determines their consciousness. At a certain stage of their development the material forces of production in society come into conflict with the existing relations of production, or – what is but a legal expression for the same thing – with the property relations within which they had been at work before. From forms of development of the forces of production these relations turn into their fetters. Then comes the period of social revolution. With the change of the economic foundation the entire immense superstructure is more or less rapidly transformed. In considering such transformations the distinction should always be made between the material transformation of the economic conditions of production, which can be determined with the precision of natural science, and the legal, political, religious, aesthetic, or philosophic – in short, ideological – forms in which men become conscious of this conflict and fight it out.[2]**

As Humpty Dumpty remarked to Alice when asked to explain the poem *Jabberwocky*, 'That's enough to begin with ... there are plenty of hard words there'. So, let us see if we can unravel Marx's ideas and put them in a more straightforward way. To be fair, he was writing with a specialist readership of political economists in mind. First, there is a label (provided by Engels) to attach to his fundamental approach: *historical materialism*. This means that economic (material) conditions shape everything significant in human society. So, change in history must come about because of changes in economic conditions. It is vital to understand the importance of this point. Marx spoke of 'material powers of production' (or 'productive forces', as he often termed it) and 'relations of production'. 'Productive forces' are simply those things needed to produce the food and the goods required by a given society, such as technology and tools, the raw material and the labour needed to use them. The 'relations of production' are the relations (generally between classes of people, or a relationship between a person and property) which make that production happen – such as factory boss and worker, landlord and tenant, noble and serf, owning, renting, wage-earning. Marx argued that relations of production must correspond to (and are shaped by) the powers of production. He put this with a kind of brutal simplicity in *The Poverty of Philosophy* (1847) where he said:

> **The handmill gives you society with the feudal lord; the steam mill, society with the industrial capitalist.**[5]

Marx added that the economic base or foundation of society rests upon these relations of production. Crucially, he argued that all the visible aspects of society – its superstructure above these foundations – are shaped by the relations of production. So, our political institutions, our legal systems, our religious beliefs, our value-systems, our media, our ideologies, our educational institutions, are determined by the economic base – hence the phrase often used to describe such ideas: economic determinism. In other words, what we are in any given society is shaped by economic relationships. We might assume that we can come up with political ideas just by inspiration or abstract theorizing, but they are, in fact, the creation of that economic base. This is why Marx talked of the consciousness of men being created by their social existence, rather than the consciousness of men creating that social existence.

Perhaps an example would help. We can take the time of the 'steam mill and the industrial capitalist' and see how Marx's concept of the base/superstructure applies. The economic base rests upon the relations of production, which are – in Marx's terminology – the bourgeoisie, or middle-class property owners, led by industrial capitalists, who control and exploit for their own profit the industrial workers (the proletariat). And so, all the visible aspects of society serve the needs of this relationship – dominated, as it is, by the bourgeoisie. The political system which suits the bourgeoisie is parliamentary democracy, because this takes power away from the feudal landowning classes and monarchs but does not give it directly to the workers. Religious values also serve the needs of this relationship, because

Christianity is used by the bourgeoisie to encourage deference amongst the workers and to distract them from their sufferings and exploitation on earth by offering the promise of reward in Heaven. Even the type of Christianity serves the needs of the bourgeoisie. The Catholic Church, with its alleged emphasis on rather indiscriminate charity and good deeds and its world-denying model of salvation (in which the monastic way was seen as the best route to salvation) was of little use to the aggressive profit-making of the nascent capitalist. Nor was its hierarchical structure, with its clear links with feudal monarchy. But Protestantism was a different matter. Its emphasis on an individual relationship with God matched the individualism needed to forge one's way in a competitive world. Some Protestants – particularly Calvinists – discouraged indiscriminate charity, extravagance and ostentation, and so accumulated the capital necessary for industry. The education system was geared to the needs of industry, aiming to turn out deferential workers with appropriate skills or middle-class entrepreneurs with a competitive spirit.

Now, what did Marx mean when he talked about the period of social revolution, when the productive forces come into conflict with the relations of production? Take the feudal period, characterized by hand or horse-powered technology and static relationships between a landowning aristocracy and a landless peasantry. Then, productive forces start developing and the machine age dawns. Steam power demands factories, towns for workers – but landowners try to preserve the old ways, and conflict arises with the growing capitalist class of the bourgeoisie as they create the new relations of production (factory owner and worker) demanded by the new productive forces. So, the old relations of production of the landowner/serf variety try and fail to hold back the developing productive forces of capitalism. Marx suggested a contradiction (in philosophical terms, a *dialectic*) between the relations of production and forces of production which leads to major historical change. For those who like to bandy about historical terms, Marx's ideas can be called *dialectical materialism*. In his use of the dialectic, we see Marx's adaptation of the thought of the philosopher Hegel, who saw in ideas the motive force behind history. Each age, according to Hegel, was characterized by a dominant idea (or thesis) which nevertheless contained within itself a directly opposing idea (or antithesis). From the resulting contradiction and conflict (the dialectic) came a new synthesis – itself, of course, the dominant idea of the next age. As a materialist, Marx was replacing the concept of the dominant idea with the economic base.

There are three important points to make here. Firstly, it seems that Marx claimed that the economic transformations he had identified have the status of laws explaining the workings of nature. Secondly, it is clear that Marx offered a fundamental structure to history, based upon the forces and relations of production (which taken together he termed 'modes of production').

These modes of production were, in order: Asiatic, ancient, feudal and capitalist. And thirdly, Marx attached considerable importance to social classes – feudal, bourgeois, proletarian – within that structure. To help us with the two last points, I need to refer in some detail to *The Communist Manifesto*:

> **The history of all society up to now is the history of class struggles. Freeman and slave, patrician and plebeian, lord and serf, guildmaster and journeyman, in short, oppressor and oppressed stood in continual conflict with one another, conducting an unbroken, now hidden, now open struggle, a struggle that finished each time with a revolutionary transformation of society as a whole, or with the common ruin of the contending classes ...[4]**

Marx continued by arguing that the system of capitalism, like the system of feudalism before it, brings about its own destruction:

> **... with the development of industry the proletariat not only increases; it is forced together in greater masses, its power grows and it feels it more ... machinery increasingly obliterates different types of labour and forces wages down to an almost equally low level. The increasing competition of the bourgeois amongst themselves and the crises emerging therefrom make the worker's wage ever more fluctuating ...[5]**

However, class conflict was, in Marx's view, by no means never-ending. The proletariat would indeed overthrow the bourgeoisie and, through using the state as its instrument of control, would transform the relations of production by abolishing private ownership and therefore class conflict for ever. And, since human characteristics like greed and acquisitiveness are not innate but the products of a particular economic base, then cooperation would replace competition and the state would simply dissolve, since its coercive purpose had vanished with the end of class conflict.

What Marx is doing is offering a new periodization of history based on changes in productive forces and also – crucially – a projection into the future. The basic outline of his theories is, I hope, reasonably clear, but there are aspects of it which are problematic. As presented so far, they seem to be rigidly determinist: productive forces shape relations of production and the resulting economic base of society shapes its ideologies, political and legal structures and so on. So, there seems to be no place for the human free will, or ideas derived independently of the base. To put it another way, the superstructure cannot affect the base in any meaningful way. This seems most unlikely. Are we to dismiss the view that religious belief – or ethics, for that matter – can be arrived at independently of economic relationships, or that such beliefs cannot in themselves shape a society? What about Marx's own ideas? Should they not emerge from a proletarian as a reflection of his experience under the grinding economic Leviathan of capitalism, rather than a middle-class intellectual with a distinctly bour- geois lifestyle? Also, the relationship between class struggle and historical change is arguably rather unclear. If the motive force for change is the development of productive forces, then where does the political behaviour of, say, the proletariat, have a part to play? Why set up Communist Leagues and agitate at all? Why not simply wait upon the inevitable demise of capital- ism, which comes from within? Peter Singer puts this problem very well:

> ... if neither thought nor politics has any real causal significance, what is the meaning of Marx's dedication, intellectually and politically, to the cause of the working class?[6]

Quite. Of course, one should reflect that Marx was not a cloistered academic but a political activist whose sense of outrage at aspects of his society com- bined with his background in philosophy to produce a vision which was more complex than any brief outline – including his own – could hope fully to reflect; a vision which had its claims to be scientific, but which is clearly informed by a moral and ethical sense. The dispassionate social scientist would not write *The Communist Manifesto*, and would certainly not con- clude it with the ringing cry:

> Let the ruling classes tremble at a communist revolution. Proletarians have nothing to lose in it but their chains. They have a world to win. *Proletarians of all countries unite!*[7]

Crude economic determinism is, as we have seen, a relatively easy target. But, despite the evidence from the *Critique of Political Economy* (and from several other of Marx's comments), it is possible to argue that Marx did not intend to claim that the superstructure could not affect the base, and so deny that political or religious ideas had their effect on the mode of produc- tion. After Marx's death, Engels claimed that neither he nor Marx had ever taught an iron law of economic determinism. In one letter of 1890, Engels wrote:

> According to the materialist conception of history, the *ultimately* deter- mining element in history is the production and reproduction of real life. More than this neither Marx nor I have ever asserted. Hence if somebody twists this into saying that the economic element is the *only* determining one he transforms that proposition into a meaningless, abs- tract, senseless, phrase. The economic situation is the basis, but the

various elements of the superstructure ... also exercise their influence upon the course of the historical struggles and in many cases preponderate in determining their *form*. There is an interaction of all these elements in which, amidst all the endless host of accidents ... the economic movement finally asserts itself as necessary ... Marx and I are ourselves partly to blame for the fact that the younger people sometimes lay more stress on the economic side than is due to it.[8]

There is some support for Engels' stance in some of Marx's writings. In the introduction to the *Grundrisse*, for example, Marx said:

It is known in the case of art that specific times of artistic flowering by no means stand in a proportional relation to the general development of society, therefore (they do not stand in a proportional relation) to the general development of the material basis.[9]

This appears to suggest that art can sometimes be independent of the base – although it has to be said that the form of the *Grundrisse* hardly lends itself to clarity of explanation. More helpful, perhaps, is the concept of class consciousness. Marx argued that it was vital for the proletariat to be aware of its destiny as the agent of the downfall of the bourgeoisie; once the class became conscious of its need for solidarity and its strength, then, given the appropriate crisis in the mode of production, social revolution would follow. In other words, the timing and perhaps the immediate shape of the revolution was not precisely dictated by impersonal laws. Ordinary men (and women, we might add) had to do that. In *The Eighteenth Brumaire of Louis Bonaparte* (1852), Marx made the comment:

Men make their own history, but they do not make it just as they please in circumstances they choose for themselves; rather they make it in present circumstances, given and inherited.[10]

This statement is usually taken by modern commentators to suggest that Marx was at least giving human agents a subsidiary role in historical change. Well, perhaps he was doing that, but there is a danger in taking the passage out of context. In *The Eighteenth Brumaire*, Marx did not follow up the remarks with a discussion of any such role, but instead talked about how revolutionaries nervously summon up names and titles from the past to justify their actions. It all goes to show that coming to a firm decision on the extent of Marx's economic determinism is anything but easy. But it may be that a closer look at *The Eighteenth Brumaire* will help, since it is, after all, Marx writing contemporary history.

Louis Bonaparte was a nephew of the great Napoleon and had been elected president of the French Republic established after the overthrow of the king, Louis Philippe, in 1848. In 1851, Bonaparte staged a coup, overthrew the Republic and was proclaimed emperor. Marx's title, the 'eighteenth brumaire', is an ironic reference to the coup staged by the first Napoleon – an incomparably more impressive figure than his nephew. Now, one can admire Marx for tackling this subject, because it appeared to run counter to his class struggle analysis. It was undeniable that Louis Napoleon was supported by considerable numbers of the bourgeoisie, and some of the workers – in defiance, it would seem – of their class interests. After all, the Marxist model would suggest that the middle classes would aim for a parliamentary-style democracy and the workers for state control in the name and interests of the proletariat.

Terrell Carver's recent introduction to *The Eighteenth Brumaire* is very enthusiastic, suggesting that:

> **It must count as the best argued defence ever of the view that 'history is the history of class struggles', even if in it not all action in politics is traceable to social class, nor all outcomes to revolutionary action presented as advances towards communism ... In the light of *The Eighteenth Brumaire* it cannot be said that Marx's understanding of politics was reductionist and determinist.**[11]

I find myself a little less enthusiastic. The work is wonderfully lively and contains some splendid invective against the bourgeoisie and Bonaparte himself. Marx offered a detailed political analysis of the complex events and interest groups and seems to have taken into account the effect of Bonaparte's personality and cunning on what happened – perhaps not the most obvious line of attack if one was to expect historical determinism and class struggle analysis. But, having said all this, I would argue that *The Eighteenth Brumaire* is firmly anchored in economic determinism. For example, when discussing the different factions amongst the pro-royalists, Marx remarked:

> **What kept the two factions apart was not any so-called principles, it was their material conditions of existence ... On the different forms of property, the social conditions of existence, arises an entire superstructure of different and peculiarly formed sentiments, delusions, modes of thought and outlooks on life. The whole class creates and forms them from the material foundations on up ...**[12]

Marx also suggested that the action of the bourgeoisie in destroying its own political power and handing it over to what appeared to be a lackey of the old feudal classes was the result of fear of proletarian revolution. He then accounted for the support for Bonaparte amongst some of the workers by claiming that they represented the unthinking riff-raff of society – the *lumpenproletariat* – who were manipulated by the bourgeoisie. And, for good measure, he completed the class analysis by claiming that:

> **Bonaparte represents a class, indeed the most numerous class in French society, the *small-holding peasants*.**[15]

So, what we have in *The Eighteenth Brumaire* is an extremely vigorous political narrative without any pretence at being a dispassionate work of history. It rests upon economic determinism as expressed through the shape of its class-based analysis; an analysis which does not dominate the content in a blunt and unsophisticated way, but which very much reflects Engels' view that, ultimately, it is the economic base which counts. And it has to be said that Marx provided little by way of supporting evidence for his contentions – his analysis of the classes engaged in the conflict remains unencumbered by proof.

One final point on the issue of economic determinism. Let us look at the implications of accepting (however tentatively) Engels' argument that he and Marx were agreed that elements of the superstructure might influence in some way the base, but that, in the end, the base remained the real shaper of history. But what does 'in the end' mean? It is difficult to see how one can accept a two-way (reciprocal) action between base and superstructure but also insist that, ultimately, the base is more important. In what circumstances? Or in every circumstance? If so, how can there be true reciprocity?

The impact of Marx on historiography

There are really three ways in which Marx's ideas might have an impact on historiography. The first is when a country becomes Communist and upholds Marxism as the political, philosophical and historical truth. The second is where historians in a non-Communist country are themselves Communist. The third is the possible influence of Marxist historiography on non-Communist historians in a non-Communist country. These three channels of influence can be considered separately, but we also need to examine the differing ways in which the fraught issue of base/superstructure was received.

As one would expect, historical materialism became the official history of the Communist states of Europe. And, generally speaking, where the historians of these countries were subject to the greatest degree of party and state control (such as in the former East Germany and the USSR), then rigid determinism – sometimes called 'crude' or 'vulgar' Marxism by its opponents – was expected and imposed. This meant that it was accepted that Marx's view of the periodization of history and the crude base/super-structure model had the status of natural laws, and therefore any work of history utilizing them did not need to offer balanced arguments and supporting evidence in their justification. The history of the working classes was, of course, a feature one would expect from Marxist historiography, but, in the official histories, it tended to be distorted into an institutional history concentrating on the deeds and thoughts of party leaders – so serving the ruling party's political needs.

What of the Communist historians in the non-Communist countries? To make this issue manageable, it might be best to take one case study, and my choice would be the work of the British Marxist historians from the period of the setting up of the British Communist Party's Historians' Group in the aftermath of the Second World War. There are a number of reasons for this choice. A significant number of the historians associated with this group are generally accepted as fine practitioners of their discipline even by those who do not accept their political views. Their work has, at the very least, been impossible to ignore. Christopher Hill, George Rudé, E.P. Thompson and Eric Hobsbawm spring immediately to mind. Second, I have been able to take advantage of the work in this field of Harvey Kaye, whose desire to appropriate such historians for his own brand of democratic socialism has by no means compromised the value of such books as *The British Marxist Historians* and *The Education of Desire*. And finally, the British Marxist historians have much to say on the relationship between Marxist historiography and economic determinism.

Eric Hobsbawm has commented that, before the Historians' Group, there had been 'no tradition of Marxist history in Britain'.[14] For radical members of the student generation of the 1930s, Communism and Marxism had had many attractions. The Wall Street Crash of 1929 had shaken confidence in capitalism, and, given the supine attitude of the Western democracies towards Hitler, Soviet Russia appeared to represent the only meaningful alternative to the growing power of Fascism. The uncharacteristically harsh tone of Christopher Hill's short work *The English Revolution 1640*, which first appeared in 1940, can be taken to reflect a deep sense of anger at the West's failure to stand up to Hitler and to prevent a world war. The Historians' Group was formally established in 1946, and Hobsbawm speaks with affection of the sense of intellectual excitement and commitment to the cause at this time: 'Our work as historians was therefore embedded in our work as Marxists, which we believed to imply membership of the Communist Party'.[15] However, the events of 1956 broke the unity of the group. In that year, the Russian leader Khrushchev launched an attack on his feared predecessor Stalin and the excesses of Stalinism at the Congress of the Communist Party of the Soviet Union. But the British Communist Party failed to respond to it, and also failed to condemn the Russian invasion of Hungary later in the year. The result was a mass exodus from the party, and the Historians' Group was similarly hit. Although Hobsbawm remained, Hill and Thompson were among those who left. Even so, this should not be taken as a sign that their commitment to Marxism itself had changed in any way.

I now want to look at the way in which the British Marxist historians responded to the issue of economic determinism. Two useful comments should set the scene. The first is Hobsbawm, referring to the work of the Historians' Group:

> **A third advantage of our Marxism – we owe it largely to Hill and to the very marked interest of several of our members ... was never to reduce history to a simple economic or 'class interest' determinism, or to devalue politics and ideology.**[16]

The second is from George Rudé. In his essay 'The Changing Face of the Crowd', Rudé comments:

> **What I learned from Marx was not only that history tends to progress through a conflict of social classes ... but that it has a discoverable pattern and moves forward ... broadly from a lower to a higher phase of development. I learned also that the lives and actions of the common people are the very stuff of history, and though 'material' rather than the institutional and ideological factors are primary, that ideas themselves become a 'material force' when they pass into active consciousness of men.**[17]

Although the materialist conception is perhaps more strongly stressed in Rudé than in Thompson, it seems from both statements that one should not expect from the most influential British Marxist historians a crude economic determinism, but instead that factors usually referred to as part of the superstructure can be derived independently of the base and themselves affect it in some way. Is this contention justified when we look at their work? By and large, it is. Of course, one can point to exceptions. Hill's early essay on the English Revolution presents a simplistic explanation of it as a class war led by the bourgeois parliament against the essentially feudal classes of monarch and major landowners; a war in which religious ideas are seen as the cloak for economic needs:

> **... those who wanted to overthrow the feudal state had to attack and seize control of the Church. That is why political theories tended to get wrapped up in religious language ... But the fact that men spoke and wrote in religious language should not prevent us realising that there is**

> **a social content behind what are apparently purely theological ideas.
> Each class created and sought to impose the religious outlook best
> suited to its own needs and interests. But the real clash is between these
> class interests: behind the parson stood the squire.**[18]

The later Hill would be less ready to label the landowning classes as essentially feudal and much less ready to present arguments with a minimum of
supporting evidence in references. There are one or two signs even within
The English Revolution 1640 that Hill is unhappy with his style of presenta-
tion, which suggests that religious ideas were a blatant cover for class interest. Later in the essay, he accepts that 'The Parliamentarians thought they
were fighting God's battles'.[19] Now, it is the contention of Kaye – and I
accept his argument – that Hill's later work retains the view that the English
Revolution was bourgeois, but in the sense that its outcome favoured the
development of capitalism,[20] rather than being a revolution caused by
capitalism. Richardson agrees,[21] commenting that Hill is judging it to be
bourgeois in terms of consequences rather than origin. As confirmation, we
can simply cite one example among many – Hill's 1988 lecture 'The place of
the seventeenth-century Revolution in English History'[22] – in which he
argues that the English Revolution was neither planned nor willed, but that
its political implications meant that governments were able to give priority
to economic growth, leading to the Industrial Revolution. Kaye also points to
other key developments or changes of emphasis. In his later work, Hill is
keen to stress (and demonstrate) that it is wrong to limit an analysis of class
to economics, or to see ideas as the product of economic circumstances in a
simplistic way. In his *Intellectual Origins of the English Revolution* (1965),
Hill comments:

> **Marx himself did not fall into the error of thinking that men's ideas
> were merely a pale reflection of their economic needs, with no history of
> their own; but some of his successors ... have been more economic-
> determinist than Marx.**[23]

Indeed, in an earlier essay – 'Recent Interpretations of the Civil War' (1956)
– Hill is clearly unhappy with simplistic economic motives behind religious
belief or political behaviour. Talking of religion and the government of the
seventeenth-century English Church, he says:

> **We must have a better explanation of their importance for contempo-
> raries than the theory that Puritanism helps landowners to balance their
> income and expenditure, or encourages the bourgeoisie to grind the
> faces of the poor ... The connections of religion, science, politics, and
> economics are infinite and infinitely subtle. Religion was the idiom in
> which the men of the seventeenth century thought. One does not need**

to accept the idiom, or to take it at its face value, to see that it cannot be ignored or rejected as a simple reflex of economic needs.[24]

Strictures against simplistic base/superstructure Marxism notwithstanding, it is clear that Hill remains wedded to class struggle as central to the process of history – a fundamental tenet, of course, of Marxism. The marked characteristic of much of Hill's more recent work has been a mastery of an extraordinary quantity and range of written sources as he places the emphasis on the significance of culture to class-struggle analysis. Culture is, of course, not to be seen as the mere product of economic relationships. This is clearly stated in Hill's 1989 book *A Turbulent, Seditious and Factious People: John Bunyan and his Church.* In seeking the answer to the question of why changes took place in popular culture in early modern Europe, Hill comments:

> **Phrases like 'the rise of individualism', 'of capitalism' are groping towards an answer, but a merely economic definition is too narrow. For England our answer must include – among many other things – an explanation of the decline of magic, of hell, of Calvinism as a dominant intellectual system ...[25]**

Even so, I can see no evidence that Hill is rejecting the *primacy* of material factors in class-struggle analysis. After all, he talks of the economic definition being too narrow, rather than inappropriate. And, in 'A Bourgeois Revolution?',[26] he significantly defines a class as the position its members have in relation to other classes and to the *productive process* – in other words, a definition which offers a fundamentally economic basis for class. Elsewhere, Hill comments that historians of culture need economic history, 'because culture is a class phenomenon'.[27] So, to study class, economic history appears to have primacy of place, even if it is not the only significant factor.

This has been a complex discussion, but a necessary one. What we seem to see in Hill is a Marxist whose early polemic *The English Revolution 1640*, with its rather crude, relatively unsupported economic determinism focused on causes, has been replaced by work of far greater sophistication, in which the bourgeois revolution thesis is redirected at the consequences of the revolution. That work displays a historicity which the early essay lacked – in other words, a desire to see the seventeenth century from the inside, accompanied by a mastery of written sources and a recognition of the need to cite evidence. Hill does not accept the vulgar Marxist view that the superstructure is entirely the product of the economic base. But I believe there remains a commitment to economic determinism, even though that commitment is worn rather lightly as Hill pursues his interest in studying class struggle through culture. I recall hearing Hill say that his vocabulary had changed since his earliest published work, but that his ideas were essentially the same. His stance, in fact, is not dissimilar to that of Engels. Significantly, in an early article (1948) for *The Modern Quarterly*,[28] Hill states bluntly that Marxism is not determinist, but then backtracks by quoting the passage from Engels discussed above (see pp.132–3) and arguing that even ideas *ultimately* originate in economics. Hill faces, perhaps, the same problem as other Marxists who accept a reciprocal action between base and superstructure: to what extent can the superstructure really affect the base given that primacy of economic factors?

Hill's approach to Marxism is paralleled in the work of other former members of the Historians' Group. E.P. Thompson's *The Making of the English Working Class* (1963) offers an approach to class which is openly critical of those who write as if the working classes were created purely by the productive processes of the Industrial Revolution. He starts by accepting that what the working class is obliged to experience is determined by the forces of production. However, he then points to the resulting temptation to see the workers merely as data – as examples to prove a point, in fact. Thompson insists that the historian must consider how the workers actually handle those experiences and mediate them in terms of their traditions and existing values – mediate them, in fact, in terms of their own culture. Thompson is keen – even desperate – to ensure that any definition of class allows for the contribution and experience of real human beings, not merely the responses of someone who matters only because he is representative of a particular class. After all, Thompson's involvement in contemporary politics (particularly with CND, the Campaign for Nuclear Disarmament) must surely imply that change can take place through the agency of ordinary people. As with his politics, so with his history. With wonderful eloquence, Thompson makes his case for writing about the working classes:

> I am seeking to rescue the poor stockinger, the Luddite cropper, the 'obsolete' hand-loom weaver, the 'utopian' artisan ... from the enormous condescension of posterity. Their crafts and traditions may have been dying. Their hostility to the new industrialism may have been backward-looking. Their communitarian ideals may have been fantasies. Their insurrectionary conspiracies may have been foolhardy. But they lived through these times of acute social disturbance, and we did not. Their aspirations were valid in terms of their own experience; and, if they were casualties of history, they remain, condemned in their own lives, as casualties.[29]

'Experience' is certainly a key word in our understanding of Thompson, but it has to be said that what he means by it is less than clear. One possible interpretation is that he is not denying that the mode of production gives shape to society, but may be saying that the mode of production is not merely defined by economics; that the experiences of men and women, the way in which they mediate their experiences into their existing culture and their growing consciousness of class are really part of that mode of production and shaping force. On the other hand, some of his comments appear to imply that experience is a medium whereby the fundamental concepts (including, perhaps, determinism) are made real. In *The Poverty of Theory*, for example, he comes up with the oblique statement that he and his fellow British Marxist historians

> ... explored, both in theory and in practice, those junction-concepts (such as 'need', 'class', and 'determine') by which, through the missing term, 'experience', structure is transmuted into process, and the subject re-enters into history.[30]

I am relieved that William Sewell, in his work on Thompson's theory of working-class formation, is as uncertain about the meaning of this as I am.[31] Sewell quite rightly, I think, identifies passages from *The Poverty of Theory* which are clearly intended to distance 'experience' from being determined by the mode of production but, by tying 'experience' into 'class experience' and accepting that class is itself determined by the mode of production, Thompson ends up contradicting himself. Whether this is the case or not matters less than the fact that Thompson is *trying* so hard to bring human agency into Marxist history. This explains the virulence of his response (in *The Poverty of Theory*) to the Marxist philosopher Louis Althusser, whose concentration on the supposedly scientific aspects of Marx's works virtually led him to deny the importance of independent human action in history. In so doing, Althusser implicitly sabotaged the work of historians who claimed to be using historical evidence on which to base their propositions. It is important to note that the British Marxist historians certainly accepted the need for the standard scholarly techniques of analysis to be applied to evidence. Hobsbawm makes this point very clearly when commenting on Marx's model of historical development:

> It is right that it should be debated, and in particular that the usual criteria of historical verification should be applied to it. It is inevitable that some parts of it, which are based on insufficient and misleading evidence, should be abandoned.[32]

Thompson, in fact, uses the term 'empiricism' to describe what he sees as the necessary testing of the theory (be it Marxist class struggle or whatever) against the evidence. Heyck[33] offers an excellent discussion of Thompson's criticism of two other British Marxists, Perry Anderson and Tom Nairn. Thompson accused them of a slavish use of base/superstructure without understanding that the action between base and superstructure was recip-rocal, and of distorting evidence to fit their over-rigid model. An interesting charge, and one which has been frequently levelled at Thompson and Hill themselves by non-Marxists.

To conclude. Thompson's route is different from that of Hill, but the intention is similar. Both historians are ultimately unwilling to shed deter-minism, but are equally unwilling to see human beings as victims of histor-ical forces rather than being responsible in some way (however limited) for their own lives. The difficulties of this stance have been the subject of the last few paragraphs.

What, then, do historians owe to Karl Marx? This question is an adapta-tion of a chapter title in Hobsbawm's *On History*, so it seems only fair to start with Hobsbawm's comments. He himself starts by reminding us of the con-tribution and limitations – mainly the latter – of the Rankean tradition. In particular, professional history following Ranke tended to restrict itself to politics, war, diplomacy and the concerns of the élites. In Hobsbawm's view, Rankean-style history contributed little to the understanding of human society, past or present. Elsewhere, Hobsbawm expands somewhat on this by arguing that the British Marxist historians in the early 1950s were part of a general movement against

> **'old fashioned' politico-constitutional or narrative history. 'Namierism', against which we polemised, had enormous prestige among our British academic colleagues.**[34]

So, what type of history has Marx stimulated? It seems very obvious to say that social and economic history owes much to Marx, and this is true within limits. After all, Marx offers a way of relating economic history to social history (and to political history, for that matter) through historical material-ism and class struggle. This is very seductive. In short, Marxism offers the historian not only a fundamental approach akin to a methodology, but also a purpose. As Hill puts it in his *Modern Quarterly* article, 'the historian himself must have a vision of society and the social process as a whole: he must have a philosophy'.[35] Marxism therefore makes it possible for histor-ians to tackle some of the 'big issues' – change through time, the impact of industrialization, the causes and effect of imperialism, political and social revolution – by offering hypotheses on what is likely to be most significant in an otherwise daunting avalanche of historical data. One need only con-sider the scale and breadth of Hobsbawm's *Age of* books to appreciate this point: *The Age of Revolution* (1962); *The Age of Capital* (1975); *The Age of Empire* (1987). *The Making of the English Working Class* and Hill's textbook

The Century of Revolution, 1603–1714 (1961) are similarly wide-ranging and – crucially – offer interpretations which subsequent historians of whatever persuasion simply cannot ignore.

The relationship between Marxism and the discipline of economic history is less direct and more tenuous than one might expect. It would certainly be untrue to say that economic history owed its being to Marx. After all, the experience of the Industrial Revolution itself was likely to arouse interest in economics. This, rather than Marx, explains the growth of economic history in the USA at the end of the nineteenth century. Significantly, American economic history and mainstream history tended to drift apart – hardly a characteristic of Marxist historiography. Nor does the economic history practised in late twentieth-century America owe much to Marx; the so-called New Economic History or 'cliometrics', which offers explanations based not on class struggle and historical materialism but – according to one of its chief practitioners, Fogel – on 'explicit behavioural models ... and quantitative evidence'.[36]

Marxist class analysis has, as we have seen, helped to stimulate an interest in cultural history. In particular, the study of popular culture has increasingly developed into an accepted branch of academic history from the late 1970s onwards. This is not to say that those involved in the study of popular culture owe their discipline or methodology purely to Marx. Interest in popular culture was a feature of growing nationalism in Europe in the late eighteenth and nineteenth centuries and, if we look at it historiographically, then the dissatisfaction with traditional, event-based political and diplomatic history was not restricted to Marxists. In any case, those who now study popular culture are as likely to be influenced by the French *Annales* school (whose origins owe little to Marxism – see p.156) and/or anthropology as they are by Hill, Thompson or Marxist theoreticians like Gramsci. The latter offered a class-based concept of culture in which the dominant class uses culture as a control mechanism ('hegemony'). But popular culture does not have to be defined in class-struggle terms. If we take Peter Burke's definition in his *Popular Culture in Early Modern Europe* (1978), (derived from the anthropologist Robert Redfield), we are told that popular culture was, to some extent, shared by both the élite and the majority, rather than being imposed by the former on the latter:

> **There were two cultural traditions in early modern Europe, but they did not correspond symmetrically to the two main social groups, the élite and the common people ... the crucial cultural difference in early modern Europe (I want to argue) was that between the majority, for whom popular culture was the only culture, and the minority, who had access to the great tradition but participated in the little tradition as a second culture.[37]**

The 'great tradition' was the culture formally transmitted through university and other élite education.

One area where Marxist influences are more clearly identifiable is 'History from Below': the attempt to recapture the experiences, attitudes, value-systems and perspectives of those left out of traditional history (and most published primary sources). After all, one would expect Marxist historians to show an interest in those classes whose exploitation had left so few records. We can see their interest in so-called grass-roots history, of course, in Rudé's comments above (see p.137), in Thompson's *Making of the English Working Class* and in Hill's *The World Turned Upside Down* (1975). Hill, for example, deliberately takes what he calls 'the worm's eye view'[38] as he looks at radical ideas during the period of Oliver Cromwell. However, Hobsbawm admits to some limitations to the Marxist contribution to 'History from Below'. He accepts that Marxists – or, in fact, socialist historians in general – were tempted to study ordinary people as and when they could be seen as contributors to the forward march of the labour movement. This led to a concentration on institutions and organizations which represented the workers, rather than the workers themselves;[39] a point echoed forcefully by Paul Thompson who, in advocating the value of oral history, points to the way in which too much history of the working classes has concentrated on trade unions and working-class political groups.[40] Similarly, George Rudé's attempt to recover the mentalities of the crowd is less a desire to explore the world-view and feelings of ordinary people than to examine the attitudes of those people in potentially revolutionary situations. He says as much in his introduction to *Ideology and Popular Protest*:

> **In my earlier work, I have often been concerned with establishing the identity ... of the common people in history that have taken part in demonstrations, riots and revolutions occurring mainly in a 'pre-industrial society' ...**[41]

There are other limitations to the influence of Marxism. Peter Burke is full of praise for the two books by Hill and Thompson cited above, but he has one major worry which echoes the point just made: that the 'ordinary people' chosen are there because they were suitably exploited, or suitably radical. Thompson, he argues, comes close to excluding the very real phenomenon of the working-class Tory; Hill tends to forget that not all radicals were ordinary people, and that not all ordinary people were radicals. In Orwellian phraseology, Burke comments that, to Thompson and Hill, 'some people are considered as more people than others'.[42] We might add that Hill is understandably fascinated by the ideas of proto-Communists like the Diggers or the remarkably subversive, blaspheming and outrageous Ranters.[43] But this is not really 'People's History' or 'History from Below' in the sense of recapturing the experiences of ordinary people. Particularly in the case of Hill, we see an historian out to recapture those who were excluded from traditional histories because he finds their ideas stimulating and – crucially – of use to us today. They are recaptured on his terms, and his net is not spread for those who had less interesting things to say. However, one should accept that the Marxist historians have done much to recover the thoughts and actions of radical groups languishing in undeserved obscurity.

The relationship between Marxism and women's history is somewhat problematic. As we have seen, Marxism certainly played a part in the attack on élitist (and male-dominated) political and diplomatic history, and so helped to open the door to a much wider definition of what constituted the discipline of history. Practitioners of Marxist and feminist history wish to make their contribution to political and social change. Both Marxism and women's history share an awareness of exploitation, but also frequently wish to point to achievement; in other words, to demonstrate the extent to which those discriminated against were able, against all the odds, to make their own histories. However, women's history is offering an alternative way of structuring the past to that offered by class analysis and economic determinism. In one form, it seeks to recapture the experience of women and so offer 'her-story' as opposed to 'his-story'. On the other hand, in the form of gender history, it seeks to explore how the power relationships in society reflect relationships between women and men. Joan Scott's useful summary of the approaches towards women's history[44] significantly makes no mention of Marx, barely refers to class and instead discusses what women's history/gender history might stand to gain from the pluralism of poststructuralism and discourse analysis (see Chapter 1).

How can we summarize the contemporary value of Marxism to historiography? Marxist history has certainly been both shaken and stirred by politics, economics, philosophy and, not least, by the writing of history itself. Its status as a scientific exposition of laws of history, promulgated in its crudest form in Communist countries, has not really survived the collapse of Communism as a political and economic power in Europe and beyond. A theory which rests upon a particular line of progress which projects into the future is clearly vulnerable when the future turns out to be an unanticipated one. Economic determinism, with all the provisos attached to it, remains, ultimately, a fundamental precept of Marxism. It is not, however, verifiable as such. The political breakdown of Communism and the apparent triumphs of pluralistic capitalism encouraged a deep suspicion of the grand explanations (the metanarratives) which sometimes expressed itself as postmodernism or, for practising historians, as the kind of revisionism which downplays the idea of revolution. J.C.D. Clark's book on state and society in seventeenth and eighteenth-century England is significantly titled

Revolution and Rebellion. Clark comments: 'Rebellion rather than revolution is thus the crucial explanatory category for revisionist historians'.[45] He refers to Hill, Thompson, Rudé and Hobsbawm as the 'Marxist Old Guard'; a not-very-subtle ploy to suggest that their day – along with Marxists in general – has gone. But has it? I think not. Had the British Marxists written in the manner of East German or Soviet party-men, then we would be waving them goodbye. But their blend of a sophisticated use of class-struggle analysis, their refusal to offer crude versions of the base/superstructure model, their willingness to subscribe to the need to provide evidence for their contentions, their frequent mastery of an astonishing range of sources – all these suggest that their influence is likely to remain and that Marxist history is anything but dead. Were it so, then Clark and those of his ilk would have no need to write as revisionists. In general, Marxist history is a great stimulus to historians of every type to consider some of the most fundamental ideas. What is the place of theory in the writing of history? How far are men and women free agents or the product of impersonal forces? Is there a pattern to history? Are we to reject the thought that the writing of history serves a political purpose? Of course, it is easy enough to say that Marxists (or any other historians who employ a model to structure their analysis) select evidence which fits the model and ignore evidence which conflicts with or seems inappropriate to it. In Chapter 5, I discuss the case of the Marxist historian David Abraham, who fell into this very trap (see p.178). And we have expressed concern about what is meant by the economic base ultimately creating the superstructure. Distortions will and do occur for these reasons. But we have already seen that distortion occurs in many ways in the writing of history: in the selection of a particular type of source, or the omission of another; or in claiming not only objectivity, but also neutrality as well. So, although it is possible to overestimate the importance of Marxism for twentieth-century (and no doubt twenty-first century) historiography, it would be quite wrong to downplay it too.

THE EMERGENCE OF THE *ANNALES* SCHOOL AND 'TOTAL HISTORY'

∎

The massive economic, political and social changes of the nineteenth century were, as we have seen, instrumental in generating distinctive types of history. The legacy of Ranke could be applied to the history of nation-states and, if sufficiently distorted, serve the needs of self-confident new nations like Germany. The growth of Marxist history and economic history similarly reflected those changes. In Britain, the belief in the superiority of British institutions and the British way of liberal parliamentary democracy stimulated 'Whig history' (see pp.114–20). The dreadful impact of the First World War and the subsequent economic depressions led a number of historians to question historical writing which fed the needs of nation-states. For some, this of course led to an espousal of Marxism; for others, it led to an increasing dissatisfaction with traditional 'event-centred' history and a desire to widen the scope of history both in terms of methodology and in subject-matter. In France, even before the First World War, there was a movement against what was seen as a German obsession with the grubbing up of facts and/or theories of development and dominance (sometimes in defence of the kind of expansionism which had lead to the seizing of Alsace and Lorraine from France in 1871). In some cases, French historians became interested in interdisciplinary approaches – using, say, human geography or the relatively new discipline of sociology. An interdisciplinary approach does not fit very well with a history dominated by the narration of 'great events', often shaped by 'great men'. It would suit an approach focusing on structures underpinning events and on problems rather than description.

These, in fact, are essential characteristics of the so-called *Annales* historians. The name comes from the journal founded by the medievalist Marc Bloch and the sixteenth-century specialist Lucien Febvre in 1929: *Annales d'histoire économique et sociale*. Peter Burke[46] identifies a first phase of the movement in the period from the 1920s to 1945, where we see a radically subversive attack on traditional French political narrative history.

Marc Bloch (1886–1944)

Marc Bloch operated on the basis that history meant the study of the past, not the study of documents. This is not to deny his expertise in documentary analysis, but to recognize that he saw such inquiries as only one aspect of an historian's work. An early (1913) study of the area around Paris, the Ile-de-France, emphasized the importance of geography. Specifically, Bloch used a study of landscape and townscape to help establish the characteristics of the region. Already, Bloch was approaching history by setting himself a question to answer, rather than simply taking an accepted historical period and describing the doings of the élites therein. Bloch certainly liked his questions to be broad ones, and his later works are a case in point. In 1924, whilst a professor at the University of Strasburg, he wrote *Les rois thaumaturges* (literally, 'Miracle-working kings'; English title, *The Royal Touch*), which asked the question 'how could people believe in the illusion that kings had a healing touch?' This book displayed his interest in group psychology (or more specifically 'collective mentalities') and a willingness to show how those mentalities interconnected with political institutions. He did not restrict himself to France, but tackled the way in which kingship was given a supernatural character in England too. In 1931, his short book *French Rural History* explored the links between landscape, rural customs, political and social institutions. He divided France into three regions based on the differences in terrain, soil and climate and argued that rural life was the product of these and other interrelated factors (including religion, attitudes, royal policies and monetary developments) over an impressive timescale (early medieval to the French Revolution). Class was by no means ignored, but not seen as a determinant in the Marxist sense. Bloch, in fact, had no time for historians who clearly wrote with a predetermined thesis in mind, and was more than prepared to admit when his own conclusions were tentative. The range of evidence used was inevitably very broad, and included archaeology, place names and modern estate maps. Bloch exploited his modern sources by reading them backwards into the past (the so-called 'retrogressive method') to help fill in the inevitable gaps in knowledge. Bloch's *Feudal Society* (1939–40) also tackled the study of society through time, covering the period AD900–1300 throughout Europe (and beyond). It is vital to understand that Bloch was not writing the standard type of institutional or legalistic history of feudalism, but instead a work which explored social structure through a veritably polymathic range of skills: in language, literature, group psychology, geography, economics and, of course, the critical evaluation of a variety of sources both documentary and visual. At the heart of *Feudal Society* was Bloch's examination of feudal culture through a discussion of modes of thought, feeling and attitude – in short, mentalities. Bloch, for example, explored the medieval concept of time: an obvious interest for an historian who spoke of history as the 'science of men in time'. Carole Fink, an understandably enthusiastic biographer of Bloch, accepts the shortcomings of the work, including the way in which it fails to discuss the roles of the middle class and clergy. One might add that Bloch's handling of the political background was sketchy, and that his attempt to locate modern nationalism in a feudal past was less than convincing. Nevertheless, as a wide-ranging and innovative analysis of the development of social relationships, it has great merit to this day.

Equally appealing, perhaps, is the way in which Bloch's vision of history – with its demands for probing questions and an unfettered spirit of enquiry – coalesced with his commitment to the liberal values of twentieth-century France. As a Jewish teenager, he had seen the defeat of the army and anti-Semitic elements in French society in the infamous Dreyfus case, where a Jewish army officer had been accused and found guilty (on forged evidence) of passing military information to Germany. Dreyfus was exonerated by the courts in 1906, and it is not too fanciful to see Bloch's insistence on critical method, the interrogation of evidence and a delight in exposing forgeries as a reflection of his interest in and regard for the processes of law. His commitment to France was certainly unequivocal. He fought in both world wars, joined and became a leader of the Resistance (code-name 'Narbonne'), was captured, tortured and shot. Carole Fink comments:

> **In the persona of 'Narbonne', Marc Bloch entered history itself, wrestling with the angel who stands guard over the age-long quest for knowledge and self-knowledge. Perhaps he won.**[47]

Lucien Febvre (1878–1956)

One man who embarked on the sad search for the missing Bloch in 1944 was his colleague Lucien Febvre. Febvre's career ran parallel with that of Bloch when they both taught at the University of Strasburg, but his rise through the ranks of the French historical profession was significantly smoother and faster (in part because he did not have to cope with the anti-Semitism which baulked Bloch all too often). In 1933, he was appointed one of the professors to the highly prestigious research institution, the Collège de France; despite all his efforts, Bloch was never able to follow him there. Febvre interpreted his success in getting a chair at the Collège de France as an endorsement of the approach championed by Bloch and himself through the founding of the *Annales* journal. It was no such thing, but Febvre was a consummate propagandist and advocate, and he used his combative personality and skills to ensure that the *Annales* approach became the single most dominant force in French historiography. After the end of the Second World War, he was made president of the so-called Sixth (social sciences) section of the Ecole Pratique des Hautes Etudes – the ideal base from which to shape the French historical establishment.

What, then, were Febvre's aims? He stuck firmly to the manifesto of the very first *Annales* issue: namely, the emphasis on the need for interdisciplinary work, the adopting of a problem-solving approach and a desire to move beyond political narrative. His early work reflected a particular interest in geography. His *Philippe II et la France-Comté* (1912) opened with a geographical outline of this region of France, and he followed it up with a work on historical geography in general: *La terre et l'évolution humaine* (1922). Subsequent work on Reformation history concerned itself with religious attitudes rather than focusing, in the traditional manner, on the churches as institutions. The very title of his book *The Problem of unbelief in the sixteenth century: the religion of Rableais* (1942) reflects the way in which he both structured his work around an explicit problem and also concentrated on collective mentalities (though Febvre preferred the phrase 'mental appara- tus' [*outillage mental*]). The impact of Febvre's own writings was, perhaps, restricted to France in the main, but he bequeathed the *Annales* approach to his co-worker Fernand Braudel.

Fernand Braudel (1902–85)

Braudel taught in schools in the French colony of Algeria and then in Paris before taking up a post at the University of São Paulo in Brazil (1935–8). His experience in Brazil gave him a less eurocentric perspective than most of his contemporaries. He spent the war years in a German prison camp, writing his doctoral thesis: an astonishing achievement which, in the absence of books, stretched to the limit his prodigious memory. This thesis emerged in 1949 as possibly his greatest and certainly his most influential book: *The Mediterranean and the Mediterranean World in the Age of Philip II.* To Febvre, he owed its central focus – the sea itself. It was originally envisaged as a study of Philip II's foreign policy, but Febvre encouraged him in his distaste for traditional accounts of the sixteenth century based on battles and 'great leaders'. In the preface to the first edition, and speaking of previous studies dealing with the Mediterranean area, Braudel said:

> So many of these studies speak a language of the past, outdated in more ways than one. Their concern is not the sea in all its complexity, but some minute piece of the mosaic, not the grand movement of Mediter- ranean life, but the actions of a few princes and rich men, the trivia of the past, bearing little relation to the slow and powerful march of history which is our subject.[48]

Instead, this huge book (six times the size of the standard volume) was divided into three parts, each with a different use of the concept of time and each with a different approach to the subject-matter of history. The first part was what Braudel called 'geo-history', and concentrated on the way in which geographical features underpin all other history. The relationship between the environment and humankind is intimate, but inevitably change is virtually imperceptible: 'almost timeless', as Braudel put it.[49] Mountains, for instance, shape cultures and attitudes. They isolate, create psychological and social barriers between those who live there and those who live in the more productive valleys. The second part ('Collective destinies and general trends') concerned the history of the

slow but perceptible rhythms ... studying in turn economic systems,
states, societies, civilizations and finally, in order to convey more clearly
my conception of history, attempting to show how all these deep-seated
forces were at work in the complex arena of warfare.[50]

What we have here is the history of the structures without which the actions
of people make little sense: communication systems, supply of raw materials and currency. The third and final part 'gives a hearing', as Braudel put it,
to traditional history – namely, the fast-moving but superficial history of
events and individuals:

> ... what Paul Lacombe and François Simiand call *'l'histoire évenémen-
> tielle'*, that is, the history of events: surface disturbances, crests of foam
> that the tides of history carry on their strong backs ... Resounding
> events are often only momentary outbursts, surface manifestations of
> these larger movements and explicable only in terms of them.[51]

Significantly, Braudel's inaugural lecture at the Collège de France included
a dismissive reference to Ranke, narrative history and *wie es eigentlich
gewesen*:

> To the narrative historians, the life of men is dominated by dramatic
> incidents, by the actions of those exceptional individuals who occasion-
> ally emerge ... And when they speak of 'general history', what they are
> really thinking of is the intercrossing of such exceptional destinies, for
> obviously each hero must be matched against another. A delusive
> fallacy, as we all know.[52]

The Mediterranean stunned Braudel's fellow historians in France, and one
can see why. He demanded that the historian should consider time in a different way – or rather in different ways, because time is not uniform. There
is geographical time (as in Part 1); social time (as in Part 2) and individual
time, as in Part 3. But it is clear where Braudel attached the greatest importance: to *la longue durée*, or the slow, long-term changes of geographical
and social time. History of this type must cross disciplinary boundaries in
the same way as its sheer scale crosses the traditional historiographical
boundaries of borders between countries and chronology based on the contributions of individuals (like kings). The aim here is for a 'total history',
which we might define as the attempt to integrate all aspects of past human
life – cultural, social, economic, political. It is the quest for total history
which was to be perhaps the most significant characteristic of those
working within or alongside the *Annales* school as led by Braudel. 'Total
history' was certainly a term used by Braudel (as was 'global history'), but it

is as well to be aware that he meant it as an approach – almost an attitude of mind – whereby one tries to extend the boundaries of problems as far as possible, rather than a literal attempt to write the history of the totality of the human past.

Given the scope of *The Mediterranean* and the breathtaking ambition of Braudel's undertaking, it is hardly surprising that the book is open to several criticisms. Firstly, despite the influence of Bloch and Febvre, Braudel evinced little interest in collective mentalities, even though belief and value-systems must have played a significant role in an area which witnessed the confrontation between Christianity and Islam. Secondly, the third part of the book is not integrated with the other parts and perhaps reflects Braudel's relative lack of interest in events and past politics. Traditional historians certainly objected to the downgrading of politics, but Braudel was at the very least forcing them – and all historians – to justify the writing of history dominated by politics. However, it is certainly open to question whether, in downplaying the significance of individuals and political life, Braudel failed to appreciate the very real impact people can have on structures. *The Mediterranean* appears to be highly determinist, leaving little freedom for human responsibility and action. Also, the work is open to the criticism (often made by Marxists) that Braudel (and the *Annales* school as a whole) failed to explain why and how change in structures actually took place.

A further criticism is that Braudel, like his predecessors Bloch and Febvre, intended to write history based on a problem but, unlike them, he failed to do so because he was simply studying a region. This is rather unfair. Peter Burke put just this point to Braudel in an interview in 1976, and Braudel replied:

> **my great problem, the only problem I had to resolve, was to show that time moves at different speeds . . .**[53]

This is fine as far as it goes, but the reader should, perhaps, expect frequent examples of the time-levels operating together: an event, perhaps, which is clearly shaped by geo-history, by structure, and which is nevertheless part of a fast-flowing stream. If we are shown the spray on the top of the wave, then we also want to see, not only the underlying ripples, but also the slowest of slow currents beneath. The breadth of the book militates against any such precise identification, and in the same way gave Braudel no real scope for making a contribution to the uncovering of new sources. There are sections where he tended to rely heavily on secondary sources, although such sources were taken from a range of specialisms and not just the discipline of history.

Taken all in all, Braudel's book is virtually inimitable. The subsequent development of *Annales* historiography in France reflected the difficulties inherent in trying to write a global or total history on such a scale. The period of Braudel's ascendancy as president of the Sixth Section and director of the *Annales* journal was marked by the emergence of two main strands in *Annales* history: a growing emphasis on quantitative history and the attempt to write the total history of a relatively narrow area. These approaches are by no means mutually exclusive.

The growth of quantitative history within *Annales* owed more to an historian on the fringes of the movement, the Marxist Ernest Labrousse, than it did to Braudel, Bloch or Febvre. It is interesting to speculate, as Burke does, that the greater emphasis on quantitative history in the second edition of *The Mediterranean* reflected the influence of Labrousse on Braudel himself. Quantitative history complements well the emphasis on trends of the *longue durée*. It is significant that the work of one of Braudel's research students, Pierre Chaunu, should attempt to combine the massive thesis based on a huge area (in his case, the Atlantic in *Seville and the Atlantic*) with a concentration on quantitative history (in the form of economic trends). It is largely through the work of Chaunu that two words became a part of the *Annales* mind-set: *conjoncture* for the medium or shorter term and *structure* for the longer term. This is not to say that Chaunu ignored mentalities in his focus on quantitative history. He has led a research team investigating the changing attitudes to death, but through a detailed examination of thousands of wills rather than through the literary sources which provide a less statistical insight into value-systems.

Since, as we have suggested, few historians could match the mind-boggling length of *The Mediterranean* and *Seville and the Atlantic*, there developed the tendency for followers to write more restricted regional histories, focusing on a town or a well-defined province – often split into sections tackling *structure* and *conjoncture*.

Emmanuel Le Roy Ladurie

In the early work of Le Roy Ladurie, we can trace with ease the influence of both Labrousse and Braudel. His doctoral thesis, published as *The Peasants of Languedoc* (1966), was predictably huge, had a Braudel-style introduction in the geo-historical manner and settled into a detailed discussion of fluctuations in prices, birth rates and so on in the manner of Labrousse. However, it eschewed the *structure/conjoncture* framework in favour of a more chronological approach and, significantly, looked at the impact of the economy from the perspective of ordinary people. In short, Le Roy Ladurie was starting to bring people into *Annales* history in a way which was foreign to his predecessors. This vital development was made concrete in his book *Montaillou* (1975) which became a best-seller amongst general readers. Montaillou is a village in south-west France – an area which, in the fourteenth century, was heavily influenced by the heresy of the Cathars. The Cathars represented the most fundamental of challenges to the Catholic Church and to Christian belief. They denied the validity of the priesthood of the Catholic Church and its sacraments and also the Incarnation of Christ. Suspected Cathars in the Montaillou area were identified and interrogated by the local bishop, and the record of interrogations has survived (and was published in 1965). Twenty-five inhabitants of Montaillou were interrogated, and Le Roy Ladurie used the techniques of anthropology to help recreate the world of the villagers from these records. Chapter headings reveal his approach. In Part 1, 'The ecology of Montaillou', he discussed such issues as the mental outlook of the shepherds; in Part 2, 'An archaeology of Montaillou: from body language to myth', he discussed body language and sex, death, magic and so on. This is more than a study of mentalities, because he allowed the people of the village to speak, and used their words to reconstruct their world. A straightforward example would be his use of the words of the villager Alazaïs Azéma:

> *Eighteen years ago ... when I had just brought my pigs out of my house, I met Raymond Belot leaning on his stick in the square in front of the château. He said to me:- 'Come into my house'. I answered: 'No – I have left my door open.'* This passage suggests that people and pigs lived together in the same house ...[54]

Jim Sharpe, writing on History from Below, sees *Montaillou* as a landmark in that, like oral history, it allows the historian to get close to people's actual words.[55] The point is taken, and no one would deny that it is a wonderfully vivid book. But *Montaillou* is nonetheless open to major criticisms. The first is that Le Roy Ladurie treated his source in a curiously uncritical way. Why should an inquisitor's report be taken as a strict and unbiased record of the villagers' words? And where is the attempt at generalization that one usually expects from the historian? Of what, might we ask, is the village of Montaillou typical?

It would seem that, as the *Annales*-type history conquered the French historical establishment in the years of Braudel's ascendancy, its various strands developed lives of their own. Quantitative history remained an important element, and the Febvrian stress on mentalities was extended into discussions of the history of the body, dreams, and smells. To investigate this kind of history demands the multidisciplinary approach which, of course, lay at the heart of the ambitions of Bloch and Febvre. In an illuminating paper on the history of the body, Roy Porter[56] recognizes the great contribution in that field played by *Annaliste* scholarship through its demands for a total history, and also points to the need for historians of the body to exploit the insights afforded by such disciplines as cultural anthropology and sociology. And then, of course, we have the micro-history of the town or village in an attempt to make total history manageable.

However, there remains the issue of events. Reluctantly or otherwise, some *Annales* historians have displayed an increasing awareness that events cannot be ignored. In part this could be seen as a reaction against the determinism of Marxists and that of the later Braudel. Le Roy Ladurie has spoken of the 'creative event' which stimulates the transition from one structure to another, and wrote a book which had an event as its focus: *Carnival: A People's Uprising at Romans 1579–1580* (1979). The traditional Mardi Gras carnival had turned into a bloody conflict, and Le Roy Ladurie commented that, to gauge its importance, one must keep in mind the fact that it happened

> **at the juncture of two essential phases of the Wars of Religion, a bitter struggle between Protestants and Catholics involving France and much of the Western world during the second half of the sixteenth century.**[57]

He later added:

> **Although it was a strictly localized incident, the Carnival in Romans represents a deep probe into the geological stratifications of a dated culture.**[58]

Le Roy Ladurie was not leaving structures behind. He saw the carnival as an illustration of these long-term trends and social and economic systems that make up the structures of history. Let us compare his words with Braudel's comments (in two pages added to Part 3 of the second edition of *The Mediterranean*):

> **Events are the ephemera of history; they pass across its stage like fire-flies, hardly glimpsed before they settle back into darkness and as often as not into oblivion. Every event, however brief, has to be sure a contribution to make, lights up some dark corner or even some wide vista of history.**[59]

> **The Carnival in Romans makes me think of the Grand Canyon. It shows, preserved in cross section, the social and intellectual strata and structures which made up a 'très ancien régime'. In the twilight of the Renaissance it articulates a complete geology, with all its colours and contortions.**[60]

Marxism and *Annales*

What is the relationship between Marxism and *Annales*? As we have seen, Bloch and Febvre cannot be seen as Marxists or even to have been significantly influenced by Marxism. And yet, one can see the attraction for Marxists in the *Annales* attack on traditional event-centred history in favour of structural history. The *Annales* interest in social and economic history was welcome to Marxists, and it was at least possible that *la longue durée* might complement ideas of economic determinism, and vice versa. Braudel's three-volume *Material Civilisation and Capitalism* (1967–79) is as close to Marxism as he got, with 'material civilization' offered as a kind of base and 'capitalism' as a kind of superstructure. But it has to be said that he was not prepared to accept that it was predominantly economic systems and relationships which shaped society. Braudel liked the use of models in seeking to understand and write history, but had no time for a single model like that of base/superstructure. In 'The Longue Durée' essay from the *Annales* journal of 1958, he praised Marx for original and stimulating models of society, but went on to argue:

> These models have been frozen in all their simplicity by being given the status of laws ... Whereas if they were put back within the ever-changing stream of time, they would constantly reappear, but with changes of emphasis, sometimes over-shadowed, sometimes thrown into relief by the presence of other structures which would themselves be susceptible to definition by other rules and thus by other models ... Should I add that contemporary Marxism appears to me to be the very image of the danger lying in wait for any social science wholly taken up with the model in its pure state, with models for model's sake?[61]

We might also add that the concepts of the dialectic – the struggle between thesis and antithesis – and the outbreak of revolutionary action do not sit easily with the slow rhythms of *la longue durée*.

The relationship between Marxism and *Annales* is not a truly intimate one. Marxists welcomed the concept of total or global history, and some *Annales* historians were influenced by the importance attached to economic production by Marxists. Some Marxists – like Labrousse – operated on the fringes of *Annales*. Stoianovich offers a detailed discussion of the links between French Marxists and *Annalistes* and concludes that, although there has been useful dialogue enriching to both, there has been no convergence.[62]

The impact of the *Annales* historians

The impact on France of *Annales*-style history in the time of Braudel is undeniable. It took over the historical establishment. Its impact elsewhere has been variable. Peter Burke offers a convenient summary. He argues that there was little impact in Britain before the 1970s, when translations of works by *Annales* historians started to become available in numbers. The reasons are not hard to find. Fundamental words like *structure* and *conjoncture* do not translate readily, and the barrage of quantitative detail which frequently accompanied them had no real echo in the approaches of the vast majority of British historians. The British Marxists were more sympathetic and much more interested, but not particularly keen on borrowing directly from *Annales*. Eric Hobsbawm speaks of the respect felt by those who founded the left-wing journal *Past and Present* for their illustrious French counterparts – but it was a respect founded on a shared dislike for 'establishment' history rather than a desire to imitate. Nor does Hobsbawm think that those interested in mentalities in Britain owed that interest to *Annales*, but to what he calls a home-grown interest in culture in a 'quasi-anthropological sense'.[65] Neither have Germany or North America proved to be fertile ground for *Annales*. The more personal links forged by Polish historians studying in Paris or the legacy of Braudel from his work in South America have been more productive.

Even so, *Annales* history deserves to be recognized for what it is: a challenging, stimulating alternative to traditional political and diplomatic history and to the model-based history of Marxists. Perhaps we should leave the last words with Peter Burke, who sees *Annales* historians as perhaps the single most important source of inspiration for the 'New History' which has come to represent the breaking down of the restrictive, Rankean-style model of the true concerns of the historian – politics, and yet more politics. Everything and everyone has a history, and *Annales* did much to make that clear.

Conclusion

The last two chapters have taken us through over two hundred years of the writing of history. We have witnessed the development of the professional historian and a curious, almost dialectical pattern in historiography. The period of the Enlightenment was marked by the frequent attempt to use the past as evidence of the workings of laws of human behaviour. Such history was often judgemental and lacked a full methodology, but it was wide-ranging and not restricted to political history. In reaction to it, we saw the development of the Rankean method and approach whose legacy was a narrowing of history to the political and diplomatic behaviour of the élites. The heroic study of records and the PhD was born, and the pursuit of history required the detached and objective scholar who was writing history for its own sake. But alongside this immensely influential Rankean approach grew up its near antithesis, the metanarrative of Marxism. And there were other alternatives to Ranke, including the growth of the multidisciplinary *Annales* school and its call for total history. History is no longer just past politics, but past everything. And now, even within *Annales*, there are signs of a recognition that narrative, event-centred history cannot and should not be ignored. If this is confusion, at least it is healthy confusion.

5

The Value of History

In 1990, just after the Iraqi invasion of Kuwait, the British media carried an horrific story of Iraqi soldiers bursting into a Kuwaiti maternity hospital and seizing the incubators: the premature babies were therefore left to die. This account caused an understandable wave of revulsion, and I can remember the fury in the staff room of the school in which I taught. I can also remember my colleagues and I in the history department looking at each other and then suggesting to the other teachers that perhaps the story was not true. To us, it sounded like standard atrocity propaganda: a slightly more high-tech version of the bayoneting of babies supposedly carried out by the German soldiers in the First World War. Sure enough, the story was later found to be fiction, pure and simple. Perhaps we felt a little smug. But this cautionary tale at least serves to suggest some of the themes of this chapter. We would seem to have learned something useful from the study and teaching of history – so can this awareness of the manipulation of truth be seen as one of its most important values? As an extension of this, can history teach us political lessons, or perhaps moral lessons? Can it be used to guide the present? Of course, one could equally argue that the last thing a country needs is smart-alecs who try to sabotage the very propaganda which was an important part of whipping up national feeling against the Iraqi leader Saddam Hussein. Such propaganda creates myth, and it is the myth which is politically useful. After all, without that national feeling, might Saddam not have got away with naked aggression (and an apparently amoral disregard for human life which was and is a marked feature of his régime)? Either way, it seems that one can learn from something which could be called history – be it an understanding of past events as communicated by historians, an awareness of the techniques of propaganda which form part of any historian's armoury, or a myth masquerading as truth.

One has to accept that a definition of history offered by an historian is intimately linked with his view of its value. To Thucydides, we recall, history was the truthful account of near-contemporary military and political behaviour, and therefore had military and political lessons to teach. To Gibbon, it was the invitation offered by one 'man of sense' to another to engage in a dialogue with the mind of the historian, so encouraging the sharing of appropriate values. To Ranke, it was an objective, 'scientific' exploration of the past on its own terms. It therefore had no direct lessons to teach, and certainly not the impious system-building of the men of sense which had led to irreligion and the horrors of the French Revolution. To many a postmodernist, history is a shifting, problematic discourse which has, arguably, no value which transcends the needs of the individual who makes (i.e. studies) that history. Beverley Southgate's recent book *History: What and Why*[1] has therefore an eminently sensible title, recognizing as it does the relationship between the definition and perceived purpose of history. His postmodern convictions, however, lead him to concentrate much more on the 'what' than the 'why'. He argues that we need to understand the various perceptions of the past (not truths, of course) which have made us what we are. We will then be in a position to reshape those perceptions in a way which will help us move towards what we want to be in the future (see below, pp.174–5).

It follows, therefore, that I am going to take as broad a definition of history as possible to discuss the various arguments on its value. It would be quite wrong to restrict a discussion of the value of history to an examination of what contribution (if any) academic historiography can make beyond keeping historians in work. Too many historians ignore or skate over the value non-historians attach to history.

There are a number of arguments on the value of history to examine.

1 History meets a basic psychological need. None of us can redefine ourselves as we wake up each morning; we need a sense of rootedness to help us cope with our world. History is fundamental to our personal and social identity.

2 By an extension of argument **1**, history is the shaper of national identity.

3 History shapes all types of political judgement. It offers lessons (be they true or false) to which leaders, nations and peoples respond. Some of these lessons may have moral implications.

4 History is a superb intellectual discipline which has indirect benefits to all societies.

5 By a familiar extension to argument **4**, studying history is fun.

History meets a basic psychological need

It is, perhaps, crushingly obvious that we are the product of our own past: our experiences, real or imagined, help to shape the people we are. It is indeed difficult to see how self-identity can exist without the memory of such experiences. On my desk as I type are a few bits and pieces from an album I was looking at some days ago: a student railcard with the photograph of a younger me; another photograph of myself and three friends standing in St Peter's Square in Rome soaked to the skin. There is also a purloined sign which clearly belonged to a student kitchen with the word 'kitchen' erased and (for reasons I will not, perhaps, go into) the words 'Gough's Trough' rather cunningly superimposed. Around the room are other photographs: my wedding day, my daughters, a poster from a marvellous RSC production from fifteen years ago and so on.

The desire to hang on to tangible aspects of one's own past would appear to confirm the need for a sense of rootedness. The adopted child who, after many years, searches for his or her natural parents may well do so because the absence of a vital aspect of one's past produces a similar gap in the present, and perhaps a lack of direction in the future. What we were may well be a necessary part of what we are, and what we are a necessary part of what we will be.

A sense of history, then, can help to fill gaps in an individual's life and, in some cases, to restore a sense of self-worth. A few years ago, I went to conduct an oral history interview with some of my students. Its subject was an old lady, the last of her family, whose memories stretched back to the First World War and the death of her soldier-brother. We were there for three hours. Her memories came flooding back, and it was perfectly obvious that she was gaining as much as we were from the interview. At the end, she cried a little and said:

> I haven't had the chance to talk about those days for years and years. Somehow, talking about those times makes me feel worth something again.[2]

Of course, it could be argued that our discussion so far reflects personal experience rather than history as such. But every single one of the examples given so far is the product, not of purely individual experience, but of a shared culture. Can self-identity ever be defined in isolation?

David Lowenthal's *The Past is a Foreign Country* offers an unrivalled wealth of illustration on the link between the past and collective identity. He gives the example of the displaced Okies in Steinbeck's 1939 novel *The Grapes of Wrath*. Forced to leave behind their homes in Oklahoma in the desperate search for work in California, they refuse to leave behind their mementoes, however useless or trashy:

> **How will we know it's us without our past?**[5]

Actually, Lowenthal slightly overstates the case: the Okies do leave them behind, and decide to burn them. But they also, as Steinbeck puts it, burned them 'into their memories'.[4]

In *The Drowned and the Saved*, Primo Levi commented on the importance to him of his memories of studying Dante as he struggled to survive in Auschwitz:

> **Then and there they had great value. They made it possible for me to re-establish a link with the past, saving it from oblivion and *reinforcing my identity* [author's stress]. They convinced me that my mind, though besieged by everyday necessities, had not ceased to function.**[5]

Those who lost their identity became, in camp jargon, 'Muslims'; shuffling around, head bowed, unresponsive – prisoners who had given up hope.

Many people experience a desire to own the past as a confirmation of both personal and cultural identity. Those who surreptitiously chip away bits of Hadrian's Wall to keep are meeting the same need as the tourists who compulsively photograph everything old in sight. The American tourist, from a comparatively new country, comes to Europe to 'feel at home in time'.[6] The Japanese tourist, unable to acknowledge part of his country's militarist past following the trauma of the Second World War, videos Windsor Castle and the Tower of London. Those living in a country with a continuous and lengthy tradition appropriate parts of it to give their homes a sense of permanence: gas fires that look like coal fires, electric lamps that look like gas lamps, fake Tudor beams, fake Tudor houses. The trappings of modernity are concealed from view: the TV and video in a stripped pine cupboard, the videos themselves disguised as books.

A shared heritage can also be seen as a basis for a sense of national identity. In an attempt to cripple the Poles' will to resist, German forces in the Second World War destroyed much of the historic centre of Warsaw. The destruction of that shared heritage was meant to convey the stark message that a people without a past are a worthless people. After the defeat of Germany, the Poles rebuilt Warsaw – exactly as it had been before the war.

History as the shaper of national identity

So far, it has been suggested that an individual needs access to his own past to make sense of his present and to contemplate his future. In my final illustration, I also suggested that societies may have the same need. To discuss this further, we can make use of a near-contemporary cultural icon – and one which will irritate as many readers as it pleases. This icon is at once an icon of past, present and future. And the future is, in the much-imitated and much-derided phrase of Captain James T. Kirk, 'the final frontier', as presented in Gene Roddenberry's 1960s American TV series *Star Trek* (and its many successors). The scriptwriters on *Star Trek* were clearly obsessed with history. Kirk's middle name is Tiberius – the Roman commander, of course. That famous reference to 'the final frontier' deliberately echoes the American Wild West frontier. The series sets out to preach the values of a liberal America uncomfortable with both the blind antagonisms of the cold war and the overt racism of its own society. The bridge officers of the starship *Enterprise* include Americans, a Russian, and a black woman with a position of some authority. These liberal values are projected forward and backwards in time. Several episodes present what is in effect counterfactual history: the ubiquitous M-class planet whose humanoid population suffers under the yoke of a Roman Empire which never fell, or under a Nazi dictatorship which triumphed against its adversaries. The use of history gives a legitimacy to the issues that are raised, and the projection into the future provides the comforting thought (to those who share them) that the values are somehow timeless and innate to the human species. *Star Trek* is, perhaps, the ultimate Whig history. *Star teleology*, maybe.

The *Star Trek* example may seem rather an extreme one. If we accept that nations or societies have the need for a history to make sense of the present and as a guide to action for the future, then surely that history ought to bear some reasonably close resemblance to the truth as far as it can be recovered by historians? In fact, usefulness often has an inverse relationship to truth, and historians are frequently guilty of·serving up the past in whatever form suits the national need. Eric Hobsbawm puts it well:

> **... history is the raw material for national or ethnic or fundamentalist ideologies, as poppies are the raw materials for heroin addiction.**[7]

Hobsbawm's fear of the potential consequences is made clear in his imagery. Sadly, that fear can borne out by specific examples. The horrors of ethnic cleansing in the former Yugoslavia were fed by the use of what can only be called historical myth. In 1389, at the battle of Kosovo Field, a multi-national Christian force was defeated by the largely Islamic armies of the

Ottoman Empire. In the second half of the nineteenth century, the new nation-state of Serbia made use of the Kosovo defeat to proclaim the defeated leader, Tsar Lazar, as a Christian hero who preferred a heavenly to an earthly crown. His defeat was a spiritual victory, and his glory transmitted to the Serbian Orthodox Church and people: a Holy Nation, a Chosen People, God's Suffering Servant. God's chosen people proceeded to demand the 'return' of lands allegedly once belonging to the Serbs at the time of Tsar Lazar. The multinational force somehow became a purely Serbian one, and the Albanians who had actually fought on the same side as the Serbs at Kosovo were presented as usurpers who, in the nineteenth century, were treacherously in possession of land which was rightly Serbian. Significantly, the Serbs referred to the Albanians as a 'people without history'. This myth also conveniently ignored the presence of Serb Christians fighting for their Turkish overlord at Kosovo.

The dangers inherent in such a myth became apparent when it resurfaced six centuries after Kosovo. In 1986, Tsar Lazar's bones were exhumed and carried in procession through Serbian villages with the intention of mobilizing Serbs to fight their enemies. And their enemies were virtually everyone: the decadent West, the Roman Catholic Church, the USSR, the Albanians, the Muslims, the Croats. The Serbian Academy of Arts and Sciences has been accused of prostituting any academic integrity it might have possessed by supporting such dangerous xenophobia. In 1989, the six-hundredth anniversary of Kosovo, a mass rally was held on the site of the battle. President Milosevic and his generals exploited nationalist frenzy to propel Serbs into war against their former partners in Yugoslavia. The horrors of Bosnia were the direct result.

A myth serving both nationalism and religion is indeed potent. In 1992, Hindus in India destroyed a mosque in the north Indian town of Ayodhya. Violence between Hindus and Muslims spread to the great cities of Calcutta and Bombay, and further afield to Muslim Pakistan. Tension between the communities was also evident in Britain. And what had sparked it off? A myth, deliberately fostered by the Hindu nationalist Bharatiya Janata Party (BJP) of India. Building on a spurious nineteenth-century claim that Ayodhya was the birthplace of the god Ram, adding to it the equally spurious allegation that Muslims from the time of the Mughal emperors had destroyed the temple of Ram and built a mosque in its place, and capitalizing on the massive success on prime-time TV of the epic *Ramayana*, the BJP exploited resentment amongst middle-class Hindus towards Muslims. The latter were enjoying a new prosperity, fuelled as it was by jobs in the Middle East. Two thousand dead in two months in Bombay alone is enduring testimony to the power of nationalist and religious myth.

Historical myths of various types helped to create the climate which led to the Holocaust. The myth of the Jew as Christ-killer, and as an avowed enemy of Christian society, was transmuted in the nineteenth and twentieth centuries into a Jewish world-conspiracy. The so-called *Protocols of the Elders of Zion*, first published in Russia in the first decade of the twentieth century, is one of a number of fake documents purporting to be secret instructions for world domination (using a variety of contradictory political ideologies and control of media, education and financial systems).[8] Much of the appeal of Nazism itself rests upon the exploiting of myth as true history: the so-called 'stab-in-the-back' myth, where supposed traitors at the heart of German political life (mainly Jews) had betrayed the German army and surrendered to the Allies in 1918; the myth of Aryan supremacy; the myth of the 'blood-flag', consecrated by the blood of those who were killed in Hitler's abortive coup in 1923. Nor did the use of myth die out with the defeat of Nazi Germany. In 1962, following the publication in German of *If This Is A Man*, Primo Levi received the most frightful of letters from a certain Dr T. H. of Hamburg. To exculpate – or rather to deny – any sense of guilt amongst ordinary Germans for the Holocaust, this correspondent produced a convenient pseudo-religious myth, claiming that, at various times in history (such as the barbarian invasions of Rome, the massacres of the American Indians, the French and Russian Revolutions) 'the devil was unleashed'.[9] Since this was not the fault of Germans – who, in any case, could hardly be expected to defeat the devil – no blame could be attached to them for the Holocaust.

It would be unfair to see history used to foster national identity – with or without myth – as inevitably evil. In the nineteenth century, growing nationalist movements across Europe were encouraged by the writing of national histories, praising the past glories achieved when one people was united under a common rule – the Roman Empire for Italian nationalists, or the medieval German Reich for German nationalists. Similarly, the newly-independent African nations of the twentieth century demanded a history which encouraged a sense of pride and which celebrated opposition to colonialism. In 1980, the former state of Southern Rhodesia, with its white-minority government, was replaced by a state with a black-majority government. The old colonial name of the country was discarded, to be replaced by Zimbabwe: a deliberate reminder of the powerful and sophisticated black empire of medieval times.[10]

In 1707, the nation called Great Britain was established. Its origin was an Act of Union passed by Parliament in Westminster, and it marked the joining of Scotland with England and Wales to make a country which was united in law rather than in sentiment or national feeling. In 1740, however, James Thomson penned the following words:

When Britain first as heaven's command,
Arose from out the azure main,

This was the charter of the land,
And guardian angels sung this strain:

Rule Britannia, rule the waves,
Britons never will be slaves.

It is likely enough that the implied sense of unity in Thomson's words was aspiration rather than reality. In 1745, after all, Jacobite armies in support of the exiled Stuart dynasty were marching on England from Scotland. But the opening claim that Britain was founded by God was not just padding before one got to the catchy chorus. It reflected a claim that increasingly bound together the countries and peoples of Britain in a powerful historical myth: that Britain was the new Israel – a chosen people and a chosen land, united in the Protestant faith which alone conformed to God's will. As Linda Colley puts it, 'Protestantism was the foundation that made the invention of Great Britain possible'.[11] Thomson's words also, of course, reflect a sense of embattled isolation. The opposition to Protestant Britain was increasingly identified as Catholic France – Britain's imperial rival, and one whose threat persisted throughout the eighteenth century, eventually culminating in the battles of Trafalgar (1805) and Waterloo (1815). Feeding on the early history of the Reformation, this sense of election in the eyes of God operated in the manner of a particularly potent version of the Whig interpretation of history (see pp.114–17). Colley comments on the tremendous popularity of Protestant almanacs, which, as a form of calendar, combined useful information with anti-French and anti-Catholic myth. World history was served up strong and hot, with emphasis placed on Luther, Elizabeth I's accession, the defeat of the Armada, the Gunpowder Plot, the Great Fire of London (blamed on Catholics), the Glorious Revolution and so on. The eighteenth century also saw the reborn popularity of Foxe's *Acts and Monuments* (usually known as Foxe's *Book of Martyrs*), with its lurid accounts of six-teenth-century (and earlier) English Protestants and proto-Protestants who suffered and died for their faith.

The myth of Britain as God's chosen persisted in later centuries and in different guises. Kipling's oft-quoted *Recessional* (1897), a hymn for Queen Victoria's Diamond Jubilee, is both a justification for imperialism and a sombre reminder that God's favour had to be earned:

God of our fathers, known of old –
Lord of our far-flung battle-line –
Beneath whose awful Hand we hold
Dominion over palm and pine –
Lord God of Hosts, be with us yet
Lest we forget – lest we forget![12]

Nor should we forget the twentieth century. The British ability to conjure up a triumph out of the near-disaster of Dunkirk reflects the persistence of the myth of the chosen Protestant nation. It is no longer overt or clearly articulated, but it provided the necessary backdrop – the cultural resonance – to convert defeat into victory by implicitly calling up images of the embattled but finally triumphant nation under the protection of God.

So far, the examples discussed demonstrate how history might be used, perhaps through the invoking of past glories, to encourage the birth and survival of a nation. But what of a nation born either without, or in rejection of, such a past? The American Revolution of 1775–83 rested – according to the Declaration of Independence – on political theories of equality. The former colonists could hardly invoke the glories of a British past, since it was British control that was rejected by force of arms. The only bonds of unity – a common heritage of language and legal system – were those associated with the former colonial master. In the early years after Independence, the new ruling élites appealed to the newness of America and to the doctrine of natural rights of mankind as a focus around which a vigorous people might unite. However, within a generation, the Declaration of Independence had been given an historical context which it had never truly possessed. It was presented as the culmination of the efforts of the disparate groups of settlers to forge for themselves a new vision whilst struggling to escape – from the very moment of their arrival on the shores of their new land – from the constraints of the Old World. This was bad history but very good myth. In 1810 was published Benjamin Trumbull's *A General History of the United States of America*. It read backwards into history the virtues of individual liberty and democracy (for whites, at least); thirty years later, George Bancroft's *History of the United States* similarly exalted the American nation 'by revealing in its history the course of a universal democratic spirit'.[15] Fifty years later, in the time of massive industrialization, Frederick Jackson Turner looked back on the simpler days of the expanding frontier and wrote a further paean of praise to his country, emphasizing the character traits which made Americans lovers of freedom, and which freedom itself encouraged: resilience, inquisitiveness, self-reliance, energy, practicality. These traits were, of course, precisely those which complemented burgeoning American capitalism. Once more, we see a myth projected onto the past which suited the present. Moreover, the frontier myth served the needs of the many immigrants pouring into America to work in its expanding cities. It offered them a clear image of what it meant to be an American. Be self-reliant, love freedom and individual liberty; strive hard; hold fast to your family and your God. You too can enter the great melting pot and emerge as a fully-fledged American – as long as you are not black. Immigrants were encouraged to belong by adopting what Hobsbawm calls 'invented traditions' – the holidays of 4 July (the Revolution and the

Founding Fathers of the Revolution) and Thanksgiving Day (a reminder of Anglo-Saxon Protestantism which had its counterpart in the absorbing by the country of the Irish Catholic collective ritual of St Patrick's Day). The resilience of the 'freedom-loving pioneer' version of the past we have already seen. *Star Trek*, of course, is really an interstellar wagon-train.

A convenient vision of the past can also be used by a people whose national identity is under threat. In his introduction to *The Invention of Tradition*, Hobsbawm argues that, where rapid change (such as industrialization) disrupts and renders obsolete old traditions because the society which shaped those traditions is in the process of transformation, then 'new' traditions arise. Where possible, the new tradition makes use of history accepted as fact to legitimize itself – battles, strikes, heroes, great scholars. However, if these do not exist in an appropriate form, then they can be invented. Prys Morgan describes how, by the late eighteenth century, English culture and Methodism were cutting off the Welsh from their sense of national identity.[14] With the transport revolution came ever more pervasive contacts with England, and, even amongst the lower classes, rituals and customs and the Welsh language itself faded. At this point came the deliberate invention of tradition: a spurious linking of an authentic medieval bardic tradition with that of the ancient Druids, using the eisteddfod as a focus. The eisteddfod itself (meaning 'session') had a genuine history as an examination system for bards, whose skills at setting their works of music and poetry in appropriate style and metre were there put to the test. The eisteddfodau had faded in the sixteenth century and were partly revived in the early eighteenth century, but only as opportunities for amateurs to try out their abilities in front of a reasonably sympathetic audience. In the late eighteenth century, and under the influence of the extraordinary figure of Edward Williams (1747–1826), the bards were presented as heirs to the ancient Druidic tradition. This was by no means an unheard-of idea. Williams, however, wanted proof – and duly provided it himself. Taking the bardic name of Iolo Morganwg, he produced (courtesy of zealous antiquarianism and liberal potions of laudanum) an appropriate set of Druidic rituals and a theology which relied heavily on his own beliefs and expertise as a forger. But it would be most unfair to present Williams as no better than a cheat. What he was doing was trying to force his fellow countrymen to respect their own Welshness at a time when it was under the gravest of threats. If history alone could not do it, then literature and imagination would – and did.

Similar responses to similar challenges can be seen in Scotland. The Act of Union of 1707 between the crowns of England and Scotland was widely seen in Scotland as the precursor to the absorption of the Scottish way of life into that of her more powerful and rich neighbour. And, as with Wales, industrialization seemed like the agent of English economic and cultural imperialism. From today's perspective, such threats would not seem to have been realized. Hugh Trevor-Roper reminds us of the familiar way in which the Scots proclaim their national identity: the skirl of the bagpipes, the kilts and the clan tartans – the products, it would seem, of the ancient Gaelic culture of the Highlands. But they are, he claims, no such thing. Kilts and clan tartans are simply not authentic cultural artefacts; instead, they are the products of invention which, in part at least, aimed to thwart English cultural dominance. Trevor-Roper argues provocatively that the creation of

> **an independent Highland tradition, and the imposition of that new tradition, with its outward badges, on the whole Scottish nation, was the work of the later eighteenth and early nineteenth centuries.**[15]

He charts three stages to this process. The first was to reject the true origin of the Highlanders (Irish invaders of the fifth century AD) and to create the myth of the Highlanders as descendants of the Caledonians – the ancient enemies of the Romans. This was supported by the 'discovery' in the 1760s of a Caledonian epic, allegedly written by Ossian (or Oisin) but actually a specious fake by a certain James Macpherson, who used it to argue that the Irish ballads upon which he had in fact based it were simply bastardized versions of this great Scottish original uncovered by his tireless researches. The second stage was to create distinctive Highland traditions where none had existed. The best example here is the shortish belted skirt, the kilt. It was probably invented in around 1730 by an English Quaker ironmaster, Thomas Rawlinson. Working on a new site near Inverness, he noticed that the Highlanders employed on his furnaces wore a belted plaid – a one-piece garment which had the virtue of being cheap (many Highlanders lacked the income to buy trousers) but was cumbersome and dangerous when making iron. So, Rawlinson employed the services of a tailor to make the one-piece cloth into two, and so created the *philibeg* or small kilt. Out of choice, his workmen would have preferred the trousers. The plaid and the innovative kilt appear to have lost popularity as the century progressed and trousers became more affordable. But by the end of the century, a remarkable change had taken place. The Scottish upper classes began to make use of the kilt despite its association with the lower classes. But why? In the first place, the Scottish nobility was affected by the so-called Romantic movement fashionable amongst the élites of Europe. This movement was concerned with a worship of the primitive in nature and reacted against growing industrialization and political discontent by wallowing in the romance of the past. The kilt was a much more attractive version of the plaid – obviously one would not wish to carry verisimilitude too far – and it had acquired a sudden prestige from its adoption by the new Highland regiments whose exploits in India and America on the behalf of the British crown were the stuff of legend. It was not difficult to convince oneself that the kilt was indeed an ancient garment; nor that one should wear a tartan appropriate to one's clan. It comes as no surprise to note that the clan tartan was another innovation: an idea encouraged by the convenience of using different tartans to distinguish the various Highland regiments by the commercial interest of manufacturers, and by pseudo-antiquarian clubs like the Highland Society of London. The glow of the Celtic past inflamed the novelist Sir Walter Scott who, entrusted with the arrangements for George IV's state visit to Edinburgh in 1822, encouraged the attendant Scots nobility to wear the kilt of the clan. This is in fact Trevor-Roper's third stage in the invention of Scottish tradition, where the lowland and often Anglicized Scots chose to adopt it as theirs. The American tourists in our day who wander down Princes Street in Edinburgh and buy 'their' tartan are victims of the potency of this myth.

On a related point, it is often assumed that the study of a nation's past should be aimed at the fostering of patriotism (presented in many cases as 'good citizenship'). Marc Ferro points to the way in which the education systems of many countries distort the past with this in mind. An educationalist working in Communist Poland, Jósef Olszewski, duly produced a school syllabus which avoided mention of the bitter enmity over the centuries between Poland and Russia, and, when the teachers got on to Lenin, suggested that they should stress:

> the fact that Lenin always felt the wrongs that were done to the people, that his life had been entirely devoted to the revolution, that in his whole existence he delighted in the past and love of the people, that he took part in the formation of the socialist state and that he was openly in favour of Polish independence.[16]

Earlier parts of the syllabus constantly referred to the need to 'awaken patriotic sentiment' amongst the children. Similarly, the Chinese *Manual for Secondary-School Teaching* of 1958 instructed teachers to inculcate patriotism, internationalism, socialist morality ('if we uproot the poisonous weeds left by the West and capitalism; class morality is the true morality . . .') and education by work.[17]

The assumption is made, of course, by educationalists and politicians that history teaching *can* successfully inculcate patriotism and citizenship. Some participants in the acrimonious debate about the content of the National Curriculum in History for England and Wales in 1989–90 advocated a near-exclusive focus on British history with this in mind. I know of no research which challenges or proves such contentions. For what it is worth, anecdotal evidence suggests that it is as well to be cautious on such issues. It is easy to overstate the influence of the teacher in communicating effectively his goals, however well-defined. I vividly remember designing a course on the Holocaust aimed at fourteen-year-olds. I expected it to have some impact in reminding students of the evils of racism; what I did not expect was to have to deal with a tearful girl who had been bullied in the playground as a result of my lessons. Her parents were German and therefore, in the eyes of the students, anti-Semites. Trevor Grundy, brought up to hate Jews by parents whose adulation for Hitler and the Fascist leader Oswald Mosley knew no bounds, preserved his outlandish views throughout a school career amongst teachers whose ideological stances bore little relationship to his.[18]

History and the teaching of political lessons

Chapters 2 and 3 were replete with historians who believed that history could and should be used as a guide to political behaviour. On the individual level, this is easy enough to accept. Voters in a representative democracy like Britain may choose a candidate for any number of reasons, but there is a reasonable likelihood that voting is at least in part influenced by an ability to call upon an historical perspective. When a party promises to protect the National Health Service, or to reform it, or to reform it to protect it, only a sense of history can give the voter an understanding of what the National Health Service is, what its aims were and where parties traditionally stand on its well-being. Issues of privatization demand an understanding of past nationalization; issues on devolution require an understanding of past unification.

Do politicians learn from history? All believe that they do and act accordingly. Western politicians have used the issues surrounding the 1938 Munich conference on the fate of Czechoslovakia – 'the lessons of Munich' – to justify military action against opponents. Hindsight appears to suggest that the attempts made by the British prime minister Neville Chamberlain to appease Hitler up to and including the Munich conference were dangerously mistaken. Had Britain stood up to Hitler at that point (or preferably earlier, say over the remilitarization of the Rhineland in 1936), then there would have been no Second World War, no genocide, no subsequent Communist domination of Eastern Europe.

Why should such an interpretation seem unhistorical? The first reason is simply that it ignores the context in which Chamberlain was forced to operate. Appeasement was probably the only politically viable course of action up to and including 1938. British public opinion was opposed to war. The catastrophe of the First World War was fresh in many minds, and so were the new and very real dangers of the aerial bombardment of civilian targets. British interests were not directly affected by the fate of Czechoslovakia, and many were prepared to grant that Hitler had a meaningful claim over that part of Czechoslovakia called the Sudetenland, populated as it was by three million or so Germans. The very term appeasement – the attempt to resolve crises by negotiation and compromise – lacked the pejorative sense of giving in to aggression which it subsequently acquired.

Failure to contextualize the past – by no means an easy task – is particularly dangerous when accompanied by a failure to contextualize one's present. Those who were involved in the shaping of both past and present events were and are just as likely as others to fall victim to the false analogy which lies at the heart of what might be called the Munich syndrome. In 1956, the British prime minister, Sir Anthony Eden, came to the conclusion that Gamel Abdel Nasser, the ruler of Egypt, was a Middle Eastern version of Hitler. Eden's experience as foreign secretary under Chamberlain – he resigned early in 1938 – and as foreign secretary under Churchill had convinced him of the necessity to stand up to and crush any threat before it had the potential to develop. It is hardly surprising that Eden, having lived through and participated in the traumas of the Second World War, should fail to make sufficient allowances for the dilemmas facing Chamberlain. But to apply what he thought was a clear lesson to an entirely different situation was very dangerous. Eden interpreted the actions of Nasser in nationalizing the British-owned Suez Canal company (and sundry anti-imperialist statements) as the first step towards securing a stranglehold on the oil supplies of the West. Had he not lived through the perils of appeasement, then he might have taken a more balanced view. The danger of the analogy quickly became apparent. Britain and France, with the connivance of Israel, launched their infamous airborne attack on the Suez Canal zone in November 1956. In so doing, they alienated an obvious ally – the United States. Eden's attempted explanation, based on his identification of Nasser as a potential Hitler, was simply rejected. After all, how could he offer proof when his analogy was a projection into the future, and one which failed to take into account the genuine grievances of Nasser over the legacy of colonialism? Under pressure from the United States, and with threats from the USSR in the background, Britain and France were forced to withdraw. The abject humiliation and breakdown in health suffered by Eden – and the sad evasions and distortions he felt compelled to write in his autobiography, *Full Circle* – bear witness to the perils of the Munich syndrome.

It is entirely understandable that politicians should wish to use history to project likely outcomes, since this allows for meaningful planning of long-term policies. Unfortunately, if there is a clear lesson of history, it is that there are no clear lessons, courtesy of the sheer unpredictability of events. Who could have anticipated the collapse of Communism from 1989? Whose planning could have allowed for the peoples' revolution which destroyed the Berlin Wall?

However, politicians are rarely in a position which will allow the leisure to reflect on the irritating complexities of the past. The Munich episode is simply too powerful a symbol to be ignored. It has and will be used to shape relations between countries on the mistaken assumption that significant features can be identified which will repeat themselves. An analysis of the decision making of President Truman and his advisers at the time of the Korean conflict reveals that the analogy with appeasement was made unthinkingly, and that decisions on repelling 'Russian-sponsored aggression' with force were arrived at without any attempt to explore differences between 1938 and 1950. The Gulf War and subsequent relations between Iraq and the West were affected by analogies between Saddam Hussein and Hitler and the dangers of failing to stand up to him forcefully. More generally, I very much take the point of Conkin and Stromberg that, like it or not, Munich has affected the conduct of relations between powers:

> **When politicians use Munich to prove the certain results of appeasement, they almost invariably generalize nonanalogous features and assert them to be true of all diplomatic conferences.**[19]

The conclusion so far seems to be that history will be used by politicians to make crucial decisions. As with national myth, the history so used is likely to be inaccurate. Sometimes, a good might come out of it. The withdrawal of Iraqi forces from Kuwait could be seen as a good. Sometimes, the results are bad: the Suez adventure, for example. Has the professional historian any role to play in this Russian roulette? Are there any lessons from history that the historian might make use of in an attempt to influence policy making? The problem here, once again, is that it depends on the historian's view of the definition of history. As we saw in Chapter 4, the East European historian in a Communist country was, willy-nilly, supposed to operate within the context of Marxist laws of history. His work had an ideological purpose; its relationship to politics was inevitably a subservient and confirmatory one. The Whig historian, on the other hand, could offer lessons for statesmen, but the efficacy of those lessons was dependent on the acceptance and truth of the Whig liberal and democratic teleology. Once again, his role was essentially subservient and confirmatory – as long as the reader was a Whig. What we need, it seems, is a history which focuses on the differences between past and present. The Rankean tradition of history for its own sake would seem to be exactly what we are looking for. This kind of history certainly complements our view of the dangers of making analogies with the past, in that an historian in this empiricist tradition would be only too ready to identify differences between times in the past on the grounds that each age was unique to itself. What a thorough-going Rankean would not do is to embroil himself in the needs of the present – political or otherwise – on the grounds that this would imperil his objectivity. It seems to me that a most helpful comment comes from Eric Hobsbawm; a Communist, of course, but one who demands from the historian the qualities which would preclude subservience and the simplistic analogy. He comments:

> **History, even when it generalizes most effectively ... is always aware of unlikeness. The first lesson a professional historian learns is to watch out for anachronism.**[20]

He reminds us that the historian's task is often that of the warning voice: the critic of the superficial assessment, the saboteur of the myth presented as history. Hobsbawm is keen that we should not overestimate, of course, the impact of the historian's critique. His is an essentially negative role, and, in any case, he is unlikely to wield substantial political power. The strength of nationalist myth is likely to survive academic protest. The Indian historians who protested at the BJP's myth-making had little effect on the immediate events. But at least the historian can try to blunt the weapons of bad history, and refuse to act as the lackey of those who want him to serve untruth:

> **... bad history is not harmless history. It is dangerous. The sentences typed on apparently innocuous keyboards may be sentences of death.**[21]

This is not to say that the historian is to wield history as a weapon in any political struggle. Peter Burke's stance is instructive. He argues that to use history in this way also leads to bad history, since it invariably leads to 'us and them' and distortion through partisanship. Instead,

> **... the value of the study of history is surely that it reminds us of awkward truths ...**[22]

Burke's target is not so much history as distorted by politicians as history distorted by socialists and others who use it in opposing the *status quo*. As we saw in Chapter 4, there were those Marxist historians like Christopher Hill who saw the recapture of the ideas of radicals like Diggers and Ranters as an inspiration; similarly, the recapturing of the experience of ordinary people not only follows from socialist beliefs, but also serves to remind the reader of the cause for which he should fight. There is no doubt that history can be used in this way, but the dangers are clear: the temptation to write of heroes and villains means that the socialist historian falls into the same trap as the Whigs. The heroes and villains are different, but the value judgement is there all the same.

From a postmodernist perspective, the very nature of history means that value judgement is inevitable: it can never be neutral. As Keith Jenkins puts it, the question 'What is history?' is really 'Who is it for?'[23] Southgate builds upon this point by arguing that the study of history, to have any purpose at all, must have some transforming effect. It must lead to change, and therefore to a shaping of the future. The past is formless clay until moulded by the historian. He must therefore shape it in such a way that it promotes the future which he would find to his taste. The past is silent. The historian can make it speak, but it will say only what he wants it to say. It can therefore teach nothing itself. The historian can use it to teach what he wants. For example, he could use it to teach moral lessons. Southgate considers that the act of researching and writing biography could be used by the biographer himself for self-improvement, and – if I understand him aright – sees this as perhaps the key to the value of history – it has the potential to assist us in the vital task of self-examination and self-awareness:

> **For our public problems derive in the end from our personal selves, so that what is needed is a study of how we came to be the sorts of people that we are, of why we have the perceptions, the outlooks, and the attitudes that we have.**[24]

This kind of approach has its attractions. It is one possible way of accounting for, and accepting, the manner in which history is used as myth. It is enticing, in that it is empowering: the invitation to create one's own history is difficult to resist. But resist it we must. As we saw in Chapter 1, postmodernism proceeds by making a set of assumptions about modern society (or rather, postmodern society) which are questionable to say the least. Its strictures on the absence of meaning in language and the fundamental inability of the author to control that meaning contrast oddly with the traditional and logical methods of persuasion used by many postmodernists themselves. As for Southgate, there is a curious inconsistency in his discussion of biography. He advocates a detailed study of a person's life so that, through insight or empathy, one might learn to make choices oneself. But this would seem to assume that the historian is able to recover with accuracy such experiences – an odd view for an historian who generally accepts the postmodernist perspective. After all, it is hard to see what value there would be in moulding the biography to suit the already-existing needs of the biographer – and yet this would be the normal outcome of postmodernist history. There are other problems. Southgate accepts the standard postmodernist assertions that the events of the past are neutral, and so can be combined by the author 'in innumerable ways, to constitute such diverse creations as tragedy and comedy'.[25] He then adds:

> **One requirement for the postmodern future appears to be an ability to resist dogmatic pressures to accept any one single truth, or answer, or 'reality' (of past or present). Aspiration might rather point towards a**

> tolerance of many truths and answers and descriptions, without a corre-
> sponding need to deny the validity of those that fail to fit our own
> requirements.[26]

At the risk of repeating myself, I should emphasize that this form of relativism runs aground on the rocks of the Holocaust (see Chapter 1, pp.19–20).
There are references to the experiences of Primo Levi in Southgate's book,
but it is unfortunate that the issues of the Holocaust as truth (Southgate
prefers 'truth' in inverted commas) and revisionism are not directly
addressed. And, in the end, one wonders whether postmodernism really
offers an alternative to the need of human beings *in extremis* to tell that
truth about what happened. Southgate accepts that Primo Levi's desire to
tell the unvarnished truth about what he witnessed and what he endured
has survived all challenges to the possibility of doing any such thing.

So far, I have suggested that politicians frequently attempt to use the past
as a quarry for political lessons. I also suggested that historians who try to
use the past in a similar way write bad history. In both cases, the past is
seen as having a vital purpose, but the effect of using the past in this way
can be unfortunate. I argued that the historian's task is to discredit the myth
and to protest at the false analogy. I then tackled the perspective of postmodernism, which would deny historians the right to judge on the basis of
truth, but offered instead the chance to shape the future through self-awareness and a self-seeking and deliberate distortion of the past. In my view, the
postmodernist perspective founders on its relativism and inconsistency.

The value of history as an intellectual discipline

All historians would accept that the study of history is food for the mind. It
clearly demands and encourages a whole range of skills, including those of
analysis, synthesis and communication. In this sense, the study of history
has benefit for society at large, where such skills are clearly needed.
Granted, it might be argued – and with reason – that other disciplines place
similar demands on the intellect. However, history perhaps offers a unique
blending of a rigorous methodology (and often forces the mind to grapple
with frustratingly incomplete data) with a requirement to enter into mentalities which are profoundly alien to one's own. In this way, history (at its
best) stimulates both intellect and imagination, but in a way which encourages the one to feed off the other.

There are, of course, those historians who would wish to limit the value of
the study of history to such gains. As suggested in Chapter 3, the historian
writing in the historicist/Rankean tradition, perhaps conservative in

outlook, would be likely to adopt the position of 'history for its own sake'. From this perspective, since it is vital for the past to speak for itself, the historian must consider it on its own terms and not with the expectation that political or social lessons can be learned. The search for analogies will be deprecated. In *Which Road to the Past?*, G.R. Elton commented:

> Reliance on analogy – the belief that finding similarities in another set of circumstances has any force as an argument – derives at heart from the desire to set up universal laws of history ... Only the believer can work with such tools.[27]

In *The Practice of History*, Elton devoted a full chapter to the purpose of history – perhaps surprising, in that he effectively restricted it to the intellectual gain to be had in the search for truth. In fact, most of the chapter is an attack on the kinds of historical writing of which Elton disapproved. It is significant that he should oddly juxtapose the question of purpose with a question about good and bad practitioners:

> Does this then mean that there is no very positive purpose in studying history, that it really is only a matter of the student's private satisfaction? Are there no standards by which one may call historians good or bad, adequate or inadequate, right or wrong?[28]

Those looking for a brief restatement of Elton's various prejudices would be well advised to consult his short chapter in Juliet Gardiner's *The History Debate*. He also builds upon the intellectual training argument by suggesting that history can teach much about human behaviour and potential, although, inevitably worried about any general laws of behaviour being deduced from or applied to history, he is at pains to stress the 'unpredictability of the human animal'.[29] And, in the end, he gives the added justification – that history is

> exciting, rewarding, a splendid way to pass the time. Actually, it is fun.[30]

It is very difficult to know what to do with the assertion that history is fun. Elton is not, after all, referring to most peoples' sense of fascination for the past which is so marked and so well catalogued by Lowenthal. He is talking about what he admits to be one of the most complex and arduous of intellectual exercises: the academic study of history. His concluding comment reads as if he suddenly recollected that he was supposed to be providing a brief contribution to a straightforward little book which might be read by sixth-formers, and that it would be as well to suggest that academic history was really rather enjoyable. His discussion might convince the reader that history was stimulating and challenging, but fun is arguably not the most appropriate of words to describe, say, the frequently grim toil of research. The so-called Abraham affair in 1980s America is highly suggestive, not only of the considerable physical and intellectual energy needed to sustain original research and to avoid distorting sources to fit one's hypothesis, but also of the savagery of the profession when it believes it has identified fraud, gross negligence or incompetence. David Abraham, a youngish Marxist scholar, published his *The Collapse of the Weimar Republic* in 1981. It was immediately assailed for its alleged falsifying of documentary evidence to back up the thesis that German capitalism was to blame for the collapse of German democracy. Richard Evans concludes that Abraham was guilty of unacceptable and unscholarly carelessness rather than deliberate falsification.[31] Whatever the truth of the matter, Abraham was hounded out of a profession which rarely takes prisoners. What fun.

To justify the study of history on the grounds of intellectual satisfaction and stimulation – and fun – is all very well as far as it goes. But I very much like David Hackett Fischer's comment:

> **If the doing of history is to be defended by the fact that some historians are happy in their work, then its mass appeal is likely to be as broad as flagellation …**[32]

Conclusion

It has to be recognized that historians are frequently self-obsessed. Most of the works consulted in writing this chapter failed to relate discussions of the value of history to the experiences of those not involved in academia. Conversely, the few works which considered the way in which non-academics make use of the past do not relate conclusions to current academic debates. The genuine thirst for history amongst ordinary people can be attributed to psychological need, to a desire for a sense of permanence in a period of rapid change or simply to a desire to experience vicariously the romance of the different. The problem is – who will assuage that thirst? Who will answer that need? Can it be left to politicians? We have seen that they, wittingly or unwittingly, serve up the past as a justification for current policies. They are generally the victims of the dubious analogy, or the wilful exploiters of myth. This need not be dangerous, but it very often is.

I can understand that historians should fight shy of arguing that history can in any way be a guide to the present. The worst history is that which supinely serves the needs of the myth-making state; and it is often the case that those who strain to make history relevant are those who distort the past the most. Historians perform an important (and conceivably dangerous) role if they expose myths for what they are, or if they warn against analogies or generalizations based on inadequate evidence. Tómaš Masaryk, the great president of the Czech Republic from 1918 to 1935, had fought long and hard for his country's independence, but he also exposed as fakes the very manuscripts on which the popular Czech nationalist myths were based. Historians also have the responsibility to demolish the kind of enervating nostalgia for the 'good old days' which afflicts visitors to National Trust tea shops. Lowenthal warns that, if we bask in the fake but warm glow of an idealized past, then we lose the will to transcend the past and to improve the present. History packaged as 'heritage' does not allow for meaningful interaction between past and present. It fails to stimulate the intellect, and encourages the passivity of the spectator. Lowenthal prints a copy of an advertisement for Jorvik Viking Centre in York. The passengers photographed on the 'time car' have less vitality than the waxwork figures.

It is the role of the historian to challenge those who misunderstand and misapply for their own ends some of the wearier catch-phrases of history, like the 'Dunkirk spirit' or 'Victorian values'. Historians must expose official or academic silence for what it often is: a failure to come to terms with the past. The wilful amnesia affecting post-war Germany is a case in point; so is the contemporary tendency of Japanese peace studies to focus on Hiroshima and the Holocaust and not the Japanese prisoner-of-war camps.

So far, I have emphasized what is essentially a negative function of the historian. Has he no positive contribution to make? Roy Porter is adamant that he has, and is equally forthright on the dangers of failing so to do:

> **For the health of history, it is crucial that historians ... recognize their responsibilities to meeting public needs (and equally their duty to cultivate good communication skills). Otherwise we will be treated with deserved contempt, as being guilty of a prissy dereliction of duty. The AIDS crisis is only one of the many issues where the public and politicians look to history for illumination, ideas, and help. It is up to us not to let them down.**[35]

Porter's use of the example of AIDS is enormously revealing. When the AIDS crisis began to make an impact on Britain in the 1980s, the government was faced with the dilemma of what action to take. Should Draconian measures be taken? Should AIDS tests be made compulsory in the supposedly more vulnerable sections of society? What restrictions could be placed on the sexual conduct of sufferers? Given the level of public concern and alarmist stories in the media, could one learn anything from the way in which past epidemics had been tackled? Could history (and historians) help guide policy in any way? The answer was that they could. The Department of

Health and Social Security requested information and advice from various historians. It is at least possible that the government decided not to apply punitive measures because the historical perspective suggested that harsh actions stimulated public outcry. Specifically, the Contagious Diseases Acts – the mid-Victorian attempt to inspect prostitutes for sexually transmitted diseases and to imprison the carrier until cured – had to be repealed following bitter opposition from many groups in society, including doctors.

Politicians, then, constantly make – or are called upon to make – judgements which require an historical perspective. Historians might be rightly wary of providing the simplified and hasty answers that the cut-and-thrust of political life frequently demands. But this is a task in which they should not refuse to take part. The present-day approaches the past for answers, and it is surely part of the historian's responsibility to make sure that the present-day does not dictate to the past the answers it wants to hear.

Historians on History

Introduction

I think it would be a good idea to start by defending what, on the face of it, looks like an unusually peculiar chapter. It consists largely of the transcripts of interviews with two historians currently teaching and conducting research in British universities. My intention was simply to avoid some of the dangers besetting books on historiography, which all too often give the reader no feel whatsoever for the personalities of the historians or any sense of them actually at work. Historians can be labelled, slotted into their appropriate place in the development of certain historiographical traditions, can be popped into their equally appropriate intellectual and political environments and can be quoted at length so that the reader can at least see or hear their words. This is what I have done so far. But this kind of packaging is, in the end, just a little bit too neat. The comments of the two historians in my current chapter range widely and without regard for the structure of this book. In so doing, they allow readers to remind themselves of some of the main themes, but, importantly, do not fit into the very categories which neatness would require but which reality has an irritating tendency to disavow.

Perhaps I should say something of the way in which the interviews were conducted. I sent the interviewees a synopsis of the structure of this book, together with a draft of Chapter 1 so that they could get a flavour of the argument (and therefore the ideal opportunity to withdraw from the enterprise if they so wished). I provided a basic list of areas I wanted to explore and which are reflected to a greater or lesser extent in the responses in the transcripts. I tape-recorded the interviews and wrote up the transcripts with a minimum of editing (really just to rearrange some of the questions and answers and, on a very few occasions, to simplify some of the vocabulary).

Copies of the transcripts were sent to my victims for comments on accuracy, and mistakes were duly rectified.

Interview with Dr Michael Mullett

Michael Mullett teaches history, including Jewish history, the Reformation and the history of popular culture, at the University of Lancaster. His books include *Radical Religious Movements in Early Modern Europe* (1980), *Sources for the History of English Nonconformity 1660–1830* (1991) and *John Bunyan in Context* (1996). He is about to publish a study of post-Reformation Catholics in Britain and Ireland.

Do you consider that you belong to any historiographical tradition?

I wanted to address that first of all because it seemed to me there were historio-graphical, and indeed there were ideological, preconceptions to tackle ... for example, I was brought up in the classic Whig British tradition. My research supervisor was Sir John Plumb ... who was in the tradition of Trevelyan and Macaulay, and there was even a kind of hereditary baton to pass on in that they belonged in that wonderful classic English Whig libertarian, liberal optimistic tra-dition of historians' writing. And I was shaped osmotically by that kind of writing ... let's call it the great nineteenth-century Macaulian tradition that believes there is a purpose to history, that there is a political tale to tell. It's a tale to tell of the unfolding of liberty ...

I see history in optimistic terms: I'm a utopian and I believe that the present is on the whole better than the past ... now that's a very difficult thing to say at the end of the twentieth century because it's been the most ghastly century in recorded human experience and it's also been the most glorious in the human experience, and therefore as a microcosm of history, it contains all of history's contradic-tions, the contradiction between optimism and pessimism ... it's with some diffi-culty that one comes out of the ghastly dark age of the twentieth century with any sense of historical optimism, but I'm rooted in the Whig tradition, and I guess you could call me an historical optimist – for what its worth ... Macaulay took such delight in so many things ... for him writing history was part of his Chris-tian humanism – an outcome of a set of liberal and humane values. But it wasn't fully a profession yet ... but in those decades of the nineteenth century, history began to emerge as the leading discipline in the humanities ... supplanting the classics ... and all sort of things went with the professionalization of history ... the PhD is the modern equivalent of the medieval masterpiece ... the piece of work submitted to the guild for their approval – at which point the would-be entrant is admitted to the profession.

When you're talking about yourself as a historian in the Whig tradition, don't you see that as conflicting with your professional life in supervising doctoral students who are offering you that mark of professional expertise in the Rankean tradition?

Well, I want to consider the relationship between the Rankean professionalism and Whig historical writing and see whether Whig tradition has become the ideological furniture for the professional approach – the *chef d'oeuvre* of professionalism – the doctoral thesis – has to conform to certain canons in terms of length – it must be a hundred thousand words, just as a medieval broadcloth had to be a yard or whatever in length ... writing a dissertation is the entrée in to a profession whose hallmarks are attention to detail, respect for truth, concern for accuracy, respect for the sources ... the insistence on telling it like it was – *wie es eigentlich gewesen* – as it actually was. Absolute authenticity is a primary desideratum ... and a refusal to allow oneself to be thrown, skewed by prior ideological pressupositions that would distort that reverence for the incidents, the events, the facts, the narrative, the details as they actually were ... so that, for example, a pronounced Marxist bias would call into question the professionalism of the historian because he or she would be moulding the data of the past to furnish forth a conceptual and schematic overview ... this would no longer be history – this would be prophecy or historiography or the subjugation of the beloved fact to meet some kind of preordained schemata.

That was a very eloquent defence of the Rankean style of history. Is that what you believe and practise, or are you explaining it to us to try to link it up with the Whig view of history?

I want to see in what way the Whig interpretation of history is perhaps in some ways the one most consistent with the professional view ... it is the one that is least likely to be skewed by ideological bias ... the answer to that may be that the Whig view is so malleable, so subject to adjustment in the light of the evidence, that it lacks the rigidity of eschatological schemes, such as the Augustinian view of history as God's plan, or the Marxist overview ... in all these views, the prophetic end is predefined ... if I were an Augustinian – and in some ways part of me is an Augustinian – then I would believe that history is the charting of the progress of the people of God to its predetermined end ... these may well affect the way in which we look at the seventeenth century because we know the end ... I published a book in 1980 called *Radical Religious Movements in Early Modern Europe*. At that time, my brother had a hotel, and I went to the hotel bar. I'd just published the book. I was in celebratory mode, and the barmaid said, 'Michael, I understand you've just published a book.' And I said, 'yes I have.' 'Well,' she said, 'has it got a happy ending?' And I had to say, 'that's not the most intelligent question that anyone's asked me about the book, it's the *only* intelligent question anyone's asked me about the book.' If I were a Marxist I might know it had a happy ending . . . but as a Whig – a Whig might not know the end – and therefore the lightness on the tiller of his ideological touch might make him a more Plumbsian, and so more sceptical and therefore professional, historian.

But wouldn't you say that, in describing yourself as a Whig, what you've actually said is more in keeping with a Rankean? After all, the Whig tradition is very Protestant, very pro a belief in progress through Protestantism and liberty . . . but you as a Catholic historian would, one would have thought, fit better with the straight Rankean tradition of *wie es eigentlich gewesen*. Is that fair?

Well, my great hero Acton was able to combine Catholic historical writing with liberal historical writing . . . it seems to me that the Whig interpretation of history is not exclusively a Protestant interpretation; it is an optimistic view of history and in that sense can be reconciled with an Augustinian view. So – what does that make me – an Augustinian Whig? Hmmm.

Optimistic, then. But doesn't that mean that you have a view of where history is going to go – a projection into the future? After all, what might be optimism to one historian isn't necessarily optimism to another. And aren't you prophesying? In which case, are you no different from the Marxists you criticize? The prophecy might be a different one, but it's still a prophecy.

Yes – so what I'm describing now is a prophetic view and a salvationary view of history, whose ultimate end is concealed in the breast of the Almighty, because He alone has the key. But the ultimate working out of God's plan is in the mind of God, and it's not something that's made manifest to us.

You've chosen to write a book on British Catholics – why?

The obvious answer – the very superficial answer – is that Macmillan asked me to . . . partly because that's a way of being published. If the historian has something to say, I think he has to say it to a readership . . . its easier to do it this way rather than write a book and then find a publisher for it. These are matters of management. That's the simple answer . . . the book as a titular product. But the title isn't the book. Beyond that, publishers exercise varying degrees of control . . . they're open to persuasion. Generally speaking, one can write the book one wants to.

Now, let's look at in what way this book on British Catholics is influenced by current concerns, from where we are now. One of the ways it's affected is by its interest in Britishness. This is something that came about in the last twenty years through the dawning appreciation by British historians of what Britishness really is. I have to say that one of the features of the 'national' Whig tendency was an Anglo-Saxon premise . . . in so many history departments, what was called British history would not have passed muster under the Trades Descriptions Act because it was just English history writ large . . . one downside of this was a kind of national defensiveness in the Celtic rim, in which they wrote a defensive, anti-imperial British history and saw the Irish experience in terms of Irish resistance to British rule – well, that's as maybe. This department, I'm happy to say, is a pioneer in the new appreciation of the history of the British Isles . . . what I wanted to do in writing an account of Catholicism in the British Isles was to see the component entities of the British Isles in terms of their own authenticity; to consider, say, the Scottish experience in terms of the Scottish experience . . . by the way, I have great difficulty in seeing common themes in Catholic development as between my own country – Wales – where Catholicism effectively disappeared before the eighteenth century and Ireland, where Catholicism was the national identity in the eighteenth and nineteenth centuries.

So your decision to write British history is a product of this university's growing interest in it?

Yes, it's partly a product of that and partly because I want to stake my claim to write British history because I'm a Welshman of English and Irish extraction married to a wife of Scottish extraction . . . the other thing I wanted to do was to question (if not exactly to challenge or dismiss) the traditional Catholic historiography, which was defensive, introverted, and above all suffused by martyrological concerns. These were set out in the eighteenth century by the great vicar apostolic Richard Challoner, who authored a pioneer work of English Catholic martyrology called *Memoirs of the Missionary Priests* in which he wrote about the great heroism of the Tudor martyrs . . . whom he saw as being the seeds of a new church . . . I didn't want to diminish the martyrs, but perhaps to set the record straight, and perhaps to see Challoner himself as a martyr in its original meaning – the Greek word meaning 'witness'. I see the eighteenth century . . . as one in which the English Catholic community drew closer to the Protestant mainstream. In particular, the most significant force in English Protestantism was the evangelical revival of Wesley, the Methodists. There are points at which Challoner begins to look like, not a Methodist, but an evangelical. For example, he has an appreciation of the centrality of the Cross, of the atonement, and he pays less attention to the traditional Catholic agenda of the saints . . . so he's a very Christocentric thinker, and he's remarkably close to the British Protestant consensus . . . this seems to present British Catholicism in a new ecumenical light in accordance with the interests of the church at the end of the twentieth century. So I'm maybe making my small contribution to an ecumenical rewriting of British religious history.

Would this explain your interest in the Quakers and the fact that your *Lancaster Pamphlet* on Luther was in a sense a sympathetic work?

It's kind of you to say that . . . now the reason I wrote appreciatively of the Reformation is because I see it as an enormously positive force; the Vatican Council saw Luther and Protestantism as a positive force. We're moving towards a re-evaluation of Luther as a theologian who . . . restored the proper course of Christian theology after some centuries of distortion into a major theology that had not forgotten the inner realities, the Pauline realities, the Augustinian realities. I knew we'd come back to Augustine. We always do.

What makes you choose a particular topic for research?

To take the example of Bunyan. There, the reservoir of material is extant. There existed the text bases for the enquiry.

So you're saying that a central reason was because you knew that the sources were available to you in a relatively convenient form?

A convenient source, edited by Oxford University Press. I wanted to move into a slightly different area. In fact, I wanted to move back into my original intellectual home, which was the field of history with literature, and twin it with religious study . . . with this research base (the OUP volumes of Bunyan's writings) I then had to use comparative material – comparing Bunyan with other seventeenth century divines.

When you're starting off your research, do you have a hypothesis in mind or do you let the sources dictate the hypothesis?

Let's take an example – the Irish sources for my British Catholic book. I'd say that I approached the sources with a preconception that all the studies of Irish history were devoted to the view of Ireland as a suffering servant – the martyr view. All works of Irish history had green covers and usually gold harps, looking for all the world like glasses of Guinness that had gone off . . . now to what extent is this questionable in terms of Ireland's present realization of itself as a country that's more at ease with its national identity, less haunted by the vicinity of the Brits . . . it's only very recently that Ireland's been able to see itself in any terms except those of negative reaction to the Brits. Now that Ireland is comfortable, prosperous, with a mature democracy, it's time for a reconsideration of its history, the nature of its Catholic history … now that, as Mary Kenny says, Ireland is becoming post-Catholic. So – how should these new perceptions influence one's understanding of the part played by Catholicism in, say, the seventeenth century? For instance, we find that the Catholic church of the Cromwellian period was a church under the Cross. Cromwell would not allow Mass anywhere, and therefore, on the face of it, it would seem that Irish Catholicism was crushed, even though it might – Christ-like – undergo a resurrection subsequently. But the truth in history is as complex as is human life, and the reality much more confusing … in the immediate aftermath, Catholic priests and laity re-established themselves covertly in positions of power, and the Catholic tradition and influence was not exterminated in any way. The challenge of history is to get the balance right – between yesterday's excessive pessimism and today's excessive optimism. And it would do great disservice to the martyrological and national historiography to make the picture unduly glowing; nevertheless, it has to be said that Irish Catholicism did not undergo a religious holocaust in the seventeenth century, and it's in this discovery of continuity that I want to revise earlier views. I came along assuming that there would be continuity rather than discontinuity because, in history, that's the way it usually is.

Is that part of your Whig, Plumbite view?

I was wondering if it was. I could always look in the bright side. The darkest days were undoubtedly the Cromwellian times, and yet one can see new shoots in the Irish Catholic church at the time.

We've mentioned texts and the use of texts before in a Rankean sense. Do you see any value in postmodernist approaches to textuality?

I want to cop out here. This is a school which doubts the validity of the text. It seems to me to abandon one of the hallmarks of the tradition in which I was brought up: which is, in nineteenth century parlance, positivism – and the rough and ready, craftsman's acceptance of the proposition that, on the whole, texts are true and to be accepted at their face value. We have to approach texts critically, of course, but the problems are managerial and not philosophical.

So, you feel that some meaningful, craftsman-like objectivity is attainable by historians?

Well – there is the issue of liberal bias. But surely Whig centrism or consensus can't by definition be a bias; it's on the fairway, it's in the centre – so it can't be one-sided.

So, can I offer what is probably a caricature of yourself as an historian? You see yourself in the Plumb/Whig tradition, taking from that a sense of optimism and progress which you link with your religious faith – the Augustinian progress of a people moving towards, but not necessarily smoothly towards – the end predetermined by God. You accept that the historian is inevitably influenced by certain presuppositions and the state of contemporary society (such as in 'post-Catholic' Ireland, or the developing interest in ecumenism), but that nevertheless the historian is a craftsman whose task is to revere the materials – the sources – with which he is to work, and not to attempt to mould them into some sort of all-embracing theory (like Marxism).

No, no – that isn't a caricature. I can accept that.

Interview with Professor Colin Richmond

Colin Richmond is Professor of Medieval History at the University of Keele. He has published extensively on fifteenth-century England, but his range of interests and commitments is very broad – including adult education courses and the teaching of the Holocaust. For example, his 1997 publications include the editing (with Margaret Aston) of the book *Lollardy and the Gentry in the Later Middle Ages* and, for the journal *Patterns of Prejudice*, the wonderfully-titled 'Why the University Should Not be Named after de Montfort (or Why I Don't Drive a Volkswagen)'.

Can we start with the definition of history?

Well, I'm not very good at that: I tend to think of varieties of history, many of which are valid; in any case, consistency isn't something I'm all that approving of. I don't think that learning or understanding works in that sort of way; that you have to be logical, or objective, or consistently one thing or another.

I suppose I'm very keen on the reactive way of going about things, which I maybe learned from Bruce McFarlane, my supervisor at Oxford; always look for 'the other'; find the alternative to what is orthodox.

So you don't see yourself as a member of a particular historiographical tradition?

Well, I think as I grow older, I might do. I was at Leicester University, and I might characterize parts of the way I was taught as topographical – the Hoskins legacy; I was taught by Joan Thirsk, who comes out of the Hoskins, Tawney (Christian socialist) tradition. So, I think that I am very moral in my work – I've been criticized for this. Moral indignation is one thing I go by. But the other aspect is the particularity of place. I think that he [Hoskins] influenced me – I recognize the importance of visiting, say, the sites of the Holocaust; it is important to me.

In what sense is it important to you? What advantages does it have for your history?

That's more difficult to say. It gives me another dimension. I am curious about the landscape which the subjects of my work inhabit. I'm not sentimental about it.

I'm not very clear on this yet. I can see the legacy from Hoskins – *The Making of the English Landscape* – and yet it seems to be some sort of

emotional trigger as well. Does that link up with the way in which history should include moral indignation?

I suppose so. But it isn't about having feelings; if we're thinking about the Holocaust, one shouldn't go out to have feelings.

That would be voyeuristic.

Yes; you have to seek to avoid that, though being a historian is being a voyeur anyway. But there, it's an understanding of the simple topography. Let's take Belzec, [one of the extermination camps of *Aktion Reinhard*] which is a terrible place. Maps or books don't show you how it is – on a shallow hill, in full view from a road and railway.

So you're surprised by its visibility? One usually assumes that such camps are hidden away? And you can't tell how public it was until you're actually there?

Right. I'm sure you can't.

You wouldn't presumably start your research with a visit?

Very rarely – you need to know what you're looking for. A lot of my work is about art, religion. Artefacts can enlighten you about attitudes, and so can sites – this can be a trigger. But normally it's the other way round.

And this gives you another perspective, as you were saying earlier?

I think so, yes. The historian needs all the ammunition he can get. There are other ways of seeing. Sitting behind a desk with documents is not the only way.

Can we go back to the comment on moral indignation. Let's look at your work on the medieval background to the Holocaust, where the moral indignation might help to serve the history. Would you say that it helps you to put the history across?

Others would have to judge that, I think.

But moral indignation isn't something you'd guard against?

No, just the opposite. I think that complacency needs to be attacked. The fault of some historians is to think that they *know*, but really we don't know. We can just make stabs at what happened. Whenever I come across historical writing which overstates objectivity, then I am very tempted to puncture that. This also applies to oneself, but then I don't mind being self-contradictory – though I hate being wrong. But I think most work is interim work, and I don't care for words like 'definitive', 'judicious' or 'balanced'.

Are you saying that objectivity is actually inimical to the historical profession, and that the Rankean tradition of objectivity is a disadvantage to the writing of history?

That's right. This doesn't mean that all historical writing is equal in quality, of course.

Bearing in mind what you've said about objectivity – but also bearing in mind your comments about moral indignation – have you any time for postmodernist approaches?

None at all. Its moral relativism is objectionable and so is its denial of the truth and the chance to explain why things happen. You could always punch a postmodernist in the face and see if he could explain why it hurts.

So are you prepared to offer a definition of good history?

Well, yes. Things like range and the use of the imagination. A great historian is made by his imaginative use of his material.

So is Gibbon a good historian for this reason?

He is. And Tawney. And McFarlane. And Margaret Aston.

Would you say that the historian should write with passion – or is passion too strong?

I hadn't thought about passion. But yes, the historian should be passionate about certain things – doing justice to those who suffer and nailing those who make others suffer.

So simply recovering the past for its own sake is inadequate?

Yes, I think it is in the end. But you have to go through that phase as a younger or immature historian. It's a long apprenticeship in learning to recover the past, and in that phase I'm not sure that you should bother with anything beyond learning the technique of your craft.

So the traditional PhD thesis – the entrance to the profession – you'd want to remain firmly in that Rankean tradition?

Yes. Probably. I think so.

But you feel that, to merit the name, a historian should move beyond it?

Yes. You should at some point move beyond the simple recovering of the past.

By an imaginative and perhaps emotional involvement, and by one's ability to put that across to the reader?

Yes.

So a good historian is someone who has the skills to recover the past on its own terms as far as possible, but then, through a wider perspective and a genuine involvement both for himself and his readers, moves beyond that stage?

Yes. One would hope so. Mind you, I was thinking of Elton, who is certainly committed, passionate and engaged – but I don't like him in political terms.

But is one of the differences that Elton would deny that he is passionate and committed and engaged? Doesn't he claim that he is being objective, and that he is letting the truth of the past speak?

Yes, I think that's right. But I would like to add that being committed to the downtrodden – the 'done-to' – is what I'm keen on. Elton is – whatever he says – committed to the élites, the rulers, the dominators. In the end, if they do exploit, then they must be nailed. And Elton is a great supporter of the élites. I've always thought of myself as a Christian anarchist. You might ask me what that means.

What does that mean?

Well – I'm not a humanist. Any historian with any acquaintance with the Holocaust can't be a humanist in the sense of believing that we are innately good. So these historians who write up élites as if they're doing good to the community – I think you have to be a critic of that and not just a narrator.

Could we just go back to look at the point at which objectivity is necessary. You're saying that the quest for objectivity is a vital part of the training of a young historian, but you feel that the mature historian should transcend it. So, writing as a mature historian, where does the objectivity come into your work now?

I'm not sure if I like the word 'transcend' – though, oddly enough, if transcend means rising higher and higher, then that does express it rather well. Well – the mature historian moves further away from the nuts and bolts, but it's very important that you let the reader make the generalization, ask the big question – the why rather than the how. But the quality of your writing should provide the reader with the means to ask 'why', not the answer.

And yet, if your historical writing is informed by an imaginative and moral dimension, isn't this most clearly revealed in an explanation of 'why'?

Yes, but let me give you an example. Before you came in, I was looking at an old exam paper with the question 'Assess the importance of Henry II's legal reforms'. Well – your apprenticeship is in learning about the legal reforms. But when you've done years of this kind of thing and have matured as an historian, then these reforms can be seen as an exploitative measure on the behalf of the élite, to keep the lid on discontent. So now you've transcended the nuts and bolts; you're fitting into a much wider context.

And the skill in writing about these reforms would be in allowing the reader to see beyond what the sources actually state, but without you saying 'Hey, look how exploitative this is.'

Yes. Someone like Professor Alan Harding who has studied the English legal system for years is enabled to say something like 'no jury ever did anything other than acquit a gentleman'. You need those years of close study before you can come up with such a statement. You can trust that transcending statement. It's judgemental, but it isn't couched in judgemental terms.

So what he's doing is stopping short of the straight moral judgement. He's saying that juries don't convict gentlemen, but he's not adding 'and that's a bit much, isn't it?' The bit he leaves out makes it particularly good history?

I think so, yes.

So you would hope in the work you do to have transcended the craft of the historian, as it were – the necessary attempt at recovering the past through objectivity – and you are now in a position to make these vital generalizations. But the moral judgement you are leaving to the reader. But why stop? Why not just say 'Huh, how typical of kings'? Why are you unhappy with that?

Sometimes I am happy with that. Sometimes the historian should make such statements and be provocative, if only to be contradicted. Whatever you do must reflect the complexity of the past. The historian has to display that complexity and density to the reader. A provocative statement can do that, and so can allowing the reader to judge.

From what you've said, I would imagine that you object to applying some sort of model to the past – say a Marxist model – as a fundamentally unhistorical thing to do?

Yes. I'm not a determinist. If really pushed hard, then I would argue that the cultural mode underlies everything, including economic modes.

What do you mean by a 'cultural mode'?

The way in which history works on cultures – the accumulation of history as culture. If there are any constrictions on the way humans act, then it's this accumulation. Look at Polish history. Take the Warsaw rising of 1944. You could do a very good job in plotting why the decision was made to rise against the Germans at that time. But you'd also have to throw in the fact of other risings in Polish history which are ingrained in the Polish mentality.

So the rising against the invading or conquering power is part of the Polish mentality which would predispose them towards that kind of action?

Yes. And all of these risings failed. So failure is also built in.

Can we move on to look at the historian at work? I'd like the reader to get a feel for the historian actually practising the craft of history.

Perhaps I can best illustrate through an example. I'm shortly going to give a paper on the statutes of a particular Gloucestershire almshouse. I think I've chosen the title 'Victorian Values in Fifteenth-Century England'. This is because the statutes are very long and detailed and very tough on the inmates. They're intriguing in that they may even be unique in that regard. The first stage in examining these would be to look at the statutes of other hospitals at that time. One has to contextualize. The next stage is to be able to make an assessment of these statutes based on these comparisons. Then, you can say 'this is like so-and-so', but on the other hand, if you can't find where particular clauses come from, then you may well have identified what comes from the heads of these particular founders. You then begin to learn about the founders. This is hard work of a straightforward, cumulative type, but it's a stage that can never be rushed or dismissed. You can then say something you hope is significant.

How did you light on this topic?

I think you stumble on things. You are purposeful, but very often the most fertile enquiries come about almost by chance. You're maybe at a record office waiting for a document to arrive, you're flicking through a card index, and suddenly you come across something you've not noticed before ... but of course the more experience you've had, the easier it is to make these connections.

Thinking about the way in which sources are approached. It certainly isn't the case – in your maturer discoveries – that you're approaching sources with a hypothesis in mind. But on the other hand, you're not approaching them as if you're worshipping at their altar: you're not saying to yourself 'I must collect all the sources and they must speak unto me'. Neither of these things is happening – is that right?

That is right. Doing those kinds of things would be in the card-index style – fine for a PhD. This is perhaps why the PhD shouldn't generally be published. You have to be so centred and focused. When I was doing my PhD on the navy in the fifteenth century, I went through every government record, but I was only looking for the word 'ship'! Concentrating on 'ship' had to be done; you had to resist the temptation to fly off.

But as you get older, flying off gets easier because you're more aware of context and it's the flying off that can be most creative about history?

Yes. Though you have to beware that the flying off doesn't become too self-indulgent. But I've written what I wanted to write. I've never written a textbook, or a book that a publisher has approached me to write. It's a question of personality.

What do you see as the purpose and value of history?

I'm not a great thinker about this. I'm so embedded in it I tend not to theorize about it. But we must remember that history is inescapable – as with the Polish example, you can't avoid history. You are moulded by this thing called history. So when I come to think of its value, I'm a bit confused. It's there all the time.

I can see this. You are moulded by your past culture. But is there any point in studying it?

I would stand up and be counted amongst those who argue that the more knowledge you have, the more you value it. I'm tempted to hedge on whether this makes you a better person, though at heart I think it does. All intellectual pursuits are sustaining, because they're outside the self. When you enter into these disciplines, you're losing yourself.

And that is morally good for you?

It isn't good to live off your own life.

So the act of stepping outside yourself is counteracting self-obsession?

Yes. Exactly. Very exactly.

Can we compare this to George Eliot's view of why she wrote novels? After all, she stated that she wrote fiction to take the reader out of himself, to engage the sympathies in a structured way. History can do that?

Absolutely.

We've talked about how at times the history one writes could and should contain the author's moral indignation. This could be linked with what you've just said. If you wrote history merely as an intellectual pursuit which earns your keep, then it wouldn't effectively engage the sympathies. Moral indignation certainly does that, but you're wary of making it too blatant all the time?

Yes. And this is what happens in *Middlemarch*. The narrator's stance is the one I would advocate for the historian: that is, George Eliot shows through Dorothea and others what her moral indignation consists of, but she doesn't throw it in your face. It's done through the genius of expression. History written like *Middlemarch* would be wonderful.

Eliot's a great artist and doesn't offer simplistic solutions. She doesn't turn Dorothea into a goddess, but at the end she's left as the wife of an MP. And the reader thinks, is that it? But the writer is challenging the reader to consider what being selfless actually means.

Yes. All the characters have a density and complexity that ones hopes for from history itself.

Conclusion

Sometimes, when faced with a book of undeniable complexity and equally undeniable girth, readers might just possibly be tempted to turn to the conclusion in the hope that a succinct restatement of the major arguments would allow them to emerge enlightened but unscathed by the effort of reading the whole tome.

Had I ever done that myself – and it goes without saying that it has never so much as crossed my mind until now – I rather suspect that I might have been disappointed on a regular basis. It is not unknown for books swollen to vast proportions to have distinctly attenuated conclusions. One might suspect that authors are reluctant to pamper to the needs of the faint-hearted reader. As for this book, I hope it is off-putting neither in girth nor complexity. I certainly want to be helpful. But I am not going to offer a mere restatement of the main themes and arguments, which would, in my view, make a very poor conclusion. A decent conclusion should certainly be a reminder to the reader, but it should also offer something which allows for these themes and arguments to be seen from a slightly different perspective, and one which thereby encourages readers to check their understanding.

With this in mind, we might conclude by looking at the different types of explanation offered by historians. A useful and familiar starting point is to offer a distinction between history which is largely narrative and history which is largely analytical.

Narrative history can be seen as event-centred, offering an explanation of causes which focuses on human agency rather than structure – that is, on the actions of individuals (typically, members of élites) rather than on institutions, modes of thought or the fundamental economic or political shape of society itself. Narrative history, then, is unlikely to be determinist, since determinism would direct the focus away from the personal towards the impersonal and would deny that individual decisions and actions shape history. It has to be said that narrative history is offering only a limited and perhaps simplistic explanation of cause. A narrative of a major transformation in society, like the Reformation, or more particularly of social and economic changes like the Industrial Revolution, will probably be less than satisfactory in so far as it attempts to tackle the question 'Why?' Political and diplomatic history lends itself to narrative, but it is hard to see how story-style narration can cope with such issues as the history of silence, the history of the body, the mentalities of ordinary people or even the history of popular culture – all topics reflecting the extended scope of twentieth-century historical writing. Analytical history, however, tackles problems rather than story. I hesitate to foist an analogy on the reader, but perhaps we could look at the writing of a history book as a car journey. The narrative historian tells us a lot about the journey, something about the driver and a little about the car; the analytical historian is less interested in the places visited, but wants to ask questions about how the car works and how the driver's skill or otherwise reflects the workings of the car.

Narrative history emphasizing the impact of individuals was a marked characteristic of much of the work of the classical and Renaissance historians. Thucydides, a military commander himself, was fascinated by the psychology of those embroiled in a war which their actions shaped. Similarly, events happen in Sallust and Livy largely because of decisions made by individuals. The pessimistic Sallust saw history being shaped by greed for money and power; for Livy, rhetoric was a vital tool in outlining those noble deeds which should be praised and emulated and those ignoble deeds which should be censured and shunned. The narrative of their predecessor Herodotus was looser and baggier than that of Thuycides and Sallust – more of a Dickens than a Thackeray – but with an emphasis on a chain of personal obligation and revenge which the actions of the gods confirmed rather than ignored. On the face of it, Polybius, in seeking to explain the rise of Rome, appeared to offer a more analytical approach. He stressed the importance of the Roman constitution, whose judicious combination of political forms allowed it, for a time, to escape the pattern of growth and decay which Polybius claimed to have identified in history. In practice, this emphasis on structures was compromised or even contradicted, not only by an ambivalent attitude to the workings of Fortune (which at times was presented as an agent of vengeance or even as Destiny), but also by way of explaining the causes of wars which ignored deeper causes in favour of the more superficial – such as the anger of a people, or the confidence bred of success. Polybius was unable to relate the personal to the structural. He lacked a feeling for political life in Rome, and so his analysis of the constitution was not complemented by an effective discussion of its relationship to actual political behaviour and examples of decision making.

The cyclical pattern of growth and decay was generally anything but congenial to medieval Christian historians, whose vision of history was inevitably linear: from the creation to Christ, and from Christ to His anticipated Second Coming. Explanation was, in the case of Bede, harnessed to the need to evangelize the pagan and to feed the faith of the converted. God intervened directly in the world to reward the faithful and punish His enemies. The later medieval historians did not need to counter the long-vanished threat of paganism, but continued to root descriptions of causes of major and minor events in a providential world-view.

The Renaissance historians were generally able to translate their devotion to the classical historians into a fundamentally Christian moral framework; but, in Machiavelli, we see a writer who challenged both the classical tradition and the assumptions of his own society. He explained the success of Rome as being based on a widely-held regard for civic good, which overrode both personal interest and the dictates of morality. One must be prepared to do whatever is necessary for the wider good: if, as is all too likely, the masses lack that sense, then they can and should be forced by the terror inspired by a ruthless leader into appreciating its virtues. Machiavelli's explanation of the rise and fall of polities was therefore profoundly secular and political. In the *Discourses on Livy*, he analysed the advantages of the mixed constitution in the manner of Polybius and, like Polybius, advocated the use of religion by civic leaders as a military and political tool to inspire confidence in battle and to prevent selfish and antisocial behaviour. Christian teaching, Machiavelli complained, frequently lacked that vital political utility, since it praised the humble and world-denying. Indeed, he reversed the standard Christian homily on the positive good that was peace by praising class conflict as a mechanism for maintaining political stability:

> **I must say that it appears to me that those who condemn the disturbances between the nobles and plebeians condemn those very things that were the primary cause of Roman liberty ... good examples arise from good training, good training from good laws, and good laws from those disturbances that many people thoughtlessly condemn ...[1]**

Machiavelli's ill-repute amongst his contemporaries ably reflects how unrepresentative his work was, both in terms of its secularism and in the way it made some attempt to focus on the structure of society and the political theories which illuminated it. Nevertheless, the explanation offered by Machiavelli remained wedded to the classical and humanist assumption that human nature did not change as society changed through time – the much-lauded Renaissance sense of anachronism was inadequate to the task of fully contextualizing the past.

Like their Renaissance forebears, most of the *philosophes* who wrote history did so by making assumptions about unchanging human nature. And they did so without worrying too much about the tiresome inconvenience of demonstration and proof. 'Woe to details!' cried Voltaire in a letter on the writing of his history *The Age of Louis XIV*.[2] Enlightenment historical explanation, however, converted these assumptions into optimistic generalizations about the human spirit and, in effect, laws of human behaviour: a right understanding of such laws – and the freedom from clerical obfuscation which hampered understanding – would lead to progress for humanity. The great motor of progress was the development of the faculty of reason. The *philosophe* Condorcet (1743–94), writing just before his execution during the Terror in revolutionary France, commented:

> … progress [of the human mind] is subject to the same general laws that can be observed in the development of the faculties of the individual, and it is indeed no more than the sum of that development realized in a large number of individuals joined together in society.[3]

Since the *philosophe* was no longer attempting to use history in the Renaissance manner as an illustration of certain *exempla* for the use of political leaders, writers of history could afford to move beyond classical and humanist obsession with political, military and diplomatic narrative into structural analyses of manners, laws and customs.

A comparison of Machiavelli's comments from the *Discourses* with a passage from Gibbon is most instructive:

> The temperate struggles of the patricians and plebeians had finally established the firm and equal balance of the constitution, which united the freedom of popular assemblies with the authority and wisdom of a senate and the executive powers of a regal magistrate.[4]

The similarities are evident, but we note how Gibbon, with the self-confidence of the Enlightenment 'man of sense' and the citizen of a country with a relatively stable political system, prefers 'temperate struggles' to 'disturbances'.

Although Gibbon certainly offered the 'balanced constitution' as the political theory and practice which alone could preserve and encourage the progress of a state, one should not overstate the extent to which Gibbon's writing of history was based upon typical Enlightenment generalizations, laws or models as such. *The History of the Decline and Fall of the Roman Empire* is not a fundamentally analytical work focused on causation: it is largely a narrative in which Gibbon invites the reader to enjoy precision and detail and to enter into a dialogue – mind to mind – in an exploration of the events and personalities of the past, albeit distorted through his anticlericalism and willingness to judge his characters by the enlightened standards of the *philosophe*.

Leopold von Ranke's distaste for Enlightenment theorizing led him reject any history which sought to impose 'modern' values on the past. This had the effect of short-circuiting Enlightenment-style interest in structures and the *philosophes*' tendency to raid the past for examples of the laws of human behaviour in society. In Ranke's view, each age was unique: it bore the imprint of God's providence, but one must not presume to detect the providential plan. Reverence dictated that one must recover the past on its own terms, and not distort it to fit the kind of sacrilegious ideological system-building that had led to the horrors of the French Revolution. The historian's explanation must therefore rest on the sources, and not on his own needs. Given the nature of the extant sources and the conservative and nationalist predilections of many of Ranke's followers, the result was often narrative histories of the political élites.

In Britain, the Rankean legacy revealed itself in the attacks on the so-called Whig interpretation of history – that sweeping political narrative which imposed on the past assumptions about material, moral and ideological progress culminating in liberal parliamentary democracy. The determinist philosophy of Marxism was similarly rejected as a fundamentally unhistorical imposing of present-day theories on a past which must be allowed to explain itself. Suspicion of teleological narrative (Whigs) and teleological analysis of structures (Marxists) led to the heavily-detailed monograph, narrow in scope, and generally focused on the motivations and behaviour of the élites – in Butterfield's terminology, 'technical history'. Namier's detailed scholarship might be rather misleadingly known as 'structural analysis', but it essentially relied upon analysis of the aggregate of the behaviour of individuals and not of economic, social or ideological structures *per se*. Those who wrote and write in the conservative tradition of Namier are therefore inclined to reject explanations of revolutions which are based on the impact of ideas or the structural instability of society in favour of explanations resting on chance (or mischance) and personality.[5]

At the heart of Marxist historiography lies historical materialism. As we saw in Chapter 4, the attraction of Marxism is very real: it offers an explanation of the shape of all human societies past, present and future, an explanation of fundamental change past, present and future – and an ethical system with a firm set of practical goals which embraces past, present and future. The damage to the credibility of such an all-embracing system by the collapse of Communism in Eastern Europe in 1989 is considerable. However, as I suggested earlier, Marxism has forced – and will continue to force – historians to explain and interpret the past in terms of a broader context than the actions of élites and individuals; to consider, in fact, the relationship between a society's institutions, its value-systems, culture and its economic base. One can reject such structural explanations, but, to reject them, one has to offer a critique of them.

Marxism is, of course, heavily analytical, although, in seeking answers to problems, it has the effect of dictating both the questions and answers. For instance, a Marxist scholar studying the culture of a particular society would consider the question of the extent to which a dominant culture reflected the needs of the dominant class: how far, for example, bourgeois culture in a capitalist epoch exerted control over proletarian culture. The more rigid the Marxist, the more likely he would be to answer that bourgeois culture successfully manipulated working-class culture.

An attack on narrative from a different perspective is a feature of the so-called *Annales* school of historians. As we saw in Chapter 4, *Annales* historians advocated an interdisciplinary approach which analysed the shaping of society by long-term trends (*structure*) and rejected event-centred history as essentially ephemeral, or, at best, of value only when illustrating the workings of those trends. In the search for 'total history', the traditional narrative had little part to play. We noted that the third part of Braudel's groundbreaking work *The Mediterranean* did indeed include a narrative account, but one that was simply not integrated with Braudel's chief love, *la longue durée*.

If one dared to cite a 'typical' *Annales* work, then it would be not be a bestseller like Le Roy Ladurie's *Montaillou*. It would be a regional study, yes, but one which relied heavily on quantitative history as a means of elucidating *structure* and *conjoncture*. It would therefore be profoundly dull to all but the believer and utterly inaccessible to the non-academic reader, for whom history generally means narrative history. And there are other, more significant, objections to the type of explanation offered by the *Annales* historians. Failing to integrate traditional history with structural history meant that the role of the individual simply disappeared; such history appeared determinist, but without the kind of theoretical basis for determinism which Marxism possesses. Unlike Marxism, *Annales* history rarely offers an explanation for change. We noted in Chapter 4 the response by Le Roy Ladurie to these kinds of strictures: the so-called 'creative event' which stimulates the transition from one structure to another. But does Le Roy Ladurie offer a precise explanation of the nature of such events? The answer has to be no. His attachment to the deeper layers of history remains intact. We recall that even the creative event in his *Carnival* is described using geological imagery (see p.155).

It is tempting to assume that the various problems of narrative and analytical history might be solved by a combination of the two. This practice is common enough in academic history. Sometimes, the historian offers a narrative of events followed by an 'analytical' chapter or two. It is, perhaps, open to doubt how well this works. Narrative is unlikely to be devoid of explanation, and analytical passages unlikely to be devoid of narrative; readers may be uncertain as to the relative status of what they are reading. Blending the two may be the better way, and a recognition that explanation needs both events and structures, but with a discussion of how the two interconnect.[6]

There is, however, a more fundamental problem which may render the discussion of narrative and analytical history meaningless. This conclusion has, after all, rested on the assumption that history has an essentially explanatory role. This may seem self-evident, but those made wary by postmodernism may at least wish to register it as less self-evident than it appears. Chapter 1 offered an introductory guide to the challenge of Hayden White and others who see history as a fundamentally fictional discourse. To postmodernists, the distinction made between narrative and analysis, between event-centred history and structural history, is more of a distinction of style than one of relative proximity to a 'true' explanation. One cannot come closer to a true explanation by combining narrative with analysis, any more than one can come closer by keeping them separate.

Our discussion of postmodernism concluded that its denial that history could claim to recover at least an approximate truth about the past was overstated; that it attempted to use methods of reason and logic it denied to others; that it sought to exploit linguistic theories which were open to challenge and countenanced a relativism which was morally and philosophically unacceptable. But I also suggested that historians stood to gain from recognizing the extent to which all texts, including their own, are the subject of silences, evasions and metaphors akin to fictional narrative. This leads us to two conclusions. Firstly, we need not cast aside our discussion of narrative and analytical history. Secondly, we might build upon the postmodernist insight into the fictive elements in texts to at least consider a new style of historical writing. Peter Burke suggests[7] that historians should consider the offering of contrasting viewpoints to represent different types of collective experience and, of course, a contribution from the historian himself in his own voice. The best example of just such a book is Richard Price's *Alabi's World*. Price wishes to write about the interaction between the inhabitants of the Dutch colony of Suriname: Moravian missionaries, Dutch officials, and escaped slaves (the Saramaka Maroons). He therefore offers a tapestry of four interweaving voices, representing the three groups and himself as the historian. Each voice has a separate type style. But does it work? As an evocation of cultural conflict, it is powerful and moving. In his prologue, the author invites the reader to imagine the sound of the voices and even the appearance of the speakers;[8] many would feel that the reader is indeed drawn into Alabi's world. And Price gives a voice to those who would be ignored by traditional, document-based history. But the problem is that the voices do not truly interweave. The author's own narration tells the voices when to speak, and reminds the reader of what has been said; he is the conductor, and they respond to his baton. Arguably, there is also a fundamental problem with the structure of the book. The more the author attempts to withdraw, the more the book loses its coherence. The fact that Price decided to include a massive 'Notes and Commentary' section may well be a recognition of the need to compensate for this problem.

And yet, for all these criticisms, *Alabi's World* challenges historians to think, not only about their role in manipulating the past, but also about the reader, who, in my view, has the right to expect to be engaged by what he reads. Neither analytical nor narrative history has a monopoly on inviting the reader to enter into a dialogue, but perhaps the great works of history are indeed those which combine the two: combine, perhaps, an appeal to the intellect with an appeal to the imagination, and so encourage the reader to participate in the historian's enjoyment of the mind at work. I vividly recall just such a book, and I also recall that it inspired me to study history at university: Sir Richard Southern's *The Making of the Middle Ages*.[9] It offers analysis of structures, it offers an absolutely riveting narrative – it offers the best that history can afford.

One should conclude with the happy thought that the writing of history is – and will remain – a subject of contentious debate and likely experimentation. On the other hand, I am afraid that those who only like questions with definite answers will find this an uncomfortable thought. In fact, this book has asked lots of questions; answers have been less apparent. We have considered the nature and value of history, and have discussed how historians past and present have tackled the task of making intelligible that which has gone for ever. We have made the acquaintance of those who wanted to restrict history to the doings of the political and military élites; we have met those who wanted to write the history of everything. We have studied those who have claimed that history is no better – or worse – than fiction, and we have studied those who claim that, whilst it cannot recover the whole truth, it gets mighty close. We have seen how history which is demonstrably false might do great good – and great harm. We have seen that history is inescapable, but have warned of the dangers of escaping to it as a refuge from the present. We have looked at the many ways in which the past has been explained: by those who claim to make use of theories with the status of scientific laws, and by those who want to let the past speak without the alleged distortion of present-minded theory.

Disagreement is surely the life-blood of the subject called history. It is an argument about the past, and an argument that can only die if either of the following occur:

1 An explanation of the past is imposed upon a society and accepted as universally valid.

2 If history is seen as an activity which merely serves the immediate needs or prejudices of particular groups, and an activity which therefore cannot be judged as true or false.

On this basis, I see no reason to anticipate, and so to mourn, the imminent demise of history.

Further Reading

There is an absolute obligation in an introductory book of this type to offer suggestions on further reading, but this should be tempered by an awareness that to offer readers new to the themes of *The Past and its Presenters* a deluge of titles would be off-putting and counter-productive. I have therefore concentrated in this section on works which I have found most helpful, instructive, thought-provoking or downright irritating. The full bibliography can then be used for further help, instruction, stimulation and irritation.

The astute reader will have noticed the number of times Eric Hobsbawm, Roy Porter, Peter Burke, E.P. Thompson and Geoffrey Elton have been referred to in this book. It is a sign of the importance of debates on the nature and purpose of history and the study of historiography itself that such eminent practitioners should engage in them. And one should, of course, read their own historical works. At the risk of imposing my own preference, I would suggest the following:

Eric Hobsbawm, *The Age of Revolution: Europe 1789–1848* (London, 1962).
Roy Porter, *A Social History of Madness: Stories of the Insane* (London, 1996).
Peter Burke, *Popular Culture in Early Modern Europe* (London, 1978).
E.P. Thompson, *The Making of the English Working Class* (Harmondsworth, 1968).
G.R. Elton, *Reformation Europe 1517–1559* (London, 1963).

I should say a few words on this final choice. Those familiar with Elton's works might have expected other titles. *Reformation Europe* provides an excellent example of Elton's method of tackling causation. Direct causes, he argues, are those resulting from the exercise of human volition (and can be identified from close study of the documents). Longer-term causes (such as the state of the pre-Reformation Church) are not seen as fundamentally structural, but largely as the result, once again, of human action. They are less significant than the direct causes in explaining why an event occurred. There is an article by Geoffrey Roberts in *The Historian* 51 (Spring 1998) which I came across when in the process of writing this section: 'Geoffrey Elton and the Philosophy of History', pp.29–31. It is well worth consulting.

Elton's emphasis on the absolute requirement to base interpretations on the extant evidence can also be seen in his *Tudor Revolution in Government: Administrative Changes in the Reign of Henry VIII* (Cambridge, 1953). Its central thesis – more or less, that a centralized and bureaucratic state emerged in Henry VIII's time due to the activities of Thomas Cromwell – has been seen more as a reflection of Elton's conservative predilections and a biographer's attachment to his subject than the result of a supposedly value-free empirical inquiry.

There are a number of large – in some cases, very large – general works on historiography. Edited by John Cannon, *The Blackwell Dictionary of Historians* (Oxford, 1988) tackles schools of history, historical terminology and over 400 individual historians from the classical period to the 1980s; contributions from its multiple authorship are inevitably variable in depth of treatment and usefulness. It is a handy source of reference and a convenient starting-point. The even vaster Routledge *Companion to Historiography* (London, 1997) came too late for me to make much use of it. It offers an impressive range of essays covering historical writing from both Western and non-Western traditions. Perhaps inevitably, the relatively specialized themes of many of the contributors militate against the overall coherence of the book. The introductory essays to the various sections do, however, place emphasis on providing the necessary context for the succeeding essays, and are therefore particularly valuable.

Ernst Breisach's *Historiography Ancient, Medieval, and Modern* (Chicago, 1983) arguably tries to do too much: its range is vast, and one rarely gets a feel for the many historians discussed. I was disappointed that I was not able to make more use of it.

As far as possible, I have tried to include reasonably lengthy extracts from the historians featured in Chapters 2, 3 and 4. There are a number of useful compilations of historical writings from various periods, although one should really do the writer the courtesy of reading him rather more widely than such compilations (or this book in particular) allow. Readily available are:

Michael Grant, *Readings in the Classical Historians* (New York, 1992).
Donald R. Kelley, *Versions of History from Antiquity to the Enlightenment* (New Haven and London, 1981).
Peter Burke, *The Renaissance Sense of the Past* (London, 1969).
Fritz Stern, *The Varieties of History: From Voltaire to the Present* (London, 1970).

There are a number of introductory textbooks which cover some of the same ground as *The Past and its Presenters*. Arthur Marwick's *The Nature of History* (London, third edition 1989) is deservedly popular, but, with a very broad content – including controversy in history, types of source and the relationship between history and other disciplines – it cannot always offer a satisfactorily detailed coverage of historiography. John Tosh's *The Pursuit of History: Aims, Methods and New Directions in the Study of Modern History* (London, second edition 1991) is a shorter, clearly written and thematic book which is, as its title would suggest, strongest on twentieth-century approaches. The chapter 'History and theory' offers a very good discussion of Marxist history. There are brief surveys of the history of historical writing in chapters of *Studying History* by Jeremy Black and Donald MacRaild (London, 1997) and in Richard J. Evans' *In Defence of History* (London, 1997). Evans provides the more bracing gallop.

Simon Hornblower (ed.) *Greek Historiography* (Oxford, 1994) and Denys Hay's *Annalists and Historians* (London, 1977) offer a more detailed study of groups of historians. Anything by Arnaldo Momigliano can be strongly recommended – particularly his *Studies in Historiography* (London, 1966). So can the two volumes on medieval and early modern historiography in England by Antonia Gransden, *Historical Writing in England* (London, 1974 and 1982).

Edited by John Cannon, *The Historian at Work* (London, 1980) has a number of very accessible chapters on individual historians, including Gibbon, Ranke, Macaulay, Marx, Bloch, Namier, Butterfield and Braudel. All are good, those by Burke (Braudel), Cannon (Namier) and Ramm (von Ranke) particularly so. I disagree with Richard Evans' dismissive view of Peter Burke's *The French Historical Revolution: The Annales School, 1929–89* (Oxford, 1990). It is a well-structured survey and can be supplemented by the earlier and more detailed *French Historical Method: The Annales Paradigm* by T. Stoianovich (Ithaca, 1976). The relationship between Marxist historical writing and *Annales* (from a British perspective) is summarized with dispatch by Eric Hobsbawm in *On History* (London, 1997), pp.178–85.

Twentieth-century British historians are discussed in the collection of essays edited by Walter Arnstein, *Recent Historians of Great Britain* (Iowa, 1990); the chapter by Heyck on E.P. Thompson is the most useful. *The British Marxist Historians* (Oxford, 1984) by Harvey J. Kaye is very helpful on Hill, Thompson *et al.*; it is very sympathetic in tone, but manages to offer a balanced analysis despite the author's pronounced 'democratic socialist' views. Kaye's *The Education of Desire: Marxists and the Writing of History* (London, 1992) is perhaps a book too far on the same subject, but there is a useful discussion of Rudé in particular. John Kenyon's *The History Men: The Historical Profession in England since the Renaissance* (London, second edition 1993) fills in the background on personalities admirably; Christopher Parker's *The English Historical Tradition since 1850* (Edinburgh, 1990) is much more analytical and cooler in tone.

Individual studies to be recommended include those in the generally admirable *Historians on Historians* series, published by Weidenfeld & Nicolson. Roy Porter's *Edward Gibbon: Making History* (London, 1988) is a model of what a scholar who clearly loves his subject can do. The same is true of John Gould's *Herodotus* (London, 1989). Linda Colley's *Namier* (London, 1989) does a wonderful job of integrating an analysis of the historian with an assessment of his personality without ever descending into psycho-babble. G.R. Elton's *F.W. Maitland* (London, 1986), Owen Dudley Edwards' *Macaulay* (London, 1988) and Hugh Tulloch's *Acton* (London, 1988) are also helpful. Learning is worn lightly in the excellent little books in the Oxford *Past Masters* series: Quentin Skinner's *Machiavelli* (Oxford, 1981), J.W. Burrow's *Gibbon* (Oxford, 1985) and Peter Singer's *Marx* (Oxford, 1980). All have the virtue of exemplary clarity and genuinely encourage the reader to explore further.

On Leopold von Ranke, Georg Iggers and Konrad von Moltke offer a superb short analysis of Ranke's background, works and impact on later historians in their introduction to an invaluable collection of his writings in *The Theory and Practice of History: Leopold von Ranke* (Indianapolis, 1973), pp.xv–lxxi. There are several essays of value in Iggers and Powell, (eds) *Leopold von Ranke and the Shaping of the Historical Discipline* (New York, 1990), particularly those by Burke, Benzoni, Goldstein and Iggers himself, which deal respectively with Ranke's conservatism, his use of sources, his impact on the universities of Oxford and Cambridge and the blunting of Ranke's impact on twentieth-century historiography. Leonard Krieger's *Ranke: The Meaning of History* (Chicago, 1977) requires a certain dedication given its distinctly turgid style.

On the value of history in its broadest sense, one can do no better than to start with David Lowenthal's *The Past is a Foreign Country* (Cambridge, 1985). Eric Hobsbawm's *On History* (London, 1997) offers salutary thoughts on the dangers of the misuse of history and reminders of the historian's responsibilities. The use of history to cement national identity is discussed in Hobsbawm and Ranger (eds), *The Invention of Tradition* (Cambridge, 1992); by Linda Colley in *Britons: Forging the Nation 1707–1837* (New Haven and London, 1992) and in Joyce Appleby *et al.*, *Telling the Truth about History* (London, 1995) – see Chapter 3 in particular. Juliet Gardiner's *The History Debate* (London, 1990) offers brief but revealing essays by G.R. Elton (on the value and necessity of learning history for its own sake) and Roy Porter (on the need for historians to respond to the questions the present asks of the past). The postmodernist perspective on the value of history (such as it is) is outlined by Beverley Southgate in *History, What and Why: Ancient, Modern, and Postmodern Perspectives* (London, 1996).

In Chapter 1, 'Defining History', I used the challenge of the postmodernist perspective as the main focus for the discussion. Since I wrote that chapter, Keith Jenkins has edited *The Postmodern History Reader* (London, 1997) and brought together in a thoroughly admirable way extracts from many of the works and writers referred to in 'Defining History'. Not the least of his services is to enable the faint-hearted to experience the doubtful pleasures of postmodernist prose in small doses. In particular, he has included the debate on postmodernism in the pages of *Past and Present* and some of the major contributors to the debate on postmodernism and the Holocaust. The *Reader* should be supplemented by the formidable onslaughts against post-modernism in Alex Callinicos' *Theories and Narratives: Reflections on the Philosophy of History* (Oxford, 1995) and Richard J. Evans' *In Defence of History* (London, 1997). I would also recommend Hayden White's compara-tively accessible response in the *Journal of Contemporary History* 30 (1995), pp.233–46 to Arthur Marwick's attack on postmodernism in the same journal, pp.5–31.

Keith Jenkins' own books, *Re-thinking History* (London, 1991) and *On 'What is History': From Carr and Elton to Rorty and White* (London, 1995) are supposedly student introductions to postmodernism, but I would imagine that his extraordinary prose – a mixture of colloquialism and obfus-cation – offers little encouragement to the reader.

For those who wonder what postmodernist historical writing (as opposed to theory) might be like, Richard Price's *Alabi's World* (Baltimore and London, 1990) is a useful example. For a comment on the value of this approach, see Eric Hobsbawm, 'Postmodernism in the Forest', *On History*, pp.192–200.

The battleground of postmodernism must not be allowed to obscure the continuing usefulness of G.R. Elton's classic restatement of the empiricist viewpoint in *The Practice of History* (London, 1969) and, even more to the point, the insights of E.H. Carr in *What is History*? Sadly, Carr died in 1982 before he could complete a revised edition of his book: R.W. Davies has edited some of Carr's notes for the 1987 edition. Carr in particular continues to cause controversy. Nor can the arguments of E.P. Thompson be ignored. As a contribution to the debate over the nature of the historical discipline, his essay 'The Poverty of Theory or An Orrery of Errors' is essential reading. It can be found in *The Poverty of Theory and Other Essays* (London, 1978).

Notes and References

Chapter 1: Defining History

1 R.J. Evans, *In Defence of History* (London, 1997).
2 G.R. Elton, *Return to Essentials: Some Reflections on the Present State of Historical Study* (Cambridge, 1991), p.41.
3 J. Appleby, L. Hunt, M. Jacob, *Telling the Truth about History* (New York, 1995).
4 R. Barthes in S. Sontag (ed.), *A Barthes Reader* (London, 1982), p.459.
5 J-F. Lyotard, *The Postmodern Condition* (Manchester, 1984), pp.xxiv.
6 R. Young, *White Mythologies: Writing History and the West* (London, 1990), pp.1–2.
7 S. Monas in H. Kozicki (ed.), *Developments in Modern Historiography* (London, 1993), p.3.
8 M. Foucault *Power/Knowledge: Selected Interviews and Other Writings, 1972–1977* (Brighton, 1980), pp.131–3.
9 M. Foucault, quoted by L. Hunt, 'History, Culture and Text' in Hunt (ed.), *The New Cultural History* (Berkeley, 1989), p.8.
10 See in particular the disciple-like comments of Keith Jenkins, *On 'What is History?' From Carr and Elton to Rorty and White* (London, 1995) and the distinctly adversarial and splenetic comments of Arthur Marwick, 'Two Approaches to Historical Study: The Metaphysical (including 'Postmodernism') and the Historical', *Journal of Contemporary History* 30, 1 (Jan 1995), pp.5–31.
11 Georg G. Iggers, 'Rationality and History' in Kozicki (ed.), op.cit., p.28.
12 P. Joyce, 'History and Post-Modernism', *Past and Present* 133 (1991), p.208. This article is a response to a brief note from Lawrence Stone in *Past and Present*, 131 (May 1991) critical of postmodernist approaches. Stone duly responded to Joyce – 'I am sorry that Patrick Joyce is so cross with me' – in the same journal, no.135 (May 1992), pp.189–94. Perhaps the most useful and least polemical article in the series on postmodernism is that by Gabrielle Spiegel, also in no.135, pp.194–208.
13 E.H. Carr, *What is History?* (Harmondsworth, second edition 1987), p.11.
14 ibid., pp.12–13.
15 G.R. Elton, *The Practice of History* (London, 1969), p.76.
16 J. Tosh, *The Pursuit of History: Aims, Methods and New Directions in the Study of Modern History* (London, second edition 1984), p.148.
17 G.R. Elton (1991), op.cit., p.43.
18 A. Marwick in Kozicki, op.cit., p.136.
19 A. Marwick, 'Two Approaches to Historical Study: The Metaphysical (Including 'Postmodernism') and the Historical', *Journal of Contemporary History* 30, 1 (1995), p.19.
20 Hayden White, 'Response to Arthur Marwick', ibid., pp.233–46.
21 R.J. Evans, op.cit., p.106.
22 E.W. Said, *The World, the Text and the Critic* (Cambridge, Mass., 1983), pp.4–5.
23 R.J. Evans, op.cit., p.124.

24 H. White, 'Historical Emplotment and the Problem of Truth', in S. Friedlander (ed.), *Probing the Limits of Representation: Nazism and the 'Final Solution'* (Cambridge, Mass., 1992), p.40.

25 Alex Callinicos, *Theories and Narratives. Reflections on the Philosophy of History* (Oxford, 1995), p.73.

26 K. Jenkins, op.cit., p.192.

27 Simon Schama, *Dead Certainties (Unwarranted Speculations)* (London, 1991). It has sometimes been suggested that Francis Fukuyama's *The End of History and the Last Man* (Harmondsworth, 1992) can be seen as a postmodernist work of history. In his original 1989 article 'The End of History?', Fukuyama generated considerable controversy over his contention that the supposed evolution of human society could progress no further than Western liberal capitalist democracy. His dismissal of metanarratives like Marxism – easy enough in 1989 – appeared to imbue his work with postmodernist characteristics, but it should really be seen as the ultimate Whig history for the late twentieth century. Fukuyama's work is evaluated in Frank Füredi's *Mythical Past, Elusive Future* (London, 1992), pp.218–24.

28 K. Jenkins, *Re-thinking History* (London, 1991), p.70.

29 J. Appleby, op.cit., p.236.

30 Joan W. Scott in Peter Burke (ed.), *New Perspectives on Historical Writing* (Oxford, 1991). See in particular pp.57–61.

31 For a rather strident postmodernist perspective on time, see Elizabeth Deeds Ermarth, *Sequel to History: Postmodernism and the Crisis of Representational Time* (Princeton, 1992). The legions of the unconvinced are led by Richard Evans, op.cit. (particularly pp.140–4), and Appleby *et al.*, op.cit.(particularly pp.205–7).

32 A. Cameron, 'Virginity as Metaphor: women and the rhetoric of early Christianity' in Cameron: (ed.), *History as Text: The Writing of Ancient History* (London, 1989), p.194.

33 E. Said, *Orientalism* (Harmondsworth, 1995).

34 E. Said, 'Orientalism Reconsidered', in Francis Barker *et al.* (eds), *Europe and Its Others* (Colchester, 1985) 2 vols, vol.1, p.15.

35 R. Young, op.cit. See pp.132–4.

36 G.R. Elton (1991), op.cit., p.43.

37 E.P. Thompson, *The Poverty of Theory and Other Essays* (London, 1978), p.231.

38 Joan W. Scott, quoted in P. Novick, *That Noble Dream: The 'Objectivity Question' and the American Historical Profession* (Cambridge, 1988), p.598.

39 G.R. Elton (1991), op.cit., p.41.

40 K. Jenkins (1991), op.cit., p.26.

41 R.J. Evans, op.cit., p.205. Evans comments that Jenkins' view of university historians could be seen as a reflection of the latter's resentment at being 'only a lecturer in an institute of higher education' and therefore excluded from the prestigious and wealthy universities. 'Doubtless this would be an unfair charge', says Evans – in other words, I didn't really mean it, folks – but the comment is, at best, unfortunate and unnecessary. By the same argument, as a school teacher and therefore not a member of the higher education establishment, I should be a thoroughly rabid postmodernist.

Chapter 2: From the Birth of Historiography to the Renaissance

1 Herodotus, *The Histories*, trans. Aubrey de Sélincourt (Harmondsworth, 1972), p.41.
2 ibid., p.43.
3 John Gould, *Herodotus* (London, 1989), p.17.
4 ibid., p.49.
5 Herodotus, op.cit., pp.151–2.
6 Detlev Fehling, *Herodotus and his 'Sources': Citation, Invention and Narrative Art* (Liverpool, 1989).
7 Herodotus, op.cit., p.536.
8 D.M. Lewis, 'Persians in Herodotus' in Lewis (ed.), *The Greek Historians – Literature and History: Essays presented to A.E. Raubitschek* (Stanford, 1986). Lewis' insight in discussed in Gould, op.cit., pp.113–14.
9 Gould, op.cit., p.41.
10 Herodotus, op.cit., p.177.
11 ibid.
12 ibid., pp.375–6.
13 Gould, op.cit. Gould offers a most informative discussion of Herodotus' problems with other tongues. See especially pp.26–7.
14 Herodotus, op.cit., p.77.
15 Beverley Southgate, *History: What and Why? Ancient, Modern, and Postmodern Perspectives* (London, 1996).
16 Herodotus, op.cit., p.451.
17 Peter Derow, 'Historical Explanation: Polybius and his Predecessors' in Simon Hornblower (ed.), *Greek Historiography* (Oxford, 1994), p.76.
18 Herodotus, op.cit., p.486.
19 ibid., p.54.
20 Gould, op.cit., p.65.
21 Simon Hornblower, 'Thucydides and Herodotus' in Hornblower (ed.), op.cit., p.31.
22 François Hartog, *The Mirror of Herodotus* (Berkeley, 1988), p.379.
23 Fehling, op.cit., p.249.
24 Herodotus, op.cit., p.43.
25 Arnaldo Momigliano, *Studies in Historiography* (London, 1966), p.130.
26 Thucydides, *History of the Peloponnesian War* (London, 1910), p.1. I have used the translation by Richard Crawley in Dent's *Everyman* series. There is also the translation by Rex Warner for Penguin Classics, which some readers may find more readily available. I have therefore also included page references to Warner, in this instance, p.35.
27 ibid., pp.14–15. Warner, pp.47–8.
28 ibid., pp.352–3. Warner, pp.363–4.
29 ibid., p.439. Warner, p.444.
30 ibid., p.299. Warner, p.314.
31 Simon Hornblower, *Thucydides* (London, 1987), p.79.
32 Arnaldo Momigliano, *The Classical Foundations of Modern Historiography* (Berkeley, 1990). See pp.44–5 in particular.
33 Thucydides, op.cit., p.524. Warner, p.522.
34 Virginia Hunter, *Thucydides: The Artful Reporter* (Toronto, 1973).
35 Thucydides, op.cit., p.532. Warner, p.530.
36 F.W. Walbank, *Polybius* (Berkeley, 1972).
37 Polybius, *Histories* in C.A. Robinson (ed.), *Selections from Greek and Roman Historians* (New York, 1957), pp.136–7. The translation is by Evelyn

Shuckburgh and reads, I think, very well. Penguin Classics also do an abridged version with a translation by Ian Scott-Kilvert. Once again, I have included page references to a text which may be more readily available. In this case, the passage can be found on pp.302–3.

38 ibid., p.139. Scott-Kilvert, p.305.
39 Walbank, op.cit., p.71.
40 Polybius, op.cit., p.137. Scott-Kilvert, p.303.
41 ibid., pp.143–4. Scott-Kilvert, pp.309–11.
42 Walbank, op.cit., p.135.
43 Arnaldo Momigliano, *Essays in Ancient and Modern Historiography* (Oxford, 1977), p.76.
44 Polybius, op.cit., p.158. Scott-Kilvert, p.349.
45 ibid., p.159. Scott-Kilvert, p.349.
46 Derow, op.cit., p.88.
47 Walbank, op.cit., p.44.
48 Roger Ray, 'The Triumph of Greco-Roman Rhetorical Assumptions in Pre-Carolingian Historiography' in C. Holdsworth and T.P. Wiseman (eds), *The Inheritance of Historiography 350–900* (Exeter, 1986), p.70.
49 Cicero, *De Oratore*, trans. Sutton and Rackham (London, 1959) 2 vols, vol.1, p.225.
50 ibid., pp.243–5.
51 Livy, *The Early History of Rome*, trans. Aubrey de Sélincourt (Harmondsworth, 1971), p.34.
52 ibid., p.69.
53 Ronald Syme, *Sallust* (Berkeley, 1964).
54 Sallust, *The War with Catiline* in *Sallust*, trans. J.C. Rolfe (London, 1960), p.9. The Penguin Classics version is translated by S.A. Handford. This passage can be found on p.177.
55 ibid., p.139. Handford, pp.37–8.
56 ibid., pp.311–23. Handford, pp.117–22.
57 Ronald Martin, *Tacitus* (London, 1981), p.21.
58 For the link with Thomas More, see Alistair Fox, *Thomas More: History and Providence* (Oxford, 1982), p.82 and in his *Politics and Literature in the Reigns of Henry VII and Henry VIII* (Oxford, 1989), pp.119–20.
59 Tacitus, *The Annals of Imperial Rome*, trans. Michael Grant (Harmondsworth, 1959), p.29.
60 ibid., p.89.
61 ibid., p.272.
62 Ronald Syme, *Tacitus* (Oxford, 1958), vol.1.
63 Martin, op.cit., p.213.
64 Denys Hay, *Annalists and Historians: Western Historiography from the VIIIth to the XVIIIth Centuries* (London, 1977), p.10.
65 ibid., p.11.
66 Beryl Smalley, *Historians in the Middle Ages* (London, 1974), p.42.
67 *Cuthbert's Letter on the Illness and Death of the Venerable Bede, Priest* in Bede, *Ecclesiastical History of the English People*, trans. Leo Sherley-Price (Harmondsworth, 1990), p.359.
68 ibid., pp.41–3.
69 Walter Goffart, *The Narrators of Barbarian History (A.D. 550–800): Jordanes, Gregory of Tours, Bede, and Paul the Deacon* (Princeton, 1988), p.235.
70 Antonia Gransden, *Historical Writing in England, c.550–c.1307* (London, 1974).
71 Bede, op.cit., p.267.
72 ibid., p.43.

73 J.H. Dahmus, *Seven Medieval Historians* (Chicago, 1982), p.48.
74 N.J. Higham, *An English Empire. Bede and the Early Anglo-Saxon Kings* (Manchester, 1995), p.9.
75 Bede, op.cit., pp.241–2.
76 ibid., pp.281–2.
77 ibid., p.54.
78 ibid., p.266.
79 Antonia Gransden, op.cit., p.22.
80 Bede, op.cit., p.117.
81 ibid., p.107.
82 ibid., p.324.
83 ibid., pp.300–6.
84 ibid., p.342.
85 Ray, op.cit. See in particular pp.80–1.
86 Bede, op.cit., p.41.
87 Ray, op.cit., p.80.
88 Bede, op.cit., pp.129–30.
89 Gransden, op.cit., p.25.
90 Smalley, op.cit, p.55.
91 *The Anglo-Saxon Chronicle*, trans. G.N. Garmonsway (London, 1972), p.82.
92 William of Malmesbury, *History of the Kings of England* in J. Stevenson (ed.), *The Church Historians of England* (London, 1854), vol.III, p.4.
93 Orderic Vitalis, quoted in Smalley, op.cit., p.88.
94 Peter Burke, *The Renaissance Sense of the Past* (London, 1969), pp.12–13.
95 Jacob Burckhardt, *The Civilization of the Renaissance in Italy* (New York, 1960), p.148.
96 Peter Burke, *The Renaissance* (London, 1987), pp.1–3.
97 Peter Burke, 'The Spread of Italian Humanism' in Anthony Goodman and Angus MacKay (eds), *The Impact of Humanism on Western Europe* (London, 1990), p.1.
98 George Holmes, 'Humanism in Italy', ibid., p.118.
99 Petrarch (Francesco Petrarca), sonnet from *Epistolae metricae* in Donald R. Kelley (ed.), *Versions of History from Antiquity to the Enlightenment* (New Haven and London, 1991), pp.220–1.
100 Antonio Filarete, 'Treatise on Architecture' in Burke, 1969, p.27.
101 Lorenzo Valla, 'Declamation on the Donation of Constantine' in Kelley, op.cit., pp.250–1.
102 Petrarch, 'Familiar Letters' in Burke (1969), p.22.
103 Leonardo Bruni quoted in Burke, ibid., p.119.
104 Felix Gilbert, *Machiavelli and Guicciardini: Politics and History in Sixteenth-Century Florence* (Princeton, 1965). See in particular pp.212–18.
105 Niccolò Machiavelli, *Discourses on Livy* (Oxford, 1997), p.45.
106 ibid., p.254.
107 ibid., p.56.
108 ibid., p.60.
109 Niccolò Machiavelli, *Florentine Histories* (Princeton, 1988). See in particular pp.90–104.
110 ibid., p.105.
111 ibid., p.227.
112 Gilbert, op.cit., p.219.
113 Machiavelli (1988), op.cit., pp.172–3.
114 ibid., p.362.
115 Francesco Guicciardini, *History of Italy* in Burke (1969), p.82.
116 ibid., in particular p.107.
117 Gilbert, op.cit. See pp.220–1 for Gilbert's discussion of Bruni's technique.

Chapter 3: From the Enlightenment of the Eighteenth Century to von Ranke and the Rankean Tradition

1 J-J. Rousseau, *The Social Contract* (Harmondsworth, 1968), p.49.
2 Roy Porter, *The Enlightenment* (London, 1990), p.14.
3 '... car, comme les hommes ont eu dans tous les temps les mêmes passions, les occasions qui produisent les grands changemens sont différentes, mais les causes sont toujours les mêmes.' Montesquieu quoted in David Womersley, *The Transformation of 'The Decline and Fall of the Roman Empire'* (Cambridge, 1988), p.11.
4 David Hume, from *Essays and Treatises on Several Subjects*, quoted in Womersley, ibid., p.20.
5 ibid., p.34.
6 David Hume, commenting to his friend Henry Mackenzie, and quoted in Nicholas Phillipson, *Hume* (New York, 1989), p.80.
7 ibid., p.140.
8 Edward Gibbon, *The History of the Decline and Fall of the Roman Empire*, Betty Radice (ed.) (London, 1983), vol.1, p.31.
9 ibid., p.40.
10 ibid., p.51.
11 ibid., p.220.
12 ibid., p.117.
13 ibid., p.177.
14 ibid., p.209.
15 ibid., p.210.
16 ibid., vol.2, pp.111–2.
17 ibid., vol.2, pp.113–4.
18 ibid., vol.2, p.119.
19 ibid., vol.2, p.120.
20 ibid., vol.2, p.275.
21 ibid., vol.3, p.352.
22 ibid., vol.4, p.64.
23 ibid., vol.5, p.80.
24 ibid., vol.6, p.194.
25 ibid., vol.8, p.317.
26 ibid., vol.7, p.100.
27 Edward Gibbon, *Memoirs of My Life* (Harmondsworth, 1984), p.80.
28 Arnaldo Momigliano, *Studies in Historiography* (London, 1966), p.52.
29 Edward Gibbon (1984), op.cit., p.159.
30 Gibbon (1983), op.cit., vol.4, p.372.
31 ibid., vol.4, p.344.
32 Momigliano, op.cit., p.51.
33 Gibbon (1983), op.cit., vol.4, pp.372–4.
34 Gibbon (1984), op.cit., p.151.
35 Alexander Pope, *The Poetical Works* (London, 1885), p.60.
36 Roy Porter, *Edward Gibbon: Making History* (London, 1988).
37 Gibbon (1984), op.cit., p.158.
38 See J.W. Burrow, *Gibbon* (Oxford, 1985) for a discussion of this stylistic device (particularly p.80).
39 Womersley, op.cit., p.71.
40 G.R. Elton, *The Practice of History* (London, 1969), p.14. Elton's view is echoed by Eric Hobsbawm – hardly the most likely pairing, perhaps. Hobsbawm says, 'We don't read Gibbon as we still read Kant or Rousseau, for their relevance to our own problems. We read him ... for his literary merits;

that is to say most practising historians don't read him at all, except in their leisure hours'. See 'Has History made Progress?' in Hobsbawm, *On History* (London, 1997), pp.57–8.

41 Momigliano, op.cit., p.40.

42 Burrow, op.cit., p.109.

43 John Clive, *Not by Fact Alone. Essays on the Writing and Reading of History* (London, 1990).

44 Gibbon (1983), op.cit., vol.4, p.301.

45 Leopold von Ranke, *The Theory and Practice of History*, G.G. Iggers and Konrad von Moltke (eds) (Indianapolis, 1973). Ranke, of course, wrote no book on historical methodology as such. Iggers and Moltke have usefully collected and translated extracts from prefaces, introductions to lectures and manuscripts to provide a convenient insight into Ranke's ideas on the study and writing of history. Their introduction is an excellent and succinct assessment of Ranke.

46 Historicism (or 'historism', if one insists on a closer translation of the original German term 'Historismus') is a much used, misused and derided term which one devoutly wishes could be ignored. Unfortunately, it resurfaces like a bloated corpse. It seems odd that one could use the term for an historian like von Ranke whose work rests on the assumption that texts reflect reality and again, under the label 'New Historicism', for a group of late twentieth-century cultural historians – or literary scholars – with postmodernist views on the nature of texts. The dubious career of the word was suddenly shunted into a cul-de-sac by the philosopher Karl Popper, who decided in rather an arbitrary way that it could be used of determinist philosophies like Marxism. This had the effect of turning it into a term of abuse, and a particularly convenient one at that, since it could be invested with virtually any meaning. I have used historicism in the sense of 'a critical movement insisting on the prime importance of historical context to the interpretation of texts of all kinds'. This definition comes courtesy of Paul Hamilton, whose book *Historicism* (London, 1996) brings the use of the term up to date by looking at its relevance to scholars in a number of disciplines.

47 Peter Hanns Reill, 'History and the Life Sciences in the Early Nineteenth Century' in G.G. Iggers and James M. Powell (eds), *Leopold von Ranke and the Shaping of the Historical Discipline* (New York, 1990), p.34.

48 Peter Hanns Reill, *The German Enlightenment and the Rise of Historicism* (Berkeley, 1975), p.3.

49 Leopold von Ranke, preface to the first edition of *Histories of the Latin and Germanic Nations* in Iggers and von Moltke, op.cit., p.137. For a significantly different translation, see Fritz Stern (ed.), *The Varieties of History. From Voltaire to the Present* (London, 1970), p.57. The translation by G.P. Gooch, from his *History and Historians in the Nineteenth Century* (London, 1952), p.74, is a familiar one and cited by both Tosh and Marwick, although Marwick mistakenly refers to Gooch but appears to make more use of Stern.

50 Iggers and Moltke, op.cit., pp.xix–xx.

51 Ranke, preface to the first edition of *Histories of the Latin and Germanic Nations* in Iggers and Moltke, ibid., p.137.

52 Leonard Krieger, *Ranke: The Meaning of History* (Chicago, 1977), p.14.

53 Ranke, quoted in Krieger, ibid., p.5.

54 J.E.E.D. Acton, *Lectures on Modern History* (London, 1960), p.22.

55 Ranke, in Iggers and Moltke, op.cit., p.138.

56 Leopold von Ranke, *History of the Popes* in Iggers and Moltke, ibid., p.195.

57 ibid., p.496.

58 ibid., p.lix.

59 Gino Benzoni, 'Ranke's Favorite Source – The Venetian *Relazioni*: Impressions with Allusions to Later Historiography' in Iggers and Powell, op.cit., pp.45–57.
60 Ugo Tucci, 'Ranke and the Venetian Document Market', ibid., pp.99–107.
61 Ranke, quoted by Agatha Ramm, 'Leopold von Ranke' in John Cannon (ed.), *The Historian at Work* (London, 1980), p.49.
62 Ranke, in Iggers and Moltke, op.cit., pp.30–1.
63 ibid., pp.li–lii.
64 Ranke, preface to *Universal History*, in Iggers and Moltke, ibid., p.162.
65 Ranke, preface to *History of France*, ibid., p.150.
66 Peter Gay, *Style in History* (London, 1975), p.62.
67 Ranke, quoted in Gay, ibid., p.60.
68 Acton, op.cit., pp.32–3.
69 Josef L. Altholz and Damian McElrath (eds), *The Correspondence of Lord Acton and Richard Simpson* (Cambridge, 1971) 3 vols, vol.1, p.142.
70 Herbert Butterfield, *The Whig Interpretation of History* (London, 1931), p.109.
71 T.B. Macaulay, *The History of England from the Accession of James II* (Harmondsworth, 1979), p.52.
72 ibid., pp.97–8.
73 ibid., pp.82–3.
74 T.B. Macaulay, *The Works of Lord Macaulay Complete* (London, 1866), 8 vols, vol.1, p.376.
75 T.B. Macaulay, 'History', *Edinburgh Review* (May 1928), p.361.
76 Owen Dudley Edwards, *Macaulay* (London, 1988), p.131.
77 Macaulay quoted in Edwards, ibid., p.126.
78 Butterfield, op.cit., p.7.
79 ibid., p.24.
80 J.H. Plumb, *The Death of the Past* (London, 1969), p.42.
81 R.H.C. Davies, 'The Content of History', *History* LXVI (1981), p.364.
82 H. Butterfield, 'God in History' in C.T. McIntyre (ed.), *God, History, and Historians: An Anthology of Modern Christian Views of History* (New York, 1977), p.193.
83 H. Butterfield, *Christianity and History* (London, 1957), p.87.
84 ibid., p.35.
85 ibid.
86 Butterfield in Ved Mehta, *Fly and the Fly-Bottle: Encounters with British Intellectuals* (London, 1963), p.196.
87 Lewis Bernstein Namier, *England in the Age of the American Revolution* (London, 1961), p.4.
88 Linda Colley, *Namier* (London, 1989), pp.21–2.
89 Lewis Namier quoted in Colley, ibid., p.6.
90 John Cannon, in Cannon (ed.), *The Historian at Work* (London, 1980), pp.136–53.
91 Lewis Namier quoted in Cannon, ibid., p.144.
92 R.J. Evans, *In Defence of History* (London, 1997), pp.33–4.
93 G.R. Elton, *F.W. Maitland* (London, 1986), p.28. See Doris S. Goldstein, 'History at Oxford and Cambridge: Professionalization and the Influence of Ranke' in Iggers and Powell (eds.), op.cit. Goldstein charts the establishing of schools of history at Oxbridge characterized by a belief that history was an autonomous discipline, and 'scientific' in the sense that it had a specific methodology based on the critical evaluation of documents. These sources were exploited, not to claim a practical utility for history or to illustrate the general laws characteristic of other disciplines, but to recognize the uniqueness of the past. It is clear that the Rankean influence contributed immeasurably to the establishing of modern history as a prestigious field of study.

94 Peter Burke, 'Ranke the Reactionary' in Iggers and Powell (eds), op.cit. pp.36–57.
95 Ernst Mayr, 'When is Historiography Whiggish?', *Journal of the History of Ideas* (1990), pp.301–7.
96 Pieter Geyl, *Debates with Historians* (London, 1962), pp.28–9.
97 ibid., p.29.

Chapter 4: Historiography from Marx to the *Annales* School

1 Friedrich Engels, preface to the 1888 English edition of K. Marx and F. Engels, *The Manifesto of the Communist Party* in Lewis S. Feuer (ed.), *Karl Marx and Friedrich Engels: Basic Writings on Politics and Philosophy* (London, 1969), p.46.
2 Karl Marx, *A Contribution to the Critique of Political Economy* in Feuer, ibid., pp.84–5.
3 Karl Marx, *The Poverty of Philosophy* quoted in Peter Singer, *Marx* (Oxford, 1980), p.36.
4 Marx and Engels, *Manifesto of the Communist Party* in Terrell Carver (ed.), *Marx: Later Political Writings*, pp.1–2.
5 ibid., p.9.
6 Singer, op.cit., p.38.
7 Marx in Carver, op.cit., p.30.
8 Feuer, op.cit., pp.436–7.
9 Karl Marx, *Grundrisse* in Carver, op.cit., p.155.
10 Karl Marx, *The Eighteenth Brumaire of Louis Bonaparte* in Carver, ibid., p.32.
11 ibid., pp.xii–xiii.
12 Marx, *The Eighteenth Brumaire*, ibid., p.56.
13 ibid., p.116.
14 Eric Hobsbawm, 'The Historians' Group of the Communist Party' in Maurice Cornforth (ed.), *Rebels and their Causes: Essays in Honour of A.L. Morton* (London, 1978), p.22.
15 ibid., p.26.
16 ibid., p.38.
17 George Rudé, 'The Changing Face of the Crowd' and quoted in Harvey J. Kaye, *The Education of Desire: Marxists and the Writing of History* (London, 1992), p.58.
18 Christopher Hill, *The English Revolution 1640* (London, 1940), pp.17–18.
19 ibid., p.57.
20 Harvey J. Kaye, *The British Marxist Historians* (Oxford, 1984). See in particular pp.99–130. The outline of Kaye's argument is on pp.108–9.
21 R.C. Richardson, *The Debate on the English Revolution Revisited* (London, 1977). See in particular pp.117–22.
22 Christopher Hill, 'The place of the seventeenth-century Revolution in English History' in Hill, *A Nation of Change and Novelty: Radical Politics, Religion and Literature in Seventeenth-Century England* (London, 1993), pp.19–37.
23 Christopher Hill, *The Intellectual Origins of the English Revolution* (Oxford, 1965), p.3.
24 Christopher Hill, 'Recent Interpretations of the Civil War' in Hill, *Puritanism and Revolution* (London, 1968), pp.37–8.
25 Christopher Hill, *A Turbulent, Seditious, and Factious People: John Bunyan and his Church* (Oxford, 1989), p.348.

26 Christopher Hill, 'A Bourgeois Revolution?' in J.A.G. Pocock (ed.), *Three British Revolutions: 1641, 1688, 1776* (Princeton, 1980), pp.109–39.
27 Christopher Hill, 'Partial Historians and Total History', *Times Literary Supplement* 24 November 1972 and quoted in Kaye (1984), op.cit., p.117.
28 Christopher Hill, 'Marxism and History', *The Modern Quarterly*, New Series 3 (1948), pp.52–64.
29 E.P. Thompson, *The Making of the English Working Class* (Harmondsworth, 1968), p.13.
30 E.P. Thompson, *The Poverty of Theory and Other Essays* (London, 1978), p.362.
31 William H. Sewell, Jr., 'How Classes are Made: Critical Reflections on E.P. Thompson's Theory of Working-Class Formation' in Harvey J. Kaye and Keith McClelland (eds), *E.P. Thompson: Critical Perspectives* (Philadelphia, 1990), pp.50–77.
32 Eric Hobsbawm, 'What Do Historians Owe to Karl Marx?' in Hobsbawm, *On History* (London, 1997), p.148.
33 Thomas William Heyck, 'E.P. Thompson: Moralist as Marxist Historian' in Walter L. Arnstein (ed.), *Recent Historians of Great Britain: Essays on the post-1945 generation* (Iowa, 1990), pp.121–45.
34 Hobsbawm in Cornforth (ed.), op.cit., p.38.
35 Hill quoted in Christopher Parker, *The English Historical Tradition Since 1850* (Edinburgh, 1990), pp.182–3.
36 R.W. Fogel and G.R. Elton, *Which Road to the Past? Two Views of History* (New Haven and London, 1983), p.29.
37 Peter Burke, *Popular Culture in Early Modern Europe* (Aldershot, 1988), p.28.
38 Christopher Hill, *The World Turned Upside Down: Radical Ideas During the English Revolution* (Harmondsworth, 1975), p.14. Hill explicitly compares his book with David Underdown's *Pride's Purge* (Oxford, 1971) which, he says, tackles the same period but from the viewpoint of the Whitehall élites.
39 Eric Hobsbawm, 'History from Below – Some Reflections' in Frederick Krantz (ed.), *History From Below: Studies in Popular Protest and Popular Ideology* (Oxford, 1988), pp.13–27.
40 Paul Thompson, *The Voice of the Past: Oral History* (Oxford, 1978). See in particular the chapter 'The Achievement of Oral History', pp.65–90.
41 George Rudé, *Ideology and Popular Protest* (London, 1980), p.7.
42 Peter Burke, 'People's history or total history' in Raphael Samuel (ed.), *People's History and Socialist Theory* (London, 1981), p.7.
43 See Christopher Hill's 'Abolishing the Ranters' in Hill (1993), op.cit., pp.172–218: a riposte to J.C. Davis, *Fear, Myth and History: the Ranters and the Historians* (Cambridge, 1986). Davis argues that the Ranters did not exist, but were the invention of contemporaries for their own religious/ideological purposes. Davis offers his own definition of what a Ranter might be, and then finds little evidence of any such beast. It is at least possible that this might be the fault of the definition rather than a reflection of the alleged non-existence of Ranters.
44 Joan W. Scott, 'Women's History' in Peter Burke (ed.), *New Perspectives on Historical Writing* (Oxford, 1991), pp.42–66.
45 J.C.D. Clark, *Revolution and Rebellion: State and society in England in the seventeenth and eighteenth centuries* (Cambridge, 1986), p.23.
46 Peter Burke, *The French Historical Revolution: The Annales School, 1929–89* (Oxford, 1990).
47 Carole Fink, *Marc Bloch: A Life in History* (Cambridge, 1991), p.346.
48 Fernand Braudel, *The Mediterranean and the Mediterranean World in the Age of Philip II* (London, 1975), vol.1, p.18.
49 ibid., p.20.

50 ibid., pp.20–1.
51 ibid., p.21.
52 Fernand Braudel, *On History* (London, 1980), p.11.
53 Burke (1990), op.cit., p.39.
54 Emmanuel Le Roy Ladurie, *Montaillou. Cathars and Catholics in a French Village 1294–1324* (Harmondsworth, 1980), p.40.
55 Jim Sharpe, 'History from Below' in Peter Burke (ed.), *New Perspectives*, op.cit., pp.24–41.
56 Roy Porter, 'History of the Body', in Burke, ibid., pp.206–32.
57 Emmanuel Le Roy Ladurie, *Carnival: A People's Uprising at Romans 1579–1580* (London, 1980), p.xvii.
58 ibid., p.xx.
59 Braudel (1975), op.cit., vol.2, p.901.
60 Le Roy Ladurie, op.cit., p.370.
61 Braudel (1980), op.cit., p.51.
62 T. Stoianovich, *French Historical Method: The Annales Paradigm* (Ithaca, 1979).
63 Hobsbawm (1997), op.cit., p.183.

Chapter 5: The Value of History

1 Beverley Southgate, *History: What and Why? Ancient, Modern, and Postmodern Perspectives* (London, 1996).
2 See Paul Thompson, *The Voice of the Past: Oral History* (Oxford, 1978), pp.1–18 for a discussion of the social value of oral history.
3 David Lowenthal, *The Past is a Foreign Country* (Cambridge, 1985), p.43.
4 John Steinbeck, *The Grapes of Wrath* (London, 1995), p.101.
5 Primo Levi, *The Drowned and the Saved* (London, 1989), p.112.
6 Lowenthal, op.cit., p.37.
7 Eric Hobsbawm, 'Outside and Inside History', in Hobsbawm, *On History* (London, 1997), p.5.
8 Norman Cohn, *Warrant for Genocide: The Myth of the Jewish World Conspiracy and the Protocols of the Elders of Zion* (London, 1996). Originally published in 1967, but still one of the most useful and lucid analyses of the genesis and dangers of racial myth.
9 Primo Levi, op.cit., p.145.
10 For a helpful introductory discussion of national history in black African states, see John Tosh, *The Pursuit of History: Aims, methods and new directions in the study of modern history* (London, 1984), pp.4–5.
11 Linda Colley, *Britons: Forging the Nation 1707–1837* (New Haven and London, 1992), p.54. I have made considerable use of Colley's excellent discussion of the myth of Britain as the elect nation.
12 Rudyard Kipling, *Recessional* in *The Norton Anthology of English Literature* (New York, 1968), vol.2, pp.1846–7.
13 Joyce Appleby, Lynn Hunt and Margaret Jacob, *Telling the Truth about History* (New York, 1995), p.113. The chapter 'History Makes a Nation' (pp.91–125) is useful for a discussion of the forging of national identity in the United States.
14 Prys Morgan, 'From a Death to a View: The Hunt for the Welsh Past in the Romantic Period', in Eric Hobsbawm and Terence Ranger (eds), *The Invention of Tradition* (Cambridge, 1992), pp.43–100.
15 Hugh Trevor-Roper, 'The Invention of Tradition: The Highland Tradition of Scotland' in Hobsbawm and Ranger, ibid., p.16.
16 Marc Ferro, *The Use and Abuse of History or How the Past is Taught* (London, 1984), p.173.

17 ibid., p.181.
18 Trevor Grundy, *Memoirs of a Fascist Childhood: a boy in Mosley's Britain* (London, 1998)
19 Paul K. Conkin and Roland N. Stromberg, *Heritage and Challenge: The History and Theory of History* (Arlington Heights, 1989), p.225.
20 Eric Hobsbawm, 'What Can History Tell Us about Contemporary Society?' in Hobsbawm (1997), op.cit., p.29.
21 Eric Hobsbawm, 'Identity History Is Not Enough', ibid., p.277.
22 Peter Burke, 'People's history or total history' in Raphael Samuel (ed.), *People's History and Socialist Theory* (London, 1981), p.8.
23 Keith Jenkins, *Re-thinking History* (London, 1991), in particular pp.17–18.
24 Southgate, op.cit., p.137.
25 ibid., p.132.
26 ibid., pp.133–4.
27 R.W. Fogel and G.R. Elton, *Which Road to the Past? Two Views of History* (New Haven and London, 1983), p.96.
28 G.R. Elton, *The Practice of History* (London, 1969), p.65.
29 G.R. Elton, in Juliet Gardiner (ed.), *The History Debate* (London, 1990), p.9.
30 ibid., p.12.
31 R.J. Evans, *In Defence of History* (London, 1997). The Abraham affair is discussed on pp.116–28.
32 David Hackett Fischer in Stephen Vaughn (ed.), *The Vital Past: Writings on the Uses of History* (Athens, Georgia, 1985), p.388.
33 Roy Porter in Gardiner (ed.), op.cit., pp.20–1.

Conclusion

1 Niccolò Machiavelli, *Discourses on Livy* (Oxford, 1997), pp.29–30.
2 Voltaire, letter to Abbé Jean Baptiste Dobos in Fritz Stern (ed.), *The Varieties of History. From Voltaire to the Present* (London, second edition, 1970), p.39.
3 Condorcet, 'Progress of the human mind' in Donald R. Kelley (ed.), *Versions of History from Antiquity to the Enlightenment* (New Haven and London, 1981), p.491.
4 Edward Gibbon, *The History of the Decline and Fall of the Roman Empire* (London, 1983), vol.4, p.371.
5 Rejections of explanations based on structural change can also be complemented by unusual narrative techniques exploiting the insights of postmodernism. In Simon Schama's *Citizens: A Chronicle of the French Revolution*, he comments that he had chosen narrative as the appropriate technique on the basis that: 'If, in fact, the Revolution was a much more haphazard and chaotic event and much more the product of human agency than structural conditioning, chronology seems indispensable in making its complex twists and turns intelligible. So *Citizens* returns, then, to the forms of the nineteenth-century chronicles, allowing different issues and interests to shape the flow of the story as they arise … to the extent that I have followed their precedent, what I have to offer, too, runs the risk of being seen as a mischievously old-fashioned piece of story-telling'. (pp.xv–xvi).
6 See Richard Evans, *In Defence of History* (London, 1997), pp.144–7 for a discussion of the way in which he sought to combine narrative and analysis in *Death in Hamburg*.
7 Peter Burke, 'History of Events and the Revival of Narrative' in Burke (ed.), *New Perspectives on Historical Writing* (Oxford, 1991), pp.233–46.
8 Richard Price, *Alabi's World* (Baltimore and London, 1990), p.xx.
9 R.W. Southern, *The Making of the Middle Ages* (London, 1967)

Bibliography

Acton, J.E.E.D., *Lectures on Modern History* (London, 1960)

Altholz, Josef L. and McElrath, Damian (eds), *The Correspondence of Lord Acton and Richard Simpson* (Cambridge, 1971), 3 vols.

Ankersmit, Frank and Kellner, Hans (eds), *A New Philosophy of History* (London, 1995)

Appleby, J., Hunt, L. and Jacob, M., *Telling the Truth about History* (New York, 1995)

Arnstein, Walter L. (ed.), *Recent Historians of Great Britain: Essays on the post-1945 generation* (Iowa, 1990)

Bede, *Ecclesiastical History of the English People* (Harmondsworth, 1990)

Bentley, Michael (ed.), *Companion to Historiography* (London, 1997)

Black, J. and Macraild, Donald M., *Studying History* (London, 1997)

Bloch, Marc, *The Royal Touch: Monarchy and Miracles in France and England* (New York, 1989)

Braudel, Fernand, *The Mediterranean and the Mediterranean World in the Age of Philip II* (London, 1975), 2 vols.

Braudel, Fernand, *On History* (London, 1980)

Braudel, Fernand, *The Structures of Everyday Life: The Limits of the Possible* (London, 1985)

Breisach, Ernst, *Historiography: Ancient, Medieval, & Modern* (Chicago, second edition 1983)

Burckhardt, Jacob, *The Civilization of the Renaissance in Italy* (New York, 1960)

Burke, Peter, *The Renaissance Sense of the Past: Documents of Modern History* (London, 1969)

Burke, Peter, *The Renaissance* (London, 1978)

Burke, Peter, *Popular Culture in Early Modern Europe* (Aldershot, 1988)

Burke, Peter, *The French Historical Revolution. The Annales School, 1929–89* (Oxford, 1990)

Burke, Peter (ed.), *New Perspectives on Historical Writing* (Oxford, 1991)

Burrow, J W., *Gibbon* (Oxford, 1985)

Butterfield, Herbert, *The Whig Interpretation of History* (London, 1931)

Butterfield, Herbert, *The Englishman and His History* (Cambridge, 1944)

Butterfield, Herbert, *Man on his Past* (Cambridge, 1955)

Butterfield, Herbert, *Christianity and History* (London, second edition, 1957)

Callinicos, Alex, *Theories and Narratives: Reflections on the Philosophy of History* (Oxford, 1995)

Cameron, Averil (ed.), *History as Text: The Writing of Ancient History* (London, 1989)

Cannon, John (ed.), *The Historian at Work* (London, 1980)

Cannon, John (ed.), *The Blackwell Dictionary of Historians* (Oxford, 1988)

Carr, E.H., *What is History?* (Harmondsworth, second edition 1987)

Cicero, M. Tullius, *De Oratore* (London, 1959), 2 vols.

Clark, J.C.D., *Revolution and Rebellion: State and society in England in the seventeenth and eighteenth centuries* (Cambridge, 1986)

Clive, John, *Macaulay: The Shaping of the Historian* (Cambridge, Mass., 1987)

Clive, John, *Not by Fact Alone: Essays on the Writing and Reading of History* (London, 1990)

Cogan, Marc, *The Human Thing: The Speeches and Principles of Thucydides'*
History (Chicago, 1981)
Cohn, Norman, *Warrant for Genocide: The Myth of the Jewish World Conspiracy*
and the Protocols of the Elders of Zion (London, 1996)
Colley, Linda, *Namier* (London, 1989)
Colley, Linda, *Britons: Forging the Nation 1707–1837* (New Haven and London,
1992)
Conkin, P.K., and Stromberg, R.N., *Heritage and Challenge: The History and*
Theory of History (Arlington Heights, 1989)
Craddock, Patricia B., *Edward Gibbon, Luminous Historian* (Baltimore, 1989)
Dahmus, J.H. *Seven Medieval Historians* (Chicago, 1982)
D'Amico, Robert, *Historicism and Knowledge* (London, 1989)
Davies, R.H.C., 'The Content of History', *History*, LXVI (1981), pp.361–74.
Davis, J.C., *Fear, Myth and History: the Ranters and the Historians* (Cambridge,
1986)
Edwards, Owen Dudley, *Macaulay* (London, 1988)
Elton, G.R., *Reformation Europe 1517–1559* (London, 1963)
Elton, G.R., *The Practice of History* (London, 1969)
Elton, G.R., *F.W. Maitland* (London, 1986)
Elton, G.R., *Return to Essentials: Some Reflections on the Present State of*
Historical Study (Cambridge, 1991)
Ermarth, Elizabeth Deeds, *Sequel to History: Postmodernism and the Crisis of*
Representational Time (Princeton, 1992)
Evans, Richard J., *In Defence of History* (London, 1997)
Fehling, Detlev, *Herodotus and his 'Sources': Citation, Invention and Narrative*
Art (Liverpool, 1989)
Ferro, Marc, *The Use and Abuse of History or How the Past is Taught* (London,
1984)
Feuer, L.S. (ed.), *Karl Marx and Friedrich Engels: Basic Writings on Politics and*
Philosophy (London, 1969)
Fink, Carole, *Marc Bloch: A Life in History* (Cambridge, 1991)
Fogel, R.W. and Elton, G.R., *Which Road to the Past? Two Views of History* (New
Haven and London, 1983)
Foucault, M., *Power/Knowledge: Selected Interviews and Other Writings*
1972–1977 (Brighton, 1980)
Fox, Alistair, *Thomas More: History and Providence* (Oxford, 1982)
Fox, Alastair, *Politics and Literature in the Reigns of Henry VII and Henry VIII*
(Oxford, 1989)
Fukuyama, Francis, *The End of History and the Last Man* (Harmondsworth,
1992)
Füredi, Frank, *Mythical Past, Elusive Future: History and Society in an Anxious*
Age (London, 1992)
Gagnon, Serge, *Man and his Past. The Nature and Role of Historiography*
(Montreal, 1982)
Gardiner, Juliet (ed.), *The History Debate* (London, 1990)
Garmonsway, G.N. (ed.), *The Anglo-Saxon Chronicle* (London, 1972)
Gay, Peter, *Style in History* (London, 1975)
Geyl, Pieter, *Debates with Historians* (London, 1962)
Gibbon, Edward, *The History of the Decline and Fall of the Roman Empire*
(London, 1983), 8 vols (ed. Betty Radice)
Gibbon, Edward, *Memoirs of My Life* (Harmondsworth, 1984)
Gilbert, Felix, *Machiavelli and Guicciardini: Politics and History in Sixteenth-*
Century Florence (Princeton, 1965)
Goffart, Walter, *The Narrators of Barbarian History (A.D. 550–800)* (Princeton,
1988)

Gooch, G.P., *History and Historians in the Nineteenth Century* (London, second edition 1952)

Goodman, Anthony and MacKay, Angus (eds), *The Impact of Humanism on Western Europe* (London, 1990)

Gould, John, *Herodotus* (London, 1989)

Graham, Gordon, *The Shape of the Past* (Oxford, 1997)

Gransden, Antonia, *Historical Writing in England I. c.550–c.1307* (London, 1974)

Gransden, Antonia, *Historical Writing in England II. c.1307 to the Early Sixteenth Century* (London, 1982)

Grant, Michael (ed.), *Readings in the Classical Historians* (New York, 1992)

Green, J.H., *A Short History of the English People* (London, 1915), 4 vols.

Greenblatt, Stephen, *Renaissance Self-Fashioning: From More to Shakespeare* (Chicago, 1980)

Grundy, Trevor, *Memoirs of a Fascist Childhood: a boy in Mosley's Britain.* (London, 1998)

Hamilton, Paul, *Historicism* (London, 1996)

Hartog, François, *The Mirror of Herodotus* (Berkeley, 1988)

Hay, Denys, *Annalists and Historians: Western Historiography from the VIIIth to the XVIIIth Century* (London, 1977)

Herodotus, *The Histories* (Harmondsworth, 1972)

Hexter, J.H., *Doing History* (London, 1971)

Higham, N.J., *An English Empire: Bede and the early Anglo-Saxon kings* (Manchester, 1995)

Hill, Christopher, *The English Revolution 1640* (London, 1940)

Hill, Christopher, 'Marxism and History', *The Modern Quarterly*, New Series 3 (1948), pp.52–64

Hill, Christopher, *The Intellectual Origins of the English Revolution* (Oxford, 1965)

Hill, Christopher, *Puritanism and Revolution* (London, 1968)

Hill, Christopher, *The World Turned Upside Down: Radical Ideas During the English Revolution* (Harmondsworth, 1975)

Hill, Christopher, 'A Bourgeois Revolution?' in J.A.G. Pocock (ed.), *Three British Revolutions: 1641, 1688, 1776* (Princeton, 1980)

Hill, Christopher, *A Turbulent and Seditious People: John Bunyan and his Church* (Oxford, 1989)

Hill, Christopher, *A Nation of Change and Novelty: Radical politics, religion and literature in seventeenth-century England* (London, 1993)

Hobsbawm, Eric, 'The Historians' Group of the Communist Party', in Maurice Cornforth (ed.), *Rebels and their Causes: Essays in honour of A.L. Morton* (London, 1978)

Hobsbawm, Eric and Ranger, Terence (eds), *The Invention of Tradition* (Cambridge, 1992)

Hobsbawm, Eric, *On History* (London, 1997)

Holdsworth, Christopher and Wiseman, T.P. (eds), *The Inheritance of Historiography 350–900* (Exeter, 1986)

Hornblower, Simon, *Thucydides* (London, 1987)

Hornblower, Simon (ed.), *Greek Historiography* (Oxford, 1994)

Hunt, Lynn (ed.), *The New Cultural History* (Berkeley, 1989)

Hunter, Virginia, *Thucydides: The Artful Reporter* (Toronto, 1973)

Iggers, G.G. and Moltke, Konrad von (eds.), *The Theory and Practice of History* (Indianapolis, 1973)

Iggers, G.G., *New Directions in European Historiography* (London, 1985)

Iggers, G.G. and Powell, J M. (eds), *Leopold von Ranke and the Shaping of the Historial Discipline* (New York, 1990)

Jenkins, Keith, *Re-thinking History* (London, 1991)

Jenkins, Keith, *On 'What is History': From Carr and Elton to Rorty and White* (London, 1995)

Jenkins, Keith (ed.), *The Postmodern History Reader* (London, 1997)

Joyce, P., 'History and Post-Modernism', *Past and Present*, 133 (1991), pp.204–9

Kaye, Harvey J., *The British Marxist Historians* (Oxford, 1984)

Kaye, Harvey J., *The Education of Desire: Marxists and the Writing of History* (London, 1992)

Kaye, Harvey J. and McClelland, Keith (eds), *E.P Thompson: Critical Perspectives* (Philadelphia, 1990)

Kelley, Donald R. (ed.), *Versions of History from Antiquity to the Enlightenment* (New Haven and London, 1991)

Kenyon, John, *The History Men: The Historical Profession in England since the Renaissance* (London, second edition 1993)

Kozicki, H. (ed.), *Developments in Modern Historiography* (London, 1993)

Krantz, Frederick (ed.), *History from Below: Studies in Popular Protest and Popular Ideology* (Oxford, 1988)

Krieger, Leonard, *Ranke: The Meaning of History* (Chicago, 1977)

Ladurie, E. Le Roy, *Carnival: A People's Uprising at Romans 1579–1580* (London, 1980)

Ladurie, E. Le Roy, *Montaillou. Cathars and Catholics in a French village 1294–1324* (Harmondsworth, 1980)

Levi, Primo, *The Drowned and the Saved* (London, 1989)

Lewis, D.M., *The Greek Historians, Literature and History: Essays presented to A.E. Raubitschek* (Stanford, 1986)

Livy (Titus Livius), *The Early History of Rome* (Harmondsworth, 1971)

Lowenthal, David, *The Past is a Foreign Country* (Cambridge, 1985)

Lyotard, J-F., *The Postmodern Condition* (Manchester, 1984)

Macaulay, T.B., 'History', *Edinburgh Review* (May 1828), pp.331–67

Macaulay, T.B., *The Works of Lord Macaulay Complete* (London, 1866), vols.I-IV

Macaulay, T.B., *The History of England* (Harmondsworth, 1979)

Machiavelli, Niccolò, *Florentine Histories* (Princeton, 1988)

Machiavelli, Niccolò, *Discourses on Livy* (Oxford, 1997)

Macintyre, Alisdair, *After Virtue: A study in Moral Theory* (London, second edition 1985)

Malmesbury, William of, *The History of the Kings of England* in J. Stevenson (ed.), *The Church Historians of England* (London, 1854), vol.III.

Martin, R. *Tacitus* (London, 1981)

Marwick, Arthur, *The Nature of History* (London, third edition 1989)

Marwick, Arthur, 'Two Approaches to Historical Study: The Metaphysical (including 'Postmodernism') and the Historical', *Journal of Contemporary History*, 30, 1 (Jan 1995), pp.5–31.

Marx, Karl and Engels, Friedrich, *Basic Writings on Politics and Philosophy* (London, 1969)

Marx, Karl, *Later Political Writings* (Cambridge, 1996) (ed. Terrell Carver)

Matthews, Eric, *Twentieth-Century French Philosophy* (Oxford, 1996)

Mayr, Ernst, 'When is Historiography Whiggish?', *Journal of the History of Ideas* (1990), pp.301–7.

McCullagh, C. Behan, *The Truth of History* (London, 1998)

McIntyre, C.T. (ed.), *God, History, and Historians: An Anthology of Modern Christian Views of History* (New York, 1977)

Mehta, Ved, *Fly and the Fly-Bottle: Encounters with British Intellectuals* (London, 1963)

Momigliano, Arnaldo, *Studies in Historiography* (London, 1966)

Momigliano, Arnaldo, *Essays in Ancient and Modern Historiography* (Oxford, 1977)

Momigliano, Arnaldo, *The Classical Foundations of Modern Historiography* (Berkeley, 1990)

Namier, Lewis Bernstein, *In the Margin of History* (London, 1939)

Namier, Lewis Bernstein, *The Structure of Politics at the Accession of George III* (London, second edition 1957)

Namier, Lewis Bernstein, *Vanished Supremacies* (Harmondsworth, 1958)

Namier, Lewis Bernstein, *England in the Age of the American Revolution* (London, second edition 1961)

Newman, Bertram (ed.), *English Historians: Selected Passages* (Oxford, 1957)

Novick, Peter, *That Noble Dream: The 'Objectivity Question' and the American Historical Profession* (Cambridge, 1988)

Parker, Christopher, *The English Historical Tradition since 1850* (Edinburgh, 1990)

Phillipson, Nicholas, *Hume* (New York, 1989)

Plumb, J.H., *The Death of the Past* (London, 1969)

Polybius, *The Rise of the Roman Empire* (Harmondsworth, 1979)

Pope, Alexander, *The Poetical Works* (London, 1885)

Porter, Roy, *Edward Gibbon: Making History* (London, 1988)

Porter, Roy, *The Enlightenment* (London, 1990)

Price, Richard, *Alabi's World* (Baltimore and London, 1990)

Ranke, Leopold von in G.G. Iggers and Konrad von Moltke (eds), *The Theory and Practice of History* (Indianapolis, 1973)

Ranke, Leopold von in Roger Wines (ed.), *The Secret of World History: Selected Writings on the Art and Science of History* (New York, 1981)

Reill, Peter Hanns, *The German Enlightenment and the Rise of Historicism* (Berkeley, 1975)

Richardson, Alan, *History Sacred and Profane* (London, 1964)

Richardson, R.C., *The Debate on the English Revolution Revisited* (London, 1977)

Robinson, C.A. (ed.), *Selections from Greek and Roman Historians* (New York, 1957)

Rousseau, J-J., *The Social Contract* (Harmondsworth, 1968)

Rowse, A.L. *Historians I Have Known* (London, 1995)

Rudé, George, *Paris and London in the 18th Century: Studies in Popular Protest* (London, 1974)

Rudé, George, *Ideology and Popular Protest* (London, 1980)

Said, Edward W., *The World, the Text and the Critic* (Cambridge, Mass., 1983)

Said, Edward W., 'Orientalism Reconsidered' in Frances Barker *et al.* (eds), *Europe and Its Others* (Colchester, 1985)

Said, Edward W., *Culture and Imperialism* (London, 1994)

Said, Edward W., *Orientalism* (Harmondsworth, 1995)

Sallust (Gaius Sallustius Crispus), *The War with Catiline* (London, 1960)

Sallust, *The Jugurthine War/The Conspiracy of Catiline* (Harmondsworth,1963)

Samuel, Raphael (ed.), *People's History and Socialist Theory* (London, 1981)

Schama, Simon, *Citizens: A Chronicle of the French Revolution* (Harmondsworth, 1989)

Schama, Simon, *Dead Certainties (Unwarranted Speculations)* (London, 1991).

Schwarz, Bill, 'The people in history: the Communist Party Historians' Group, 1946–56' in Richard Johnson *et al.*, *Making Histories: Studies in history-writing and politics* (London, 1982), pp.44–95

Singer, Peter, *Marx* (Oxford, 1980)

Skinner, Quentin, *Machiavelli* (Oxford, 1981)

Smalley, Beryl, *Historians in the Middle Ages* (London, 1974)

Sontag, Susan (ed.), *A Barthes Reader* (London, 1982)

Southern, R.W., *The Making of the Middle Ages* (London, 1967)

Southgate, Beverley, *History: What and Why? Ancient, Modern, and Postmodern Perspectives* (London, 1996)

Spiegel, Gabrielle, 'History and Post-Modernism IV', *Past and Present*, 135 (1992), pp.194–208

Steinbeck, John, *The Grapes of Wrath* (London, 1995)

Stephens, John, *The Italian Renaissance: The Origins of Intellectual and Artistic Change Before the Reformation* (London, 1990)

Stern, Fritz (ed.), *The Varieties of History: From Voltaire to the Present* (London, second edition 1970)

Stoianovich, T., *French Historical Method: The Annales Paradigm* (Ithaca, 1979)

Stone, Lawrence, 'History and Post-Modernism', *Past and Present*, 131 (1991), pp.217–18

Stone, Lawrence, 'History and Post-Modernism III', *Past and Present*, 135 (1992), pp.189–94

Syme, Ronald, *Tacitus* (Oxford, 1958)

Syme, Ronald, *Sallust* (Berkeley, 1964)

Tacitus, Cornelius, *The Annals of Imperial Rome* (Harmondsworth, 1959)

Thompson, E.P., *The Making of the English Working Class* (Harmondsworth, 1968)

Thompson, E.P., *The Poverty of Theory and Other Essays* (London, 1978)

Thompson, Paul, *The Voice of the Past: Oral History* (Oxford, 1978)

Thucydides, *The History of the Peloponnesian War* (London, 1910)

Thucydides, *History of the Peloponnesian War* (Harmondsworth, 1972)

Tosh, John, *The Pursuit of History: Aims, methods and new directions in the study of modern history* (London, second edition 1991)

Tuchman, Barbara, *Practising History* (London, 1983)

Tulloch, Hugh, *Acton* (London, 1988)

Vaughn, Stephen (ed.), *The Vital Past: Writings on the Uses of History* (Athens, Ga. 1985)

Veeser, H. Aram (ed.), *The New Historicism Reader* (London, 1994)

Walbank, F.W. *Polybius* (Berkeley, 1972)

White, Hayden, *Metahistory: The Historical Imagination in Nineteenth-Century Europe* (Baltimore, 1973)

White, Hayden, *Tropics of Discourse: Essays in Cultural Criticism* (London, 1978)

White, Hayden, 'Historical Emplotment and the Problem of Truth' in Saul Friedlander (ed.), *Probing the Limits of Representation: Nazism and the 'Final Solution'* (Cambridge, Mass., 1992), pp.37–53

White, Hayden, 'Response to Arthur Marwick', *Journal of Contemporary History*, 30 (1995), pp.233–46

Womersley, David, *The Transformation of 'The Decline and Fall of the Roman Empire'* (Cambridge, 1988)

Young, Robert, *White Mythologies: Writing History and the West* (London, 1990)

Index